Improving
College
Reading
FIFTH EDITION

Improving College Reading

FIFTH EDITION

LEE A. JACOBUS
University of Connecticut

HARCOURT BRACE JOVANOVICH, PUBLISHERS

San Diego   New York   Chicago   Austin   Washington, D.C.
London   Sydney   Tokyo   Toronto

Preface

Despite its similar appearance, *Improving College Reading*, Fifth Edition, is significantly different from the earlier versions. In addition to incorporating some important strains of current thinking about the teaching of reading, particularly in the emphasis on inferential reasoning from the texts, it takes a new approach to the choice of selections.

For one thing, the material in this edition is drawn entirely from primary or secondary readings assigned to students in regular college courses in a wide variety of disciplines, including literature and languages, history, sociology, anthropology, business, biology, physics, and entomology. As in previous editions, the essays are arranged in five sections of increasing difficulty.

Then, for the first time in either *Improving College Reading* or its sister text, *Developing College Reading*, the final section features nine selections from textbooks of popular freshman courses in political science, history, sociology, art history, anthropology, biology, psychology, theatre, and economics.

A number of items have been paired to permit a wider reading on key issues, such as feminism, observation in nature, childhood, problems of race and equality, the achievements of genius, the uses of language in a democracy, the nature of language and speech, the question of culture from the perspectives of the anthropologist and the sociologist, and the functioning of the brain from the perspectives of the biologist and the psychologist.

The collection covers a representative range of academic disciplines encountered by the average beginning student. In this sense, *Improving College Reading*, Fifth Edition, focuses on the kind of reading every college student must do to succeed in an academic program. The interest level of these pieces is naturally high, but the intellectual demands are high as well. The aim is to prepare students for college reading by training them to read attentively, to improve concentration and retention—and to translate those abilities into skills necessary for analyzing a reading for its main ideas and principal interpretations, and for drawing appropriate conclusions. The testing material also focuses on improving vocabulary and developing inferential abilities that involve reasoning intelligently from what has been read.

The testing apparatus is familiar to most students, and it is consistent throughout the book. The retention questions are designed to focus concentration and direct attention to important textual details. The questions concerning the main idea, interpretation, and conclusions point to large central issues. The application questions are entirely inferential, depending on questions of cause and effect, possibility, application of concepts, inferences from facts, and explanation in terms of known principles.

I have used Benjamin Bloom's evaluation techniques in the testing. Questions test for memory and understanding, application and analysis, and synthesis and evaluation. For examining the reading levels of the selections, I have relied on the useful computer program developed by Michael Schuyler, which permits comparison of all the major readability formulas currently available.

In the back of the book are several charts that may be useful. One records performance on all the testing material. Another permits students to measure their reading efficiency by presenting a simple method of calculating progress in terms of reading speed *and* exercise scores.

I would like to thank my acquisitions editor at Harcourt Brace Jovanovich, Marlane Agriesti, and my former editor, Matthew Milan. Both have been encouraging and helpful, but it is to Marlane that I am indebted for suggestions that helped shape this new edition. I am also grateful to Judith Davis Miller of Sacred Heart University, a colleague who helped once again in developing some of the testing material in this book. My thanks also to Jim Birmingham, formerly with John Tyler Community College, and Gertrude D. Laney of San Francisco State University for their suggestions. Special thanks go to Jacqueline McCurry of the University of Connecticut for help in preparing the manuscript.

Again, as in past editions, I would like to dedicate this book to the teachers and students who will use it. My hope is that it will provide them some access to the avenues of learning.

Lee A. Jacobus

Contents

SECTION THREE

Readings in Science and Sociology

SECTION FOUR
Readings in Business, Science, and Language Studies

SECTION FIVE
Readings from Popular Freshman Textbooks

SECTION
ONE

Readings in Anthropology and Popular Culture

1

ELLEN GOODMAN

Drafting Daughters

Ellen Goodman is a Pulitzer Prize-winning
columnist who writes for the *Boston Globe.*
This commentary on the prospect of women
being drafted on an equal basis with men was
published early in 1980. It is all the more
interesting because Goodman has a daughter
who might be drafted if the law is changed.
The interesting conflict is between equality
for women and the possibility that it may
mean risking military service.

My daughter is eleven, and as we watch the evening news, she turns
to me seriously and says, "I don't like the way the world is doing things." Neither
do I.

My daughter is eleven years and eight months old, to be precise, and I do not
want her to grow up and be drafted. Nor does she.

My daughter is almost twelve, and thinks about unkindness and evil, about
endangered species and war. I don't want her to grow up and be brutalized by
war—as soldier or civilian.

As I read those sentences over, they seem too mild. What I want to say is that I
am horrified by the very idea that she could be sent to fight for fossil fuel or
fossilized ideas. What I want to say is that I can imagine no justification for war
other than self-defense, and I am scared stiff about who has the power to decide
what is "defense."

But now, in the last days before President Carter decides whether we will
register young people and whether half of those young people will be female, I
wonder about something else. Would I feel differently if my daughter were my
son? Would I be more accepting, less anguished, at the notion of a son drafted, a
son at war?

Would I beat the drums and pin the bars and stars on his uniform with pride?

Would I look forward to him being toughened up, be proud of his heroism, and accept his risk as a simple fact of life?

I cannot believe it.

So, when I am asked now about registering women for the draft along with men I have to nod yes reluctantly. I don't want anyone registered, anyone drafted, unless it is a genuine crisis. But if there is a draft, this time it can't just touch our sons, like some civilized plague that leaves daughters alone to produce another generation of warriors.

We may have to register women along with men anyway. Women may not have won equal rights yet, but they have "won" equal responsibilities. A male-only draft may be ruled unconstitutional.

But at a deeper level, we have to register women along with men because our society requires it. For generations, war has been part of the rage so many men have held against women.

War is in the hard-hat yelling at an equal rights rally, "Where were you at Iwo Jima?" War is in the man infuriated at the notion of a woman challenging veterans' preference. War is in the mind of the man who challenges his wife for having had a soft life.

War has often split couples and sexes apart, into lives built on separate realities. It has been part of the grudge of self-sacrifice, the painful gap of understanding and experience between men's and women's lives. It is the stuff of which alienation and novels are written.

But more awesomely, as a male activity, a rite of passage, a test of manhood, war has been gruesomely acceptable. Old men who were warriors have sent younger men to war as if it were their birthright. The women's role until recently was to wave banners and sing slogans, and be in need of protection from the enemy.

We all pretended that war was civilized. War had rules and battlegrounds. War did not touch the finer and nobler things, like women.

This was, of course, never true. The losers, the enemies, the victims, the widows of war were as brutalized as the soldiers. Under duress and in defense, women always fought.

But, perhaps, stripped of its maleness and mystery, its audience and cheerleaders, war can be finally disillusioned. Without the last trappings of chivalry, it can be seen for what it is: the last deadly resort.

So, if we must have a draft registration, I would include young women as well as young men. I would include them because they can do the job. I would include them because all women must gain the status to stop as well as to start wars. I would include them because it has been too easy to send men alone.

I would include them because I simply cannot believe that I would feel differently if my daughter were my son.

LENGTH: 716 WORDS

1   Ellen Goodman
Drafting Daughters

SCORING: Reading time: _____ Rate from chart: _____ W.P.M.	

RETENTION	number right _____ × 3 equals _____ points	
INFERENCES	number right _____ × 5 equals _____ points	
APPLICATION	number right _____ × 5 equals _____ points	
VOCABULARY	number right _____ × 2 equals _____ points	

(Total points: 100) **total** _____ points

RETENTION   Based on the selection, which of the following statements are True (T), False (F), or Not answerable (N)?

1. _____ Society pretended that war was civilized partly because war had rules and battlegrounds.

2. _____ War splits not just couples apart, but actually splits men and women apart.

3. _____ Fortunately, war has never had a sense of maleness or mystery about it.

4. _____ The grudge of self-sacrifice refers to the fact that women have to stay home when men go to war.

5. _____ War widows were never brutalized as much as the men who went to war.

6. _____ Ellen Goodman has no son who can go off to war.

7. _____ Goodman can see no justification for war.

8. _____ If Goodman had a son, she would be proud of the toughening-up process the military would give him if he were drafted.

9. _____ Goodman's daughter is a teenager.

10. _____ Goodman assumes war brutalizes both soldier and civilian.

INFERENCES   Which four of the following eight statements, based on the selection, are most probably true? _____, _____, _____, and _____

1. Women were not drafted in the past because they were considered to be above all the ugliness that was war.

2. If women were drafted, they would change the entire character of war.
3. One reason why women may not be drafted is that war has been thought of as a test of manhood.
4. Ellen Goodman would lose the major need to protest against war if her daughter were drafted.
5. An article of this type is fairly daring for a family newspaper.
6. Women in the past have essentially been one of the reasons why men have fought wars—women have needed protection.
7. President Carter decided not to draft women because he has a daughter of his own.
8. War has been disguised under the rules of chivalry.

APPLICATION   Choose the best answer for each question.

1. _____ If there is to be a military draft:
    a. Goodman will march alongside the hard-hatters.
    b. Goodman's daughter will be one of the first to go.
    c. Goodman would want men and women to be drafted equally.
    d. women would welcome the chance to show military skills.

2. _____ Goodman's argument, if she were personally likely to be drafted:
    a. would probably be in favor of women being drafted.
    b. might be an argument against war in general.
    c. would not be printed in a general newspaper.
    d. would take on a much greater importance than it does now.

3. _____ Should a male-only draft prove unconstitutional:
    a. women would never have a chance of joining the army.
    b. women would have to be drafted on an equal basis with men.
    c. former draftees would be given immediate financial benefits.
    d. the Constitution would be changed to reflect that decision.

4. _____ Goodman feels that if women were included in the draft:
    a. they would prove ineffective warriors.
    b. they would gain status.
    c. more doors would open for them in civilian life.
    d. fewer men would be needed, and thus if she had a son, he might be spared.

5. _____ A male-only draft might be unconstitutional because:
    a. drafts in general may be unconstitutional.
    b. the word "draft" is not in the Constitution at all.
    c. it discriminates against women.
    d. it establishes a precedent that Congress did not intend.

6. ____ Veterans feel women could challenge veterans' preference:
   a. once they had been drafted.
   b. any time they wish to.
   c. if they were willing to wear American flags on their hats.
   d. if they had also experienced war.

VOCABULARY   Choose the best definition for each italic vocabulary entry.

1. ____ stripped of its maleness and *mystery*
   a. commonness
   b. appropriateness
   c. specialness
   d. heaviness

2. ____ She could be sent to fight for *fossil fuel*.
   a. old garbage
   b. easily produced electricity
   c. storage tanks and depots
   d. oil

3. ____ I have to nod yes *reluctantly*.
   a. without enthusiastic support
   b. with a shaking of the head
   c. in a guarded fashion
   d. with a note of hesitation

4. ____ I don't want anyone registered unless it is a genuine *crisis*.
   a. very dangerous situation
   b. war
   c. fully realized condition
   d. major operation recognized by the government

5. ____ Under *duress* and defense, women always fought.
   a. stressed
   b. if under strain
   c. when forced
   d. if ordered

6. ____ Women must gain the *status* to stop as well as start wars.
   a. position
   b. power
   c. situation
   d. rank

7. _____ the last *trappings* of chivalry
   a. coverings
   b. necessities
   c. characteristics
   d. supervision

8. _____ fossil fuel or *fossilized* ideas
   a. foreign, imported
   b. outmoded
   c. repugnant
   d. unpopular

9. _____ As a *rite of passage* war has been gruesomely acceptable.
   a. sign of being well traveled
   b. conditional situation
   c. initiation
   d. going for it

10. _____ war can be finally *disillusioned*
    a. eradicated
    b. suffered but not willingly
    c. stripped of illusion
    d. idealized

2

JUDY SYFERS

I Want a Wife

This is one of the most anthologized short essays of the 1970s. Judy Syfers was active in the women's movement in the late sixties, was educated as a painter at the University of Iowa, has been married, and has raised children. As a woman, she reacted to the attitudes she felt were current regarding the function and role of women in marriage. She was especially interested in what the society felt was expected of a woman in marriage, and what men really wanted from a wife.

I belong to that classification of people known as wives. I am A Wife. And, not altogether incidentally, I am a mother.

Not too long ago a male friend of mine appeared on the scene fresh from a recent divorce. He had one child, who is, of course, with his ex-wife. He is looking for another wife. As I thought about him while I was ironing one evening, it suddenly occurred to me that I, too, would like to have a wife. Why do I want a wife?

I would like to go back to school so that I can become economically independent, support myself, and, if need be, support those dependent upon me. I want a wife who will work and send me to school. And while I am going to school I want a wife to take care of my children. I want a wife to keep track of the children's doctor and dentist appointments. And to keep track of mine, too. I want a wife to make sure my children eat properly and are kept clean. I want a wife who will wash the children's clothes and keep them mended. I want a wife who is a good nurturant attendant to my children, who arranges for their schooling, makes sure that they have an adequate social life with their peers, takes them to the park, the zoo, etc. I want a wife who takes care of the children when they are sick, a wife who arranges to be around when the children need special care, because, of course, I cannot miss classes at school. My wife must arrange to lose time at work and not lose the job. It may mean a small cut in my wife's income from time to time, but I guess I can tolerate that. Needless to say, my wife will arrange and pay for the care of the children while my wife is working.

I want a wife who will take care of *my* physical needs. I want a wife who will keep my house clean. A wife who will pick up after my children, a wife who will pick up after me. I want a wife who will keep my clothes clean, ironed, mended, replaced when need be, and who will see to it that my personal things are kept in their proper place so that I can find what I need the minute I need it. I want a wife who cooks the meals, a wife who is a *good* cook. I want a wife who will plan the menus, do the necessary grocery shopping, prepare the meals, serve them pleasantly, and then do the cleaning up while I do my studying. I want a wife who will care for me when I am sick and sympathize with my pain and loss of time from school. I want a wife to go along when our family takes a vacation so that someone can continue to care for me and my children when I need a rest and change of scene.

I want a wife who will not bother me with rambling complaints about a wife's duties. But I want a wife who will listen to me when I feel the need to explain a rather difficult point I have come across in my course of studies. And I want a wife who will type my papers for me when I have written them.

I want a wife who will take care of the details of my social life. When my wife and I are invited out by my friends, I want a wife who will take care of the babysitting arrangements. When I meet people at school that I like and want to entertain, I want a wife who will have the house clean, will prepare a special meal, serve it to me and my friends, and not interrupt when I talk about things that interest me and my friends. I want a wife who will have arranged that the children are fed and ready for bed before my guests arrive so that the children do not bother us. I want a wife who takes care of the needs of my guests so that they feel comfortable, who makes sure that they have an ashtray, that they are passed the hors d'oeuvres, that they are offered a second helping of the food, that their wine glasses are replenished when necessary, that their coffee is served to them as they like it. And I want a wife who knows that sometimes I need a night out by myself.

I want a wife who is sensitive to my sexual needs, a wife who makes love passionately and eagerly when I feel like it, a wife who makes sure that I am satisfied. And, of course, I want a wife who will not demand sexual attention when I am not in the mood for it. I want a wife who assumes the complete responsibility for birth control, because I do not want more children. I want a wife who will remain sexually faithful to me so that I do not have to clutter up my intellectual life with jealousies. And I want a wife who understands that *my* sexual needs may entail more than strict adherence to monogamy. I must, after all, be able to relate to people as fully as possible.

If, by chance, I find another person more suitable as a wife than the wife I already have, I want the liberty to replace my present wife with another one. Naturally, I will expect a fresh, new life; my wife will take the children and be solely responsible for them so that I am left free.

When I am through with school and have a job, I want my wife to quit working and remain at home so that my wife can more fully and completely take care of a wife's duties.

My God, who *wouldn't* want a wife?

LENGTH: 1,000 WORDS

2 Judy Syfers
I Want a Wife

SCORING: Reading time: _____ Rate from chart: _____ W.P.M.

RETENTION	number right _____ × 3 equals _____ points	
INFERENCES	number right _____ × 5 equals _____ points	
APPLICATION	number right _____ × 5 equals _____ points	
VOCABULARY	number right _____ × 2 equals _____ points	

(Total points: 100) **total** _____ points

RETENTION   Based on the selection, which of the following statements are True (T), False (F), or Not answerable (N)?

1. _____ Wives' duties sometimes produce complaints.

2. _____ Syfers feels schooling can make her economically independent.

3. _____ Sexual infidelity could cause stress to Syfers' intellectual life.

4. _____ Syfers has classified herself as a husband.

5. _____ One duty of a wife is to sexually satisfy her husband.

6. _____ Syfers does not do ironing.

7. _____ Syfers' wife will be expected to work.

8. _____ Being able to cook a good Italian meal is a must for Syfers' wife.

9. _____ The only time a wife would get a rest is on vacation.

10. _____ Birth control is the husband's responsibility.

INFERENCES   Which four of the following eight statements, based on the selection, are most probably true? _____, _____, _____, and _____

1. The social life of a married couple is relatively uncomplicated.
2. Syfers is defining the role of a wife from the point of view of a man.
3. Syfers thinks of all this as a joke in good fun.
4. Syfers must have done all that she describes when she was a wife herself.
5. A wife, according to Syfers, should make her interests second to those of her husband.

6. The wife Syfers describes is virtually a servant, with no independent life.
7. This view of a wife is carefully balanced, objective, and accurate.
8. This essay could help husbands see what things they take for granted in their wives.

APPLICATION Choose the best answer for each question.

1. _____ If Syfers were going to marry again, she would:
   a. read this essay to her husband.
   b. use the essay as part of her marriage ceremony.
   c. behave quite differently from the wife she describes.
   d. be the ideal wife she describes in the essay.

2. _____ The husband who has the wife she describes:
   a. makes every effort to make his wife's job easier.
   b. is deeply sympathetic to the situation of women in America.
   c. really wants to change the traditional marital roles.
   d. is content with the relationship he has with his wife.

3. _____ The tone of this essay is:
   a. dead serious.
   b. light and amusing.
   c. instructive.
   d. satirical.

4. _____ This essay was stimulated by:
   a. Syfers' divorce.
   b. a friend's divorce.
   c. a rise in the divorce rate.
   d. a newspaper essay on divorce.

5. _____ Syfers repeats the phrase "I want a wife":
   a. because she wants a wife.
   b. for emphasis.
   c. to show that she really wants a husband.
   d. because that is what people always say.

6. _____ Syfers expects the readers of her essay to:
   a. give up on marriage.
   b. sit back and reflect on injustice.
   c. change some of their thinking about marriage.
   d. send copies to those whose marriages they think are in trouble.

VOCABULARY   Choose the best definition for each italic vocabulary entry.

1. _____ And, not altogether *incidentally*, I am a mother.
   a. accidentally
   b. without incident
   c. unimportantly
   d. intentionally

2. _____ I want a wife who is a good *nurturant* attendant.
   a. thoughtful, watchful
   b. helpful, supportive
   c. dietary expert
   d. nurselike and wary

3. _____ I want a wife who will not bother me with *rambling* complaints.
   a. vague
   b. occasional
   c. emotional
   d. ongoing

4. _____ Guests should be passed the *hors d'oeuvres*.
   a. drinks
   b. serviettes
   c. snacks
   d. place settings

5. _____ Their wine glasses are *replenished* when necessary.
   a. replaced
   b. restored
   c. refilled
   d. reworked

6. _____ My sexual needs may *entail* certain diversions.
   a. regard
   b. involve
   c. demand
   d. support

7. _____ strict *adherence to* monogamy
   a. attention to
   b. regard of
   c. performance of
   d. devotion to

8. _____ strict adherence to *monogamy*
   a. one woman
   b. one faith
   c. being married to one person at a time
   d. the expressly stated conditions of marriage

9. _____ an adequate social life with their *peers*
   a. friends
   b. elders
   c. dependents
   d. nurses

10. _____ I want to be *economically* independent.
   a. efficiently
   b. plainly
   c. completely
   d. financially

3

ERNESTO GALARZA

Barrio Boy

In the 1940s, Ernesto Galarza took his Ph.D. at Columbia University, after having been born in Mexico and educated in California. When he took his degree, he devoted himself to organizing agricultural workers in California. The barrio (a Mexican word for the neighborhood) was near the canneries and farms that depended on cheap Mexican labor for their existence.

Our family conversations always occurred on our own kitchen porch, away from the gringos. One or the other of the adults would begin: *Se han fijado?* Had we noticed—that the Americans do not ask permission to leave the room; that they had no respectful way of addressing an elderly person; that they spit brown over the railing of the porch into the yard; that when they laughed they roared; that they never brought *saludos* to everyone in your family from everyone in their family when they visited; that *General Delibree* was only a clerk; that *zopilotes* were not allowed on the streets to collect garbage; that the policemen did not carry lanterns at night; that Americans didn't keep their feet on the floor when they were sitting; that there was a special automobile for going to jail; that a rancho was not a rancho at all but a very small hacienda; that the saloons served their customers free eggs, pickles, and sandwiches; that instead of bullfighting, the gringos for sport tried to kill each other with gloves?

I did not have nearly the strong feelings on these matters that Doña Henriqueta expressed. I felt a vague admiration for the way Mr. Brien could spit brown. Wayne, my classmate, laughed much better than the Mexicans, because he opened his big mouth wide and brayed like a donkey so he could be heard a block away. But it was the kind of laughter that made my mother tremble, and it was not permitted in our house.

Rules were laid down to keep me, as far as possible, *un muchacho bien educado*. If I had to spit I was to do it privately, or if in public, by the curb, with

From BARRIO BOY by Ernesto Galarza. © 1971 by University of Notre Dame Press. Reprinted by permission.

my head down and my back to people. I was never to wear my cap in the house and I was to take it off even on the porch if ladies or elderly gentlemen were sitting. If I wanted to scratch, under no circumstances was I to do it right then and there, in company, like the Americans, but I was to excuse myself. If Catfish or Russell yelled to me from across the street I was not to shout back. I was never to ask for tips for my errands or other services to the tenants of 418 L, for these were *atenciones* expected of me.

Above all I was never to fail in *respeto* to grownups, no matter who they were. It was an inflexible rule; I addressed myself to *Señor* Big Singh, *Señor* Big Ernie, *Señora* Dodson, *Señor* Cho-ree Lopez.

My standing in the family, but especially with my mother depended on my keeping these rules. I was not punished for breaking them. She simply reminded me that it gave her acute *vergüenza* to see me act thus, and that I would never grow up to be a correct *jefe de familia* if I did not know how to be a correct boy. I knew what *vergüenza* was from feeling it time and again; and the notion of growing up to keep a tight rein over a family of my own was some-how satisfying.

In our musty apartment in the basement of 418 L, ours remained a Mexican family. I never lost the sense that we were the same, from Jalco to Sacramento. There was the polished cedar box, taken out now and then from the closet to display our heirlooms. I had lost the rifle shells of the revolution, and Tio Tonche, too, was gone. But there was the butterfly sarape, the one I had worn through the Battle of Puebla; a black lace mantilla Doña Henriqueta modeled for us; bits of embroidery and lace she had made; the tin pictures of my grand-parents; my report card signed by Señorita Bustamante and Don Salvador; letters from Aunt Esther; and the card with the address of the lady who had kept the Ajax for us. When our mementos were laid out on the bed I plunged my head into the empty box and took deep breaths of the aroma of *puro cedro*, pure Jalcocotán mixed with camphor.

We could have hung on the door of our apartment a sign like those we read in some store windows—*Aquí se habla español*. We not only spoke Spanish, we read it. From the *Librería Española*, two blocks up the street, Gustavo and I bought novels for my mother, like *Genoveva de Brabante*, a paperback with the poems of Amado Nervo and a handbook of the history of Mexico. The novels were never read aloud, the poems and the handbook were. Nervo was the famous poet from Tepic, close enough to Jalcocotán to make him our own. And in the history book I learned to read for myself, after many repetitions by my mother, about the deeds of the great Mexicans Don Salvador had recited so vividly to the class in Mazatlán. She refused to decide for me whether Abraham Lincoln was as great as Benito Juarez, or George Washington braver than the priest Don Miguel Hidalgo. At school there was no opportunity to settle these questions because nobody seemed to know about Juarez or Hidalgo; at least they were never mentioned and there were no pictures of them on the walls.

The family talk I listened to with the greatest interest was about Jalco.

Wherever the conversation began it always turned to the pueblo, our neighbors, anecdotes that were funny or sad, the folk tales and the witchcraft, and our kinfolk, who were still there. I usually lay on the floor those winter evenings, with my feet toward the kerosene heater, watching on the ceiling the flickering patterns of the light filtered through the scrollwork of the chimney. As I listened once again I chased the *zopilote* away from Coronel, or watched José take Nerón into the forest in a sack. Certain things became clear about the *rurales* and why the young men were taken away to kill Yaqui Indians, and about the Germans, the Englishmen, the Frenchmen, the Spaniards, and the Americans who owned the haciendas, the railroads, the ships, the big stores, the breweries. They owned Mexico because President Porfirio Díaz had let them steal it, José explained as I listened. Now Don Francisco Madero had been assassinated for trying to get it back. On such threads of family talk I followed my own recollection of the years from Jalco—the attack on Mazatlán, the captain of Acaponeta, the camp at El Nanchi and the arrival at Nogales on the flatcar.

Only when we ventured uptown did we feel like aliens in a foreign land. Within the *barrio* we heard Spanish on the streets and in the alleys. On the railroad tracks, in the canneries, and along the riverfront there were more Mexicans than any other nationality. And except for the foremen, the work talk was in our language. In the secondhand shops, where the *barrio* people sold and bought furniture and clothing, there were Mexican clerks who knew the Mexican ways of making a sale. Families doubled up in decaying houses, cramping themselves so they could rent an extra room to *chicano* boarders, who accented the brown quality of our Mexican *colonia*.

LENGTH: 1,200 WORDS

Vocabulary

barrio:	neighborhood
Se han fijado?:	Did you notice?
saludos:	greetings
zopilotes:	vultures, buzzards
un muchacho bien educado:	a well-bred young man
atenciones:	duties
respeto:	respect
vergüenza:	shame, embarrassment
jefe de familia:	head of the family
puro cedro:	pure cedar
Aquí se habla español:	Spanish spoken here
Librería Española:	Spanish bookshop
Genoveva de Brabante:	title of Spanish novel
rurales:	country people
chicano:	Mexican in the United States
colonia:	colony, settlement

3   Ernesto Galarza
Barrio Boy

SCORING: Reading time: _____ Rate from chart: _____ W.P.M.

RETENTION	number right _____ × 3 equals _____ points	
INFERENCES	number right _____ × 5 equals _____ points	
APPLICATION	number right _____ × 5 equals _____ points	
VOCABULARY	number right _____ × 2 equals _____ points	

(Total points: 100) **total** _____ points

RETENTION   Based on the selection, which of the following statements are True (T), False (F), or Not answerable (N)?

1. _____ The family still had rifle shells from the Mexican revolution.

2. _____ Ernesto was expected to ask permission to leave a room.

3. _____ Some Mexican families in the barrio were landlords.

4. _____ Ernesto felt at home in the barrio, but like an alien when he went uptown.

5. _____ Proper Mexicans did not roar when they laughed.

6. _____ Ernesto often wore his cap in the house and on the porch.

7. _____ Jalco did not have an especially large jail.

8. _____ Ernesto's mother enjoyed reading.

9. _____ Ernesto's family left Mexico because of a revolution.

10. _____ Ernesto ran errands for people other than his family.

INFERENCES   Which four of the following eight statements, based on the selection, are most probably true? _____, _____, _____, and _____

1. Ernesto's father worked in the canneries.
2. 418 L was the number of a building in the projects built by gringos.
3. Jalco is the Galarza's hometown in Mexico.
4. Ernesto had no interaction with gringos.
5. American schoolbooks pretty much ignored important Mexican heroes.

6. Ernesto's mother expected him to obey the rules even though he knew he would not be punished for breaking them.
7. Ernesto's mother seems to be the dominant figure in his family.
8. The *jefe de familia* was equivalent to the police chief.

APPLICATION   Choose the best answer for each question.

1. _____ Ernesto obviously:
   a. shared his family's values absolutely.
   b. rebelled against his family.
   c. admired some of the gringo style.
   d. thought his family was backward.

2. _____ Ernesto learned about the deeds of great Mexicans from:
   a. the other kids in the barrio.
   b. special classes in school.
   c. family conversations.
   d. his own reading.

3. _____ The language of the barrio was:
   a. used by everyone in the canneries.
   b. not the language Ernesto used in school.
   c. part English, part Spanish.
   d. that used by the gringos.

4. _____ If Ernesto were to laugh uproariously in his house:
   a. there would be sour looks.
   b. Ernesto's mother would be upset.
   c. he would be asked to leave his house forever.
   d. everyone else would laugh to put that person at ease.

5. _____ The manners of the Americans the Galarzas knew were:
   a. the ordinary manners all Americans have.
   b. those of the crass upper classes.
   c. quite like those of the Mexicans Ernesto had known.
   d. uncouth by Mexican standards.

6. _____ The Americans were thought to own the railroads, ships, stores, and breweries in Mexico because:
   a. they had worked hard for them and deserved them.
   b. they stole them with the aid of the Mexican president.
   c. nobody in Mexico could afford to own those things.
   d. that is the way the gringos always did things.

VOCABULARY Choose the best definition for each italic vocabulary entry.

1. _____ I felt a *vague* admiration for the way Mr. Brien could spit brown.
   a. intense
   b. annoying
   c. genuine
   d. uncertain

2. _____ He opened his mouth and *brayed* like a donkey.
   a. laughed
   b. cried
   c. sang
   d. honked

3. _____ I was never to fail in *respect* to grownups.
   a. concern
   b. attention
   c. responsibility
   d. high regard

4. _____ It was an *inflexible* rule.
   a. intentional
   b. unbreakable
   c. powerful
   d. firm

5. _____ *to keep a tight rein* over a family of my own
   a. hold back
   b. rule firmly
   c. establish authority
   d. suffer without revealing it

6. _____ a cedar box taken out to display our *heirlooms*
   a. precious family possessions
   b. items brought from the homeland
   c. most costly purchases
   d. things that identify us as families

7. _____ when our *mementos* were laid out on the bed
   a. gifts
   b. saludos
   c. reminders
   d. portraits

8. _____ The conversation turned to *anecdotes* that were funny or sad.
   a. jokes
   b. stories
   c. myths
   d. legends

9. _____ Only when we *ventured* uptown did we feel different.
   a. sauntered deliberately
   b. were taken against our will
   c. drove in a car
   d. took a chance on going

10. _____ The chicano boarders *accented* the brown quality of the Mexican colony.
    a. speak with a different way of pronouncing words
    b. intensified by way of contrast
    c. solidified and made whole
    d. made noticeable

4

GENE WELTFISH

The Winter Buffalo Hunt

The Pawnees were a Great Plains Indian tribe whose hunting patterns and rituals were age-old at the time of this description—the early nineteenth century. They roamed freely through their lands, following the methods that had always worked for them. They absorbed European innovations, such as horses, and learned to use them to their advantage.

For the second time within the year, the Pawnees would set out from their villages on the long journey to the buffalo hunting grounds. It was in early November and the trip lasted until the end of February or the beginning of March. This was the severest and most challenging period in the year's round. They traveled through slush and snow over hundreds of miles, braved the cold winds of the prairie plains, got their water by breaking through the ice of the river or by melting snow, and gathered their fuel from the scant supplies of timber along the streams.

The horses upon whom they depended for the chase and for transport suffered most of all, for they were unable to get food of their own. The buffaloes had small narrow feet and could push the snow aside to graze, but the horses' hooves were flat and broad and they were unable to get to the grass that lay under the cover of snow. Many of the horses died toward the end of the journey in January and February. It was hard to find enough food to give them, and the women had to gather the tenderer shoots and bark of the cottonwood for them to eat. At times they were compelled to feed them on corn.

Because of the cold, the women had to process their meat inside the tipi and often they would have to extend their working time beyond the short daylight

From *The Lost Universe: The Way of Life of the Pawnee*, Ballantine Books, 1965. Reprinted by permission of the author's estate.

hours, working by the light of the fire. They felt that, "At this time of year, things seemed to be pushing and pushing."

They moved over the land with the same order and precision as they had in summer, sending their messengers back and forth between the chiefs of the bands in order to coordinate their decisions, but their leave-taking of the villages was with less pageantry and pleasant anticipation. They knew it would be a hard and dangerous time.

The problem of the horses was especially acute and of major concern. From archaeology and written history we know that the Pawnees had acquired horses nearly two hundred years before this time. But apparently there were many essential techniques of horse care that they had not adopted from the European. For example, Lone Chief had only recently found out that they should store hay for their horses in the winter. There were no shoes for the horses. When a horse broke his hoof they tied on a "shoe" of hide.

If it snowed before they left the village or after they got back, the horses had to have special care. The young boys who took care of them in summer could not be utilized at this season for the purpose. Anyway, they were more interested in sliding on the ice. The women had to go a mile south to get whatever hay they could, and in the evening the horses were put in a corral near the lodge—a round structure of upright sticks with a gate that was closed across with five sticks. Inside there was a manger that was filled with hay when the horses were settled in for the night. They tried to economize on feed by taking them to graze at intervals during the day. In the morning, after being fed some more hay, they were taken from the corral to the bend of Beaver Creek where there was good grass. By noon they were brought back to the village and hobbled close by. Then toward evening, if snow were expected, they were again taken to Beaver Creek to graze in order to save the hay in the corral where they would have to be kept while it was snowing. If it got too cold, they would have to take the horses into the earth lodge and settle them near the wood pile. The long entrance passageway was quite large enough to accommodate them. While they were on the hunt, the horses had to be covered with an old tent skin during the night.

Some families tried to anticipate these problems by putting their horses in the best possible condition during the fall. Toward the end of September or the beginning of October, they would send them out to Grand Island for about six weeks under the care of a group of men and boys. On the island the horses could wander more or less freely, graze, rest, and water at will. Near the villages the grass was dry at this time, but here it was green and fresh and the horses would fatten. Allowed to run loose, they mated freely. No selective breeding was practiced. Some people had their horses gelded by one of the men who knew how. He tied up the horse and used certain medicines, tying up the wound with sticks which would fall off by themselves later. A buffalo robe and dry meat were paid for the operation. When he was about twelve, Otter was sent on such an expedition. He was told to take the mare, a colt, and a gray horse and join the others. They said to him, "If the Sioux overtake you, you must get on the gray horse and you will get away unless you are thrown off. Then, since you have no weapons, you will be killed." With this cheerful admonition, Otter set out about ten in the morning, taking half a sack of flour, some sugar, coffee, and baking powder as provisions. He went to the place on the Union Pacific Railroad known as Windmill and then across the sandhills on the north edge of the island, meeting the others at about two in the afternoon.

The men and boys had a good time of it on these expeditions. They built themselves dome-shaped grass houses, *kaharuut*, of big willow twigs. Their saddles served as pillows and the saddle blankets as bedding. If they wanted an especially soft bed, they put hay and willows underneath. The older men got up very early and looked around on the sandhills. Some of them cooked the bread and coffee that comprised their main diet. Otter had a cup and he shared a plate with another boy who had brought one along. Sometimes a white man having killed a beef, would give them a chunk of it. They had great times!

Considering their dependence on the horses, the Pawnees were remarkably unsentimental about them. They never called them by name, only referring to them in conversation by such names as Spotted Horse, Spotted Black Horse, Spotted Red Horse, Black Face Horse, White Hoof, Spotted on the Side, Black Nose, White Horse, Yellow Horse, Roan Horse, Red Head, High Forehead. There was no personal identification with them.

LENGTH: 1,125 WORDS

4   Gene Weltfish
The Winter Buffalo Hunt

SCORING: Reading time: _____ Rate from chart: _____ W.P.M.

RETENTION	number right _____ × 3 equals _____ points	
INFERENCES	number right _____ × 5 equals _____ points	
APPLICATION	number right _____ × 5 equals _____ points	
VOCABULARY	number right _____ × 2 equals _____ points	

(Total points: 100) **total** _____ points

RETENTION   Based on the selection, which of the following statements are True (T), False (F), or Not answerable (N)?

1. _____ The Sioux were the enemies of the Pawnees.

2. _____ Horses were free to roam on Grand Island.

3. _____ No one could teach the Pawnees how to care for their horses.

4. _____ The Pawnees hunted the buffalo only during the winter.

5. _____ While on the hunt, the horses were fed both hay and grass.

6. _____ The land along the streams on the prairies was heavily timbered.

7. _____ Each of the Pawnees had a personal relationship with a horse.

8. _____ The women often had to feed the horses while on the hunt.

9. _____ Indian boys and Indian women were equally responsible for the welfare of the horses during the winter hunt.

10. _____ Because of their special skill, Indians did not need to shoe their horses.

INFERENCES   Which four of the following eight statements, based on the selection, are most probably true? _____, _____, _____, and _____

1. The winter hunt was a highly coordinated event that required considerable organizational skills.
2. The Sioux were as interested in buffalo hunting as were the Pawnees.

3. The Pawnees described here were not in contact with Europeans.
4. The Pawnees built a fairly large earth lodge for use while on the hunt.
5. Grand Island represented a pleasant excursion, almost a party atmosphere.
6. Buffalo had an almost impossible time foraging in winter snow.
7. The Pawnees brought their houses with them when they hunted.
8. The Pawnees got their horses from the Europeans, but they had to learn how to maintain them on their own.

APPLICATION   Choose the best answer for each question.

1. _____ The winter buffalo hunt was the most challenging event of the year because:
   a. the Pawnees were weakened by hunger at this time.
   b. the buffalo herds were dwindling in size at this time.
   c. weather conditions made traveling very difficult.
   d. no one really understood the migration pattern of buffalo.

2. _____ Because of the shape of their feet, the buffalo:
   a. could run faster on the prairie than a horse could.
   b. intrigued the Pawnees, who felt they were related to a god.
   c. were more quickly satisfied when searching for grass in the snow.
   d. made life even more difficult for the Pawnees when they were on the trail.

3. _____ Apparently, when the Pawnees left their villages, their practice was:
   a. to engage in a kind of pageantry and celebration.
   b. never to incur the wrath of the gods by making their horses labor.
   c. to pretend to leave, then return for a day, then really leave.
   d. sometimes to have a complex corn ceremony with sacred music.

4. _____ While on the hunt, the Pawnees were economically minded enough to:
   a. ask for pay from the railroad workers.
   b. sense the inequities that existed between Sioux tribesmen and themselves.
   c. try to save food by having the horses forage for grass.
   d. sell the belongings they did not need on the hunt.

5. _____ The reference to the buffalo robe and dry meat paid for the gelding operation implies:
   a. that Indian doctors were rich.
   b. a special attitude toward those who have unusual skills.
   c. that the barter system was invented before money.
   d. that the Pawnees understood the concept of financial exchange.

6. _____ The fact that some families fattened their horses during the fall months means that:
   a. they were able to foresee the dangers they would face on the hunt.
   b. they were wealthier than their neighbors and could afford better horses.
   c. left alone, horses would not fatten.
   d. the tribal policy was being carried out to the letter.

VOCABULARY   Choose the best definition for each italic vocabulary entry.

1. _____ The entranceway was large enough to *accommodate* them.
   a. establish
   b. support
   c. fit
   d. make them feel at ease

2. _____ Families tried to *anticipate* the problems.
   a. sense later
   b. solve now
   c. perceive as much as possible
   d. look ahead to

3. _____ No selective *breeding* was practiced.
   a. choosing
   b. mating
   c. bedding
   d. nursing

4. _____ Some people had their horses *gelded* by one of the men.
   a. sexually sterilized
   b. hobbled
   c. artificially bred to a mare
   d. chosen for mating

5. _____ With a cheerful *admonition*, Otter set out to Grand Island.
   a. warning
   b. greeting
   c. anecdote
   d. weapon and cartridges

6. _____ Otter took sugar, flour, coffee, and baking powder as *provisions*.
   a. stuff for barter
   b. trading gear
   c. food
   d. preparations

7. _____ The Pawnees were *unsentimental* about their horses.
   a. incurious
   b. not concerned
   c. generally happy
   d. not emotional

8. _____ They gathered their fuel from the *scant* supplies of timber along the streams.
   a. inadequate
   b. slight
   c. generous
   d. unlimited

9. _____ The problem of the horses was especially *acute* and of major concern.
   a. severe
   b. painful
   c. noticeable
   d. observed

10. _____ By noon the horses were returned and *hobbled* nearby.
   a. housed
   b. cared for
   c. fed
   d. tethered

5

HELEN KELLER

The Most Important Day

Helen Keller has been an inspiration to generations of people worldwide. Although born normal, she was struck blind and deaf at the age of eighteen months. The problem of educating—virtually civilizing—her became insurmountable because in 1880, when she was born, there were no systems for educating deaf children. Anne Sullivan, however, was introduced to Helen Keller as her teacher and eventually became world famous for devising means by which to teach Helen, obviously a brilliant girl, to read and write.

The most important day I remember in all my life is the one on which my teacher, Anne Mansfield Sullivan, came to me. I am filled with wonder when I consider the immeasurable contrast between the two lives which it connects. It was the third of March, 1887, three months before I was seven years old.

On the afternoon of that eventful day, I stood on the porch, dumb, expectant. I guessed vaguely from my mother's signs and from the hurrying to and fro in the house that something unusual was about to happen, so I went to the door and waited on the steps. The afternoon sun penetrated the mass of honeysuckle that covered the porch and fell on my upturned face. My fingers lingered almost unconsciously on the familiar leaves and blossoms which had just come forth to greet the sweet southern spring. I did not know what the future held of marvel or surprise for me. Anger and bitterness had preyed upon me continually for weeks and a deep languor had succeeded this passionate struggle.

Have you ever been at sea in a dense fog, when it seemed as if a tangible white darkness shut you in, and the great ship, tense and anxious, groped her way

From Helen Keller's autobiography, *The Story of My Life* (1902).

toward the shore with plummet and sounding-line, and you waited with beating heart for something to happen? I was like that ship before my education began, only I was without compass or sounding-line, and had no way of knowing how near the harbor was. "Light! give me light!" was the wordless cry of my soul, and the light of love shone on me in that very hour.

I felt approaching footsteps. I stretched out my hand as I supposed to my mother. Someone took it, and I was caught up and held close in the arms of her who had come to reveal all things to me, and, more than all things else, to love me.

The morning after my teacher came she led me into her room and gave me a doll. The little blind children at the Perkins Institution had sent it and Laura Bridgman had dressed it; but I did not know this until afterward. When I had played with it a little while, Miss Sullivan slowly spelled into my hand the word "d-o-l-l." I was at once interested in this finger play and tried to imitate it. When I finally succeeded in making the letters correctly I was flushed with childish pleasure and pride. Running downstairs to my mother I held up my hand and made the letters for doll. I did not know that I was spelling a word or even that words existed; I was simply making my fingers go in monkeylike imitation. In the days that followed I learned to spell in this uncomprehending way a great many words, among them *pin*, *hat*, *cup* and a few verbs like *sit*, *stand* and *walk*. But my teacher had been with me several weeks before I understood that everything has a name.

One day, while I was playing with my new doll, Miss Sullivan put my big rag doll into my lap also, spelled "d-o-l-l" and tried to make me understand that "d-o-l-l" applied to both. Earlier in the day we had had a tussle over the words "m-u-g" and "w-a-t-e-r." Miss Sullivan had tried to impress it upon me that "m-u-g" is *mug* and that "w-a-t-e-r" is *water*, but I persisted in confounding the two. In despair she had dropped the subject for the time, only to renew it at the first opportunity. I became impatient at her repeated attempts and, seizing the new doll, I dashed it upon the floor. I was keenly delighted when I felt the fragments of the broken doll at my feet. Neither sorrow nor regret followed my passionate outburst. I had not loved the doll. In the still, dark world in which I lived there was no strong sentiment or tenderness. I felt my teacher sweep the fragments to one side of the hearth, and I had a sense of satisfaction that the cause of my discomfort was removed. She brought me my hat, and I knew I was going out into the warm sunshine. This thought, if a wordless sensation may be called a thought, made me hop and skip with pleasure.

We walked down the path to the well-house, attracted by the fragrance of the honeysuckle with which it was covered. Someone was drawing water and my teacher placed my hand under the spout. As the cool stream gushed over one hand she spelled into the other the word *water*, first slowly, then rapidly. I stood still, my whole attention fixed upon the motions of her fingers. Suddenly I felt a misty consciousness as of something forgotten—a thrill of returning thought;

and somehow the mystery of language was revealed to me. I knew then that "w-a-t-e-r" meant the wonderful cool something that was flowing over my hand. The living word awakened my soul, gave it light, hope, joy, set it free! There were barriers still, it is true, but barriers that could in time be swept away.

I left the well-house eager to learn. Everything had a name, and each name gave birth to a new thought. As we returned to the house every object which I touched seemed to quiver with life. That was because I saw everything with the strange, new sight that had come to me. On entering the door I remembered the doll I had broken. I felt my way to the hearth and picked up the pieces. I tried vainly to put them together. Then my eyes filled with tears; for I realized what I had done, and for the first time I felt repentance and sorrow.

I learned a great many new words that day. I do not remember what they all were; but I do know that *mother, father, sister, teacher* were among them — words that were to make the world blossom for me, "like Aaron's rod, with flowers." It would have been difficult to find a happier child than I was as I lay in my crib at the close of that eventful day and lived over the joys it had brought me, and for the first time longed for a new day to come.

LENGTH: 1,063 WORDS

Name _____ Class _____ Date _____

5   Helen Keller
The Most Important Day

SCORING: Reading time: _____ Rate from chart: _____ W.P.M.	

RETENTION	number right _____ × 3 equals _____ points	
INFERENCES	number right _____ × 5 equals _____ points	
APPLICATION	number right _____ × 5 equals _____ points	
VOCABULARY	number right _____ × 2 equals _____ points	

(Total points: 100) **total** _____ points

RETENTION   Based on the selection, which of the following statements are True (T), False (F), or Not answerable (N)?

1. _____ Helen broke her new doll when she became impatient with Anne Sullivan.

2. _____ The day that Helen describes took place in the heart of summer.

3. _____ Anne Sullivan was a loving teacher.

4. _____ Helen felt her soul was set free by the understanding of a word.

5. _____ Before she met Anne Sullivan, Helen could be aware of household activity through her senses of touch and smell.

6. _____ Helen seems to have been in an urban setting.

7. _____ Helen had a hard time distinguishing between a container and what it contained.

8. _____ Helen had not loved her doll because she had not understood tenderness or sentiment.

9. _____ Anne Sullivan eventually repaired the broken doll.

10. _____ When Helen went out, she went with a hat.

INFERENCES   Which four of the following eight statements, based on the selection, are most probably true? _____, _____, _____, and _____

1. When Helen met Anne Sullivan she did not expect her to be a teacher.
2. Most people would have reacted the way Helen did.

3. After learning the difference between *water* and *mug*, Helen was excited about the idea of learning.
4. Helen's mother was a good teacher, but did not understand language to the extent that Anne Sullivan did.
5. Before meeting Anne Sullivan, Helen was depressed and unenthusiastic.
6. Helen was, as a child, an avid sailor, interested in boats.
7. The point of this piece is that we all need an Anne Sullivan.
8. As soon as she learned a word, she wanted to go and teach it to someone else.

APPLICATION   Choose the best answer for each question.

1. _____ The fact that Helen sensed expectation from the signs of family activity means that:
   a. few things ever happened of interest in the family.
   b. it must have been a political event.
   c. Helen could learn without knowing the words for things.
   d. language is the door one opens.

2. _____ Helen questioned if some sensations were thoughts:
   a. until she met Anne Sullivan.
   b. because she did not know what a thought was.
   c. because people had challenged her on that point.
   d. because they are wordless.

3. _____ Helen began to learn letters by:
   a. intuition.
   b. imitation.
   c. individuation.
   d. illumination.

4. _____ Helen as a child took special pleasure in:
   a. thinking about the stars.
   b. spelling unusually long words.
   c. making letters correctly.
   d. bathing herself in sunshine.

5. _____ Anne Sullivan helped communicate to Helen:
   a. an overwhelming desire to excell.
   b. the excitement and satisfaction of learning.
   c. the meaning of intellectual stimulation.
   d. something about the meaning of life.

6. _____ After learning the word for water, Helen reflected on the broken doll and felt:
   a. repentance and sorrow for the first time.

b. relaxation and pleasure.

c. an agony of guilt.

d. a surprising sense of satisfaction.

VOCABULARY   Choose the best definition for each italic vocabulary entry.

1. _____ I am filled with *wonder*.
    a. hope
    b. questions
    c. curiosity
    d. surprise

2. _____ when I consider the *immeasurable* contrast between the two lives
    a. limitless
    b. grand
    c. lengthy
    d. immoderate

3. _____ I stood on the porch, *dumb*, expectant.
    a. silent
    b. moronic
    c. sullen
    d. in anticipation

4. _____ Anger and bitterness had *preyed* on me.
    a. stood forcefully
    b. waited painfully
    c. hovered tensely
    d. weighed heavily

5. _____ A deep *languor* had succeeded my anger and bitterness.
    a. depression
    b. vilification
    c. danger
    d. sorrow

6. _____ when it seemed as if a *tangible* white darkness shut you in
    a. impeachable
    b. simple
    c. solid, touchable
    d. contradictory, paradoxical

7. _____ I learned to spell in an *uncomprehending* way.
    a. without understanding
    b. insensitively
    c. with no enthusiasm
    d. with feeling, but not sense

8. _____ attracted by the *fragrance* of honeysuckle
   a. stink
   b. perfume
   c. profusion
   d. amount

9. _____ Every object I touched seemed to *quiver* with life.
   a. stir
   b. seethe
   c. breathe
   d. explode

10. _____ words that were to make the world *blossom* for me
    a. spread
    b. flush
    c. constrict
    d. open up

6

BARRY LOPEZ

My Horse

Barry Lopez is a writer and photographer
who has lived for some time in Oregon and
the American West. He has spent time with
wolves and other wildlife and is a student of
the American Indian. His discussion of his
truck has a tender quality. It is equivalent in
his life to what the horse was for the Indian.
He has a sense of attachment to it, a sense
of it possessing a heart and spirit.

It is curious that Indian warriors on the northern plains in the
nineteenth century, who were almost entirely dependent on the horse for mobility and status, never gave their horses names. If you borrowed a man's horse and
went off raiding for other horses, however, or if you lost your mount in battle
and then jumped on mine and counted coup on an enemy—well, those horses
would have to be shared with the man whose horse you borrowed, and that
coup would be mine, not yours. Because even if I gave him no name, he was
my horse.

If you were a Crow warrior and I a young Teton Sioux out after a warrior's
identity and we came over a small hill somewhere in the Montana prairie and
surprised each other, I could tell a lot about you by looking at your horse.

Your horse might have feathers tied in his mane, or in his tail, or a medicine
bag tied around his neck. If I knew enough about the Crow, and had looked at
you closely, I might make some sense of the decoration, even guess who you were
if you were well-known. If you had painted your horse I could tell even more,
because we both decorated our horses with signs that meant the same things.
Your white handprints high on his flanks would tell me you had killed an enemy
in a hand-to-hand fight. Small horizontal lines stacked on your horse's foreleg,
or across his nose, would tell me how many times you had counted coup. Horse
hoof marks on your horse's rump, or three-sided boxes, would tell me how many
times you had stolen horses. If there was a bright red square on your horse's neck

I would know you were leading a war party and that there were probably others out there in the coulees behind you.

You might be painted all over as blue as the sky and covered with white dots, with your horse painted the same way. Maybe hailstorms were your power—or if I chased you a hailstorm might come down and hide you. There might be lightning bolts on the horse's legs and flanks, and I would wonder if you had lightning power, or a slow horse. There might be white circles around your horse's eyes to help him see better.

Or you might be like Crazy Horse, with no decoration, no marks on your horse to tell me anything, only a small lightning bolt on your cheek, a piece of turquoise tied behind your ear.

You might have scalps dangling from your rein.

I could tell something about you by your horse. All this would come to me in a few seconds. I might decide this was my moment and shout my war cry—*Hoka hey!* Or I might decide you were like the grizzly bear: I would raise my weapon to you in salute and go my way, to see you again when I was older.

I do not own a horse. I am attached to a truck, however, and I have come to think of it in a similar way. It has no name; it never occurred to me to give it a name. It has little decoration; neither of us is partial to decoration. I have a piece of turquoise in the truck because I had heard once that some of the southwestern tribes tied a small piece of turquoise in a horse's hock to keep him from stumbling. I like the idea. I also hang sage in the truck when I go on a long trip. But inside, the truck doesn't look much different from others that look just like it on the outside. I like it that way. Because I like my privacy.

For two years in Wyoming I worked on a ranch wrangling horses. The horse I rode when I had to have a good horse was a quarter horse and his name was Coke High. The name came with him. At first I thought he'd been named for the soft drink. I'd known stranger names given to horses by whites. Years later I wondered if some deviate Wyoming cowboy wise to cocaine had not named him. Now I think he was probably named after a rancher, an historical figure of the region. I never asked the people who owned him for fear of spoiling the spirit of my inquiry.

We were running over a hundred horses on this ranch. They all had names. After a few weeks I knew all the horses and the names too. You had to. No one knew how to talk about the animals or put them in order or tell the wranglers what to do unless they were using the names — Princess, Big Red, Shoshone, Clay.

My truck is named Dodge. The name came with it. I don't know if it was named after the town or the verb or the man who invented it. I like it for a name. Perfectly anonymous, like Red for a dog, or Old Paint. You can't tell anything with a name like that.

The truck is a van. I call it a truck because it's not a car and because "van" is a suburban sort of consumer word, like "oxford loafer," and I don't like the sound of it. On the outside it looks like any other Dodge Sportsman 300. It's a dirty tan color. There are a few body dents, but it's never been in a wreck. I tore the antenna off against a tree on a pinched mountain road. A boy in Midland, Texas, rocked one of my rear view mirrors off. A logging truck in Oregon squeeze-fired a piece of debris off the road and shattered my windshield. The oil pan and gas tank are pug-faced from high-centering on bad roads. (I remember a horse I rode for a while named Targhee whose hocks were scarred from tangles in barbed wire when he was a colt and who spooked a lot in high grass, but these were not like "dents." They were more like bad tires.)

I like to travel. I go mostly in the winter and mostly on two-lane roads. I've driven the truck from Key West to Vancouver, British Columbia, and from Yuma to Long Island over the past four years. I used to ride Coke High only about five miles every morning when we were rounding up horses. Hard miles of twisting and turning. About six hundred miles a year. Then I'd turn him out and ride another horse for the rest of the day. That's what was nice about having a remuda. You could do all you had to do and not take it all out on your best horse. Three car family.

My truck came with a lot of seats in it and I've never really known what to do with them. Sometimes I put the seats in and go somewhere with a lot of people, but most of the time I leave them out. I like riding around with that empty cavern of space behind my head. I know it's something with a history to it, that there's truth in it, because I always rode a horse the same way—with empty saddle bags. In case I found something. The possibility of finding something is half the reason for being on the road.

The value of anything comes to me in its use. If I am not using something it is of no value to me and I give it away. I wasn't always that way. I used to keep everything I owned—just in case. I feel good about the truck because it gets used. A lot. To haul hay and firewood and lumber and rocks and garbage and animals. Other people have used it to haul furniture and freezers and dirt and recycled newspapers. And to move from one house to another. When I lend it for things like that I don't look to get anything back but some gas (if we're going to be friends). But if you go way out in the country to a dump and pick up the things you can still find out there (once a load of cedar shingles we sold for $175 to an architect) I expect you to leave some of those things around my place when you come back—if I need them.

When I think back, maybe the nicest thing I ever put in that truck was timber wolves. It was a long night's drive from Oregon up into British Columbia. We were all very quiet about it; it was like moving clouds across the desert.

Sometimes something won't fit in the truck and I think about improving it—building a different door system, for example. I am forever going to add better gauges on the dash and a pair of driving lamps and a sunroof, but I never get around to doing any of it. I remember I wanted to improve Coke High once too, especially the way he bolted like a greyhound through patches of cottonwood on a river flat. But all I could do with him was to try to rein him out of it. Or hug his back.

Sometimes, road-stoned in a blur of country like southwestern Wyoming or North Dakota, I talk to the truck. It's like wandering on the high plains under a summer sun, on plains where, George Catlin wrote, you were "out of sight of land." I say what I am thinking out loud, or point at things along the road. It's a crazy, sun-stroked sort of activity, a sure sign it's time to pull over, to go for a walk, to make a fire and have some tea, to lie in the shade of the truck.

I've always wanted to pat the truck. It's basic to the relationship. But it never works.

I remember when I was on the ranch, just at sunrise, after I'd saddled Coke High, I'd be huddled down in my jacket smoking a cigarette and looking down into the valley, along the river where the other horses had spent the night. I'd turn to Coke and run my hand down his neck and slap-pat him on the shoulder to say I was coming up. It made a bond, an agreement we started the day with.

I've thought about that a lot with the truck, because we've gone out together at sunrise on so many mornings. I've even fumbled around trying to do it. But metal won't give.

The truck's personality is mostly an expression of two ideas: "with-you" and "alone." When Coke High was "with-you" he and I were the same animal. We could have cut a rooster out of a flock of chickens, we were so in tune. It's the same with the truck: rolling through Kentucky on a hilly two-lane road, three in the morning under a full moon and no traffic. Picture it. You roll like water.

There are other times when you are with each other but there's no connection at all. Coke got that way when he was bored and we'd fight each other about which way to go around a tree. When the truck gets like that—"alone"—it's because it feels its Detroit fat-ass design dragging at its heart and making a fool out of it.

I can think back over more than a hundred nights I've slept in the truck, sat in it with a lamp burning, bundled up in a parka, reading a book. It was always comfortable. A good place to wait out a storm. Like sleeping inside a buffalo.

The truck will go past 100,000 miles soon. I'll rebuild the engine and put a different transmission in it. I can tell from magazine advertisements that I'll never get another one like it. Because every year they take more of the heart out of them. One thing that makes a farmer or a rancher go sour is a truck that isn't worth a shit. The reason you see so many old pickups in ranch country is because these are the only ones with any heart. You can count on them. The weekend rancher runs around in a new pickup with too much engine and not enough transmission and with the wrong sort of tires because he can afford anything, even the worst. A lot of them have names for their pickups too.

My truck has broken down, in out of the way places at the worst of times. I've walked away and screamed the foulness out of my system and gotten the tools out. I had to fix a water pump in a blizzard in the Panamint Mountains in California once. It took all day with the Coleman stove burning under the engine block to keep my hands from freezing. We drifted into Beatty, Nevada, that night with it jury-rigged together with—I swear—baling wire, and we were melting snow as we went and pouring it in to compensate for the leaks.

There is a dent next to the door on the driver's side I put there one sweltering night in Miami. I had gone to the airport to meet my wife, whom I hadn't seen in a month. My hands were so swollen with poison ivy blisters I had to drive with my wrists. I had shut the door and was locking it when the window fell off its runners and slid down inside the door. I couldn't leave the truck unlocked because I had too much inside I didn't want to lose. So I just kicked the truck a blow in the side and went to work on the window. I hate to admit kicking the truck. It's like kicking a dog, which I've never done.

Coke High and I had an accident once. We hit a badger hole at a full gallop. I landed on my back and blacked out. When I came to, Coke High was about a hundred yards away. He stayed a hundred yards away for six miles, all the way back to the ranch.

I want to tell you about carrying those wolves, because it was a fine thing. There were ten of them. We had four in the truck with us in crates and six in a trailer. It was a five hundred mile trip. We went at night for the cool air and because there wouldn't be as much traffic. I could feel from the way the truck rolled along that its heart was in the trip. It liked the wolves inside it, the sweet odor that came from the crates. I could feel that same tireless wolf-lope developing in its wheels; it was like you might never have to stop for gas, ever again.

The truck gets very self-focused when it works like this; its heart is strong and it's good to be around it. It's good to be *with* it. You get the same feeling when you pull someone out of a ditch. Coke High and I pulled a Volkswagen out of the mud once, but Coke didn't like doing it very much. Speed, not strength, was his center. When the guy who owned the car thanked us and tried to pat Coke, the horse snorted and swung away, trying to preserve his distance, which is something a horse spends a lot of time on.

So does the truck.

Being distant lets the truck get its heart up. The truck has been cold and alone in Montana at 38 below zero. It's climbed horrible, eroded roads in Idaho. It's been burdened beyond overloading, and made it anyway. I've asked it to do these things because they build heart, and without heart all you have is a machine. You have nothing. I don't think people in Detroit know anything at all about heart. That's why everything they build dies so young.

One time in Arizona the truck and I came through one of the worst storms I've ever been in, an outrageous, angry blizzard. But we went down the road, right through it. You couldn't explain our getting through by the sort of tires I had on the truck, or the fact that I had chains on, or was a good driver, or had a lot of weight over my drive wheels or a good engine, because it was more than this. It was a contest between the truck and the blizzard—and the truck wouldn't quit. I could have gone to sleep and the truck would have just torn a road down Interstate 40 on its own. It scared the hell out of me; but it gave me heart, too.

We came off the Mogollon Rim that night and out of the storm and headed south for Phoenix. I pulled off the road to sleep for a few hours, but before I did I got out of the truck. It was raining. Warm rain. I tied a short piece of red avalanche cord into the grill. I left it there for a long time, like an eagle feather on a horse's tail. It flapped and spun in the wind. I could hear it ticking against the grill when I drove.

When I have to leave that truck I will just raise up my left arm—*Hoka hey!*—and walk away.

LENGTH: 2,916 WORDS

6   Barry Lopez
My Horse

SCORING: Reading time: _____ Rate from chart: _____ W.P.M.

RETENTION	number right ____ × 3 equals ____ points
INFERENCES	number right ____ × 5 equals ____ points
APPLICATION	number right ____ × 5 equals ____ points
VOCABULARY	number right ____ × 2 equals ____ points

(Total points: 100) **total** ____ points

RETENTION   Based on the selection, which of the following statements are True (T), False (F), or Not answerable (N)?

1. _____ One of the most important reasons for going on the road is the chance of finding something.

2. _____ Lopez is looking forward to getting a good new truck.

3. _____ All Indians decorated their horses.

4. _____ One way for an Indian to own a horse was to name it.

5. _____ After being thrown by the badger hole, Lopez had to ride Coke High very slowly back to camp.

6. _____ Coke High was fast, but not especially strong.

7. _____ Lopez may have owned a ranch, but he never worked on one.

8. _____ Decorations on an Indian's horse provided important information.

9. _____ His cargo of timber wolves was the most chilling thing he ever put in his truck.

10. _____ The supposed power of turquoise was to keep an animal from starving.

INFERENCES   Which four of the following eight statements, based on the selection, are most probably true? _____, _____, _____, and _____

1. Lopez sees many similarities between his Dodge and Coke High.

2. Lopez's next truck will probably be a foreign pickup.
3. A good understanding of mechanics helps keep one's relationship to a truck healthy.
4. Ranchers had to name horses to keep them straight in their minds.
5. Each dent on Lopez's truck seems to trigger the memory of an incident.
6. Wolves depend on trucks for reaching their mating territories in the far north.
7. Indians counted coup in order to have more decorations put on their horses.
8. If Lopez were not such a private man, he would not have so many stories to tell.

APPLICATION   Choose the best answer for each question.

1. _____ Decorations on Indian horses:
   a. meant the same thing to different Indians.
   b. were unique.
   c. implied nothing more than a separate tribal identity.
   d. were like the painting on the side of Lopez's Dodge.

2. _____ Lopez says there are many old pickups in ranch country:
   a. several times.
   b. although he knows there are more sedans.
   c. because the new ones don't have any heart.
   d. partly because the ranchers have been having a hard time of it.

3. _____ The weekend rancher:
   a. rides around in a new pickup which often has a name.
   b. does not know the names of all his horses.
   c. avoids conversations with the wranglers.
   d. is a suburban phenomenon.

4. _____ Despite his attachment to Coke High, Lopez:
   a. prefers a good pickup.
   b. knows how stressed the poor horse was.
   c. would not decorate him the way other ranchers did.
   d. does not own a horse.

5. _____ One thing basic to a relationship with a horse is:
   a. mutual trust.
   b. mutual admiration.
   c. a healthy distance.
   d. a friendly pat.

6. _____ Lopez sees the value of something in its:
   a. use.
   b. capacity to be admired.

c. heart.

d. honesty.

VOCABULARY   Choose the best definition for each italic vocabulary entry.

1. _____ Indians were dependent on the horse for *mobility* and status.
   a. position
   b. a place in the hierarchy
   c. capacity to get around
   d. the ability to feed themselves

2. _____ a horse with a piece of *turquoise* tied to its hock
   a. blue color
   b. precious metal
   c. semiprecious stone
   d. jewelry

3. _____ Neither of us is *partial* to decoration.
   a. familiar with
   b. struck by
   c. alarmed by
   d. fond of

4. _____ I wondered if a *deviate* Wyoming farmer named him after cocaine.
   a. abnormal
   b. ordinary
   c. disturbed
   d. junky

5. _____ I never asked for fear of spoiling the spirit of my *inquiry*.
   a. purposes
   b. investigation
   c. occupation
   d. interrogation

6. _____ My truck is named Dodge. Perfectly *anonymous*.
   a. appropriate
   b. inebriated
   c. extraordinary
   d. no-name

7. _____ a colt who *spooked* a lot in high grass
   a. leaped
   b. became frightened
   c. was high-spirited
   d. took off

8. _____ It's a crazy, *sun-stroked* idea.
   a. feverish
   b. bright
   c. ludicrous
   d. lunatic

9. _____ The slap-pat on the horse's shoulder made a *bond* we started the day with.
   a. an agreement
   b. an investment
   c. a purposefulness
   d. a plan

10. _____ We drifted into Nevada with the water pump *jury-rigged* together.
   a. not working
   b. fixed for the time being
   c. perfect
   d. leaking like a sieve

Readings in Sociology, Science, Religion, and History

7

MARGARET MEAD
RHODA METRAUX

On Friendship

All of us have, or want to have, friends,
but making them is not always easy. The
situation is complicated further when the
people who are trying to make friends come
from different countries, facing the barriers
of different languages and customs. In this
essay, two renowned anthropologists explore
this special problem.

Few Americans stay put for a lifetime. We move from town to city to
suburb, from high school to college in a different state, from a job in one region
to a better job elsewhere, from the home where we raise our children to the home
where we plan to live in retirement. With each move we are forever making new
friends, who become part of our new life at that time.

For many of us the summer is a special time for forming new friendships.
Today millions of Americans vacation abroad, and they go not only to see new
sights but also—in those places where they do not feel too strange—with the
hope of meeting new people. No one really expects a vacation trip to produce a
close friend. But surely the beginning of a friendship is possible? Surely in every
country people value friendship?

They do. The difficulty when strangers from two countries meet is not a lack
of appreciation of friendship, but different expectations about what constitutes
friendship and how it comes into being. In those European countries that
Americans are most likely to visit, friendship is quite sharply distinguished from
other, more casual relations, and is differently related to family life. For a
Frenchman, a German or an Englishman friendship is usually more particular-
ized and carries a heavier burden of commitment.

But as we use the word, "friend" can be applied to a wide range of relationships—to someone one has known for a few weeks in a new place, to a close business associate, to a childhood playmate, to a man or woman, to a trusted confidant. There are real differences among these relations for Americans—a friendship may be superficial, casual, situational or deep and enduring. But to a European, who sees only our surface behavior, the differences are not clear.

As they see it, people known and accepted temporarily, casually, flow in and out of Americans' homes with little ceremony and often with little personal commitment. They may be parents of the children's friends, house guests of neighbors, members of a committee, business associates from another town or even another country. Coming as a guest into an American home, the European visitor finds no visible landmarks. The atmosphere is relaxed. Most people, old and young, are called by first names.

Who, then, is a friend?

Even simple translation from one language to another is difficult. "You see," a Frenchman explains, "if I were to say to you in France, 'This is my good friend,' that person would not be as close to me as someone about whom I said only, 'This is my friend.' Anyone about whom I have to say *more* is really less."

In France, as in many European countries, friends generally are of the same sex, and friendship is seen as basically a relationship between men. Frenchwomen laugh at the idea that "women can't be friends," but they also admit sometimes that for women "it's a different thing." And many French people doubt the possibility of a friendship between a man and a woman. There is also the kind of relationship within a group—men and women who have worked together for a long time, who may be very close, sharing great loyalty and warmth of feeling. They may call one another *copains*—a word that in English becomes "friends" but has more the feeling of "pals" or "buddies." In French eyes this is not friendship, although two members of such a group may well be friends.

For the French, friendship is a one-to-one relationship that demands a keen awareness of the other person's intellect, temperament and particular interests. A friend is someone who draws out your own best qualities, with whom you sparkle and become more of whatever the friendship draws upon. Your political philosophy assumes more depth, appreciation of a play becomes sharper, taste in food or wine is accentuated, enjoyment of a sport is intensified.

And French friendships are compartmentalized. A man may play chess with a friend for thirty years without knowing his political opinions, or he may talk politics with him for as long a time without knowing about his personal life. Different friends fill different niches in each person's life. These friendships are not made part of family life. A friend is not expected to spend evenings being nice to children or courteous to a deaf grandmother. These duties, also serious and enjoined, are primarily for relatives. Men who are friends may meet in a café. Intellectual friends may meet in larger groups for evenings of conversation.

Working people may meet at the little *bistro* where they drink and talk, far from the family. Marriage does not affect such friendships; wives do not have to be taken into account.

In the past in France, friendships of this kind seldom were open to any but intellectual women. Since most women's lives centered on their homes, their warmest relations with other women often went back to their girlhood. The special relationship of friendship is based on what the French value most—on the mind, on compatibility of outlook, on vivid awareness of some chosen area of life.

Friendship heightens the sense of each person's individuality. Other relationships commanding as great loyalty and devotion have a different meaning. In World War II the first resistance groups formed in Paris were built on the foundation of *les copains*. But significantly, as time went on these little groups, whose lives rested in one another's hands, called themselves "families." Where each had a total responsibility for all, it was kinship ties that provided the model. And even today such ties, crossing every line of class and personal interest, remain binding on the survivors of these small, secret bands.

In Germany, in contrast with France, friendship is much more articulately a matter of feeling. Adolescents, boys and girls, form deeply sentimental attachments, walk and talk together—not so much to polish their wits as to share their hopes and fears and dreams, to form a common front against the world of school and family and to join in a kind of mutual discovery of each other's and their own inner life. Within the family, the closest relationship over a lifetime is between brothers and sisters. Outside the family, men and women find in their closest friends of the same sex the devotion of a sister, the loyalty of a brother. Appropriately, in Germany friends usually are brought into the family. Children call their father's and their mother's friends "uncle" and "aunt." Between French friends, who have chosen each other for the congeniality of their point of view, lively disagreement and sharpness of argument are the breath of life. But for Germans, whose friendships are based on mutuality of feeling, deep disagreement on any subject that matters to both is regarded as a tragedy. Like ties of kinship, ties of friendship are meant to be irrevocably binding. Young Germans who come to the United States have great difficulty in establishing such friendships with Americans. We view friendship more tentatively, subject to changes in intensity as people move, change their jobs, marry, or discover new interests.

English friendships follow still a different pattern. Their basis is shared activity. Activities at different stages of life may be of very different kinds — discovering a common interest in school, serving together in the armed forces, taking part in a foreign mission, staying in the same country house during a crisis. In the midst of the activity, whatever it may be, people fall into step — sometimes two men or two women, sometimes two couples, sometimes three people — and find that they walk or play a game or tell stories or serve on a tiresome and exacting committee with the same easy anticipation of what each will do day by day or in some critical situation. Americans who have made English friends comment that, even years later, "you can take up just where you left off." Meeting after a long interval, friends are like a couple who began to dance again when the orchestra strikes up after a pause. English friendships are formed outside the family circle, but they are not, as in Germany, contrapuntal to the family nor are they, as in France, separated from the family. And a break in an English friendship comes not necessarily as a result of some irreconcilable difference of viewpoint or feeling but instead as a result of misjudgment, where one friend seriously misjudges how the other will think or feel or act, so that suddenly they are out of step.

What, then, is friendship? Looking at these different styles, including our own, each of which is related to a whole way of life, are there common elements? There is the recognition that friendship, in contrast with kinship, invokes freedom of choice. A friend is someone who chooses and is chosen. Related to this is the sense each friend gives the other of being a special individual, on whatever grounds this recognition is based. And between friends there is inevitably a kind of equality of give-and-take. These similarities make the bridge between societies possible, and the American's characteristic openness to different styles of relationship makes it possible for him to find new friends abroad with whom he feels at home.

LENGTH: 1,555 WORDS

7   Margaret Mead and Rhoda Metraux
On Friendship

SCORING: Reading time: _____ Rate from chart: _____ W.P.M.

RETENTION	number right _____ × 3 equals _____ points	
INFERENCES	number right _____ × 5 equals _____ points	
APPLICATION	number right _____ × 5 equals _____ points	
VOCABULARY	number right _____ × 2 equals _____ points	

(Total points: 100) **total** _____ points

RETENTION   Based on the selection, which of the following statements are True (T), False (F), or Not answerable (N)?

1. _____ In England, friendships are based on shared activities.

2. _____ A friend is automatically a part of family life in France.

3. _____ The word "friend" refers to several different kinds of relationships in America.

4. _____ The French group relationship among *copains* is not the same as friendship.

5. _____ Europeans have little difficulty in understanding American friendships.

6. _____ American friendships are subject to frequent change.

7. _____ The word "friendship" has no common meaning for Americans and Europeans.

8. _____ French resistance groups eventually became like families.

9. _____ German friendships are more intellectual than emotional.

10. _____ Most Americans live in the same place throughout their lifetime.

INFERENCES

1. _____ Which of the following inferences is most reasonable?
    a. Of all nationalities, a German friendship is most like a family relationship.

b. A German visitor to this country would establish a friendship with an American relatively easily.

c. An American woman is most likely to become friends with a French woman.

2. _____ Which of the following inferences is most unreasonable?
   a. An American tourist will probably be able to make one new friend in Europe.
   b. An Englishman who had not seen his friend in years would feel comfortable with him immediately.
   c. Unlike other Europeans, a Frenchman would take friendships lightly.

3. _____ Which of the following conclusions best states the main idea of the selection?
   a. Americans have relatively long-term friendships.
   b. European friendships are characterized by commitment.
   c. Although styles of friendship differ from country to country, similarities in meaning make friendships between societies possible.

APPLICATION   Choose the best answer for each question.

1. _____ My difficulty in making friends with a stranger from another country would probably be caused by:
   a. our differing political beliefs.
   b. his looking down on Americans.
   c. our different understanding of what friendship is.
   d. the fact that I am probably wealthier than he is.

2. _____ If I am a Frenchman, I am most likely to be friends with:
   a. a woman.
   b. someone who shares my deepest interests.
   c. a fellow worker.
   d. a relative I have known since I was born.

3. _____ As a German, a deep rift with my friend would probably be caused by:
   a. a significant difference of opinion on a political issue.
   b. my friend and I being attracted to the same woman.
   c. one of us taking the relationship too seriously.
   d. my friend dropping an activity we shared.

4. _____ If I call my mother's friend "Aunt M.," I am probably:
   a. English.
   b. American.

c. French.
d. German.

5. _____ As a Frenchman, I would be most likely to meet my friends:
   a. at a café.
   b. at work.
   c. in each other's homes.
   d. in large groups.

6. _____ For most nationalities, friendship does not involve:
   a. freedom of choice.
   b. recognition of individuality.
   c. kinship ties.
   d. equality of give and take.

7. _____ If a woman is American, she will probably:
   a. have only other women as friends.
   b. have mostly family members as friends.
   c. expect her friends to be nice to her family.
   d. treat fellow committee members as friends.

VOCABULARY   Choose the best definition for each italic vocabulary entry.

1. _____ what *constitutes* friendship and how it comes into being
   a. causes
   b. makes up
   c. breaks up
   d. describes

2. _____ to a trusted *confidant*
   a. sharer of secrets
   b. admirer
   c. fellow worker
   d. playmate

3. _____ the little *bistro* where they drink and talk
   a. counter
   b. theater
   c. restaurant
   d. water fountain

4. _____ *mutual* discovery of each other's and their own inner life
   a. quiet
   b. shared
   c. assured
   d. intense

5. _____ Ties of friendship are meant to be *irrevocably* binding.
   a. unnecessarily
   b. happily
   c. possibly
   d. absolutely

6. _____ some *irreconcilable* difference of viewpoint
   a. hopelessly opposed
   b. unfortunate
   c. slight
   d. inconceivable

7. _____ Friendship is quite sharply distinguished from other, more *casual* relations.
   a. predictable
   b. pleasant
   c. chance
   d. formal

8. _____ Taste in food and wine is *accentuated*.
   a. weakened
   b. seasoned
   c. punctuated
   d. sharpened

9. _____ Different friends fill different *niches*.
   a. occupations
   b. places
   c. backgrounds
   d. purses

10. _____ meeting after a long *interval*
    a. rehearsal
    b. time lapse
    c. situation
    d. circle

8

GILBERT HIGHET

How to Write an Essay

Writing an essay is a task that has
haunted millions of students and professional
writers. Using examples from writers past
and present, Gilbert Highet makes some
surprising points to show us that we are all
capable of writing an interesting and
informative essay.

At school they tried to teach me how to write an essay, and how to
draw a large brass pot full of zinnias. I grieve to say that they failed in both these
laudable aims. I am not sure why I could never draw a brass pot full of zinnias,
but I know why my schoolmasters could not teach me to write an essay. The first
reason was that they gave us rather unattractive models to study and emulate:
Charles Lamb, who is a great deal too quaint and old-fashioned for modern
youngsters; Robert Louis Stevenson, whose style is often affected and artificial;
and E. F. Benson, whose essays *From a College Window* are mild and flaccid and
middle-aged and uninspiring. The other reason was that they never explained to
us what an essay was, and what purpose we were attempting to achieve when we
wrote one.

But there are other ways of learning how to write an essay—by trial and error,
observation and meditation. There are plenty of good stimulating contemporary
models. A newspaper editorial is only a short essay; so is a review of a new book,
a play, or a concert; so are the articles of newspaper columnists. Some of the
columnists write well, some of them atrociously, but they all try to obey the first
law of the essayist: *Be interested and you will be interesting.*

Also, I now know what an essay is. One good way to get a clear idea of any
literary form is to look at its origins, and see what the men who first practiced it
thought they were doing. The first man in modern times to write essays was the
eccentric and charming Montaigne, who apparently invented the name as well
as the pattern: essay = attempt, that is, an exploration, something tentative and
incomplete, but suggestive and stimulating. He was quickly followed by the
English statesman and philosopher Francis Bacon. These men both thought in

print: they mused on subjects they considered to be important, and they allowed the public to share their thoughts by overhearing. They were not trying to teach systematically and completely, but rather to stir and interest their readers' minds and to give some instruction while doing so. In shape and method many of these early essays derive from the letters written on philosophical subjects in ancient Greece and Rome. The letters of Epicurus to his pupils and of Seneca to his friend Lucilius are really philosophical essays; some of the letters of St. Paul are religious essays; and Montaigne's essay on the education of children is set out as a letter to a lady.

An essay is a fairly short and fairly informal discussion—of what? Of any subject in the world, any topic whatever which can be discussed in public. It has two purposes—to interest its readers, and to inform them; but it is far more important that it should interest them. One of William Hazlitt's finest essays is about a champion player of handball, or fives. There are few subjects nowadays about which I care less than handball; I gave the game up when I got a heart warning thirty years ago; and I should not normally turn a single page of print in order to get information about the game and its champions. But Hazlitt writes so warmly and with such conviction that I have read his essay ("The Death of John Cavanagh") thirty or forty times, always with delight. One of G. K. Chesterton's wittiest essays is simply "On Running after One's Hat": now, there is a topic on which most people would not even waste a couple of sentences, and on which nobody (except perhaps a heart specialist) could give us any useful data; but in less than four pages Chesterton takes this piece of trivia and builds it into a fanciful little philosophical system. Essays are intended not to exhaust the subject—which usually means exhausting the reader—but rather to say a few good things about it, and to give readers the pleasure of continuing the author's thought along their own channels.

It is not hard to write an essay, if you can write decently and think a little. The first essential is to choose a subject which is clear and precise in your mind and which interests you personally—so that you really enjoy thinking and talking and writing about it. Now that it comes to mind, that was a third reason why I never learned to write essays in school: the master was inclined to choose vague and tepid subjects. For instance, "Scenery." Very few boys and girls can really appreciate scenery; and only an aesthetically trained mind can have anything rich and challenging to say about scenery in general. *Scenery*: the word fell on our minds like a thick coating of mud, chill and stifling. I remember that I once escaped from it, and infuriated my unfortunate preceptor, by writing about the unique scenic qualities of the industrial city of Glasgow, with ironically rhapsodical paragraphs about the view of the gasworks from the slag heaps, and the superb assemblage of factory chimneys, some of which (Dixon's Blazes) resembled the divine guardian of the Children of Israel in the Exodus, a pillar of smoke by day and a pillar of fire by night. At least I felt that aspect of the subject, and I knew it precisely.

The next thing is to devise a form for your essay. This, which ought to be obvious, is not. I learned it for the first time from an experienced newspaperman. When I was at college I earned extra pocket- and book-money by writing several weekly columns for a newspaper. They were usually topical, they were always carefully varied, they tried hard to be witty, and (an essential) they never missed a deadline. But once, when I brought in the product, a copy editor stopped me. He said, "Our readers seem to like your stuff all right; but we think it's a bit amateurish." With due humility I replied, "Well, I am an amateur. What should I do with it?" He said, "Your pieces are not coherent; they are only sentences and epigrams strung together; they look like a heap of clothespins in a basket. Every article ought to have a shape. Like this" (and he drew a big letter S on his pad) "or this" (he drew a descending line which turned abruptly upward again) "or this" (and he sketched a solid central core with five or six lines pushing outward from it) "or even this" (and he outlined two big arrows coming into collision). I never saw the man again, but I have never ceased to be grateful to him for his wisdom and for his kindness. Every essay must have a shape. You can ask a question in the first paragraph, discussing several different answers to it till you reach one you think is convincing. You can give a curious fact and offer an explanation of it. You can take a topic that interests you and do a descriptive analysis of it: a man's character (as Hazlitt did with his fives champion), a building, a book, a striking adventure, a peculiar custom. There are many other shapes which essays can take; but the principle laid down by the copy editor was right. Before you start you must have a form in your mind; and it ought to be a form felt in paragraphs or sections, not in words or sentences—so that, if necessary, you could summarize each paragraph in a single line and put the entire essay on a postcard.

No. Perhaps that is going too far. Reading through some of the most brilliant essays of Virginia Woolf and E. M. Forster, we realize that they have no obvious form: they often try to break away from patterns and abstract outlines. But they are held together by two factors which not all of us can use. Neither Virginia Woolf nor E. M. Forster was capable of writing a dull commonplace obvious sentence; and both of them—in spite of, and indeed because of, their eccentricities—had minds which were organic wholes, so that whatever they wrote, although sometimes apparently discontinuous, reflected the activity of a single imagination, as the same light is caught in many broken reflections from the surface of a pool. Virginia Woolf's talk and some of her novels were slightly incoherent in rather the same way; but they formed spiritual unities. However, others who cannot claim to possess minds so intense and so deeply penetrated with harmonious impulses might find it dangerous to write without a preconceived form; and their readers might find the result tedious. Never forget the immortal remark of Richard Brinsley Sheridan:

Easy writing's vile hard reading.

When you plan the shape of your essay, should you also plan its length? Yes, and no. You should always realize that whatever you write as an essay is going to be incomplete: a Sunday afternoon drive is not the Mille Miglia race. You will therefore say to yourself, thinking over the topic, that this particular subject demands forty pages or so—because you have not only to discuss the character of the man but to describe his friends and enemies and lovers; while this one—for instance, the new pleasure of aqualung diving—can have enough said about it in ten pages. But when writing (as in conversation, and even, if you are smart, in making a speech) you will always leave room for new ideas, fresh insights, "ad libs": you can cut them out later if they seem forced or extraneous. But think often of conversation and of letter writing. No one says to himself, "I am now going to talk to this attractive woman for exactly twelve minutes"; no one thinks, "I want to tell my sister about our trip to Japan: I shall take exactly four pages." An essay is a conversation between oneself and an unseen friend.

One more hint from the newspaper and magazine world. Find a good lead sentence. The opening words are important. They are far too often bungled. If they are effective, they will catch the reader's interest and start to mold his feelings. They should therefore be rather vivid, even dramatic, and contain a certain emotional charge; or else be hard and bright and factual, so that the reader knows at once what is to be discussed. There are a large number of critics writing on political and social problems, literature, music, and art, who habitually begin their essays with a sentence so long, so precious, so involved, so obscure, so filled with scholastic allusions and in-jokes and ripostes to unknown opponents that they repel every reader who is not already initiated into the clique and prepared to be impressed. Turn to the good essayists: what do you find? Bacon opens his essay on "Gardens" with the remarkable but true statement:

> God Almighty first planted a garden.

George Orwell begins a touching essay on the Moroccan city of Marrakesh with a drastic but significant sentence: "As the corpse went past the flies left the restaurant table in a cloud and rushed after it, but they came back a few minutes later." Another of Orwell's essays, written during the second world war, starts even more dramatically: "As I write, highly civilized human beings are flying overhead, trying to kill me." Once you have read such an opening, hard must be your heart and busy (or empty) your brain if you do not wish to read on. But here is the opening of an essay which, like bad antipasto, kills the appetite for anything else:

> The imbecility with which Verecundulus complains that the presence of a numerous assembly freezes his faculties, is particularly incident to the studious part of mankind, whose education necessarily secludes them in their earlier years from mingled converse, till, at their

dismission from schools and academies [= universities], they plunge at once into the tumult of the world, and, coming forth from the gloom of solitude, are overpowered by the blaze of public life.

The subject of this essay is "Bashfulness." The author is Samuel Johnson. The idea is good. Intellectuals are often uncomfortable in large groups of people. They have spent most of their time thinking, reading, and talking with other specialists—or making scientific experiments which cannot be discussed in general language; and they have few subjects of social conversation. (In a way, this essay is a remote precursor of C. P. Snow's *Two Cultures*.) But what a way to start discussing the idea! The first sentence contains seventy-one words and is made up of one principal clause with at least six subordinate clauses and phrases hanging on to it like lampreys on a lake trout. And apart from that, who is Verecundulus? Who has heard his complaints? Not I. Not you. Only Samuel Johnson. His essay is in fact a reply to an imaginary letter asking for sympathy and perhaps advice; but he might have invented a few sentences of the letter itself, to lead into the essay. As for the name Verecundulus, that is really pedantic. No one who does not know a reasonable amount of Latin will understand the word; and in Latin the word does not exist in this form: Johnson invented it. It means only "Shy little man." Addison or Steele would have produced a delightful essay on the same subject, built around a character called "Mr. Modest," or "Dr. Diffident"; but Johnson had to take the Latin *uerecundus* [= shy] and build a diminutive out of it, Verecundulus, which sounds not like a shy man but like a new kind of orchid.

I hope this does not make you feel that it is necessarily hard work to write, or even to read, an essay. If I have, then either I have mistaken the technique of writing this pleasant form of literature, or I have failed to show you how delightful it is to read a good essay. Would you like to receive an interesting letter from someone who once met you and who wants to tell you something you did not know and would like to learn? If so, you can either read or write an essay, or both.

LENGTH: 2,408 WORDS

8   Gilbert Highet
How to Write an Essay

SCORING: Reading time: _____ Rate from chart: _____ W.P.M.

RETENTION	number right _____ × 3 equals _____ points
INFERENCES	number right _____ × 5 equals _____ points
APPLICATION	number right _____ × 5 equals _____ points
VOCABULARY	number right _____ × 2 equals _____ points

(Total points: 100) **total** _____ points

RETENTION   Based on the selection, which of the following statements are True (T), False (F), or Not answerable (N)?

1. _____ Because the reader is not yet ready, the opening sentence of a newspaper article should not contain anything that is too important.

2. _____ It is not necessary to know the exact length of your essay before it is written.

3. _____ Choosing a subject that interests you is not important when writing an essay.

4. _____ Highet's own book of essays has been widely praised.

5. _____ An essay is unlike a conversation or a letter to a friend.

6. _____ A newspaper column is one form of essay.

7. _____ Highet tells us the shape our essays should take.

8. _____ A good essay fully exhausts its subject.

9. _____ George Orwell writes good introductions.

10. _____ Highet was taught about essay shape by a newspaperman.

INFERENCES

1. _____ Which of the following inferences is most reasonable?
   a. Essays written long ago are not very stimulating.
   b. Even great authors must follow the rules of writing.
   c. Essays have actually been written since the days of ancient Greece and Rome.

2. _____ Which of the following inferences is most unreasonable?
   a. It is a good idea to have a time limit in mind when starting a conversation.
   b. Knowing how to think and write is even more important than choosing a subject.
   c. Almost any subject for an essay can be made interesting.

3. _____ Which of the following conclusions best states the main idea of the selection?
   a. Writing an essay is like drawing a picture.
   b. Writing an essay is easier if you follow certain rules.
   c. The purpose of most essays is to inform.

APPLICATION   Choose the best answer for each question.

1. _____ An essay introduction should not be:
   a. factual.
   b. emotional.
   c. dramatic.
   d. lengthy.

2. _____ If you can summarize your essay on a postcard, it is probably:
   a. interesting.
   b. well shaped.
   c. too short.
   d. true.

3. _____ Highet criticizes Johnson's passage because it is:
   a. too full of imaginary characters.
   b. written in Latin.
   c. wordy.
   d. too thought-provoking for most ordinary folk.

4. _____ In his essay on bashfulness, Johnson writes about:
   a. the Romans who were too shy to speak in the Forum.
   b. Marrakesh, the home of people fleeing from civilization.
   c. scholars, who meditate upon subjects alien to most people.
   d. people in general who suffer from shyness.

5. _____ Highet's master was furious about his essay on scenery because:
   a. Highet obviously didn't appreciate scenery.
   b. he compared what he saw to the Bible.
   c. his subject choice was not beautiful.
   d. he took too long to write it.

6. _____ Highet's purpose in mentioning Hazlitt's essay on the death of John Cavanagh was to show that he:
   a. felt that it was well written.
   b. loved to play handball.
   c. knew John Cavanagh.
   d. was interested in essays on death.

7. _____ The value of an essay's shape derives from the fact that it is:
   a. like that of an S.
   b. planned ahead of time.
   c. based on answering a question.
   d. based on words and sentences.

VOCABULARY   Choose the best definition for each italic vocabulary entry.

1. _____ infuriated my unfortunate *preceptor*
   a. jailer
   b. viewer
   c. writer
   d. teacher

2. _____ This essay is a remote *precursor.*
   a. follower
   b. swearer
   c. document
   d. forerunner

3. _____ They failed in both these *laudable* aims.
   a. lowly
   b. difficult
   c. important
   d. praiseworthy

4. _____ every reader who is not initiated into the *clique*
   a. group
   b. sound
   c. fashion
   d. answer

5. _____ Some of the columnists write well, some of them *atrociously.*
   a. skillfully
   b. interestingly
   c. poorly
   d. lengthily

6. _____ filled with scholastic *allusions* and in-jokes
   a. answers
   b. references
   c. funny sayings
   d. questions

7. _____ the superb *assemblage* of factory chimneys
   a. portrait
   b. collection
   c. system
   d. appearance

8. _____ although sometimes apparently *discontinuous*
   a. unified
   b. dull
   c. interrupted
   d. interesting

9. _____ Your pieces are not *coherent*.
   a. connected
   b. meaningful
   c. careful
   d. complete

10. _____ models to study and *emulate*
    a. read
    b. educate
    c. admire
    d. imitate

9

LEWIS THOMAS

Death in the Open

Lewis Thomas, a physician and medical
researcher, often writes to bridge the gap
between the scientist and the layman. In this
essay, he connects the death of human beings
with that of other living organisms in order
to place the individual in the broader
perspective of the entire life process.

Most of the dead animals you see on highways near the cities are
dogs, a few cats. Out in the countryside, the forms and coloring of the dead are
strange; these are the wild creatures. Seen from a car window they appear as
fragments, evoking memories of woodchucks, badgers, skunks, wolves, snakes,
sometimes the mysterious wreckage of a deer.

It is always a queer shock, part a sudden upwelling of grief, part unaccount-
able amazement. It is simply astounding to see an animal dead on a highway.
The outrage is more than just the location; it is the impropriety of such visible
death, anywhere. You do not expect to see dead animals in the open. It is the
nature of animals to die alone, off somewhere, hidden. It is wrong to see them
lying out on the highway; it is wrong to see them anywhere.

Everything in the world dies, but we only know about it as a kind of
abstraction. If you stand in a meadow, at the edge of a hillside, and look around
carefully, almost everything you can catch sight of is in the process of dying, and
most things will be dead long before you are. If it were not for the constant
renewal and replacement going on before your eyes, the whole place would turn
to stone and sand under your feet.

There are some creatures that do not seem to die at all; they simply vanish
totally into their own progeny. Single cells do this. The cell becomes two, then
four, and so on, and after a while the last trace is gone. It cannot be seen as death;
barring mutation, the descendants are simply the first cell, living all over again.

The cycles of the slime mold have episodes that seem as conclusive as death, but the withered slug, with its stalk and fruiting body, is plainly the transient tissue of a developing animal; the free-swimming amebocytes use this organ collectively in order to produce more of themselves.

There are said to be a billion billion insects on the earth at any moment, most of them with very short life expectancies by our standards. Someone has estimated that there are 25 million assorted insects hanging in the air over every temperate square mile, in a column extending upward for thousands of feet, drifting through the layers of the atmosphere like plankton. They are dying steadily, some by being eaten, some just dropping in their tracks, tons of them around the earth, disintegrating as they die, invisibly.

Who ever sees dead birds, in anything like the huge numbers stipulated by the certainty of the death of all birds? A dead bird is an incongruity, more startling than an unexpected live bird, sure evidence to the human mind that something has gone wrong. Birds do their dying off somewhere, behind things, under things, never on the wing.

Animals seem to have an instinct for performing death alone, hidden. Even the largest, most conspicuous ones find ways to conceal themselves in time. If an elephant missteps and dies in an open place, the herd will not leave him there; the others will pick him up and carry the body from place to place, finally putting it down in some inexplicably suitable location. When elephants encounter the skeleton of an elephant out in the open, they methodically take up each of the bones and distribute them, in a ponderous ceremony, over neighboring acres.

It is a natural marvel. All of the life of the earth dies, all of the time, in the same volume as the new life that dazzles us each morning, each spring. All we see of this is the odd stump, the fly struggling on the porch floor of the summer house in October, the fragment on the highway. I have lived all my life with an embarrassment of squirrels in my backyard, they are all over the place, all year long, and I have never seen, anywhere, a dead squirrel.

I suppose it is just as well. If the earth were otherwise, and all the dying were done in the open, with the dead there to be looked at, we would never have it out of our minds. We can forget about it much of the time, or think of it as an accident to be avoided, somehow. But it does make the process of dying seem more exceptional than it really is, and harder to engage in at the times when we must ourselves engage.

In our way, we conform as best we can to the rest of nature. The obituary pages tell us of the news that we are dying away, while the birth announcements in finer print, off at the side of the page, inform us of our replacements; but we get no grasp from this of the enormity of scale. There are 3 billion of us on the earth, and all 3 billion must be dead, on a schedule, within this lifetime. The vast mortality, involving something over 50 million of us each year, takes place in relative secrecy. We can only really know of the deaths in our households, or among our friends. These, detached in our minds from all the rest, we take to be unnatural events, anomalies, outrages. We speak of our own dead in low voices; struck down, we say, as though visible death can only occur for cause, by disease or violence, avoidably. We send off for flowers, grieve, make ceremonies, scatter bones, unaware of the rest of the 3 billion on the same schedule. All of that immense mass of flesh and bone and consciousness will disappear by absorption into the earth, without recognition by the transient survivors.

Less than a half century from now, our replacements will have more than doubled the numbers. It is hard to see how we can continue to keep the secret, with such multitudes doing the dying. We will have to give up the notion that death is catastrophe, or detestable, or avoidable, or even strange. We will need to learn more about the cycling of life in the rest of the system, and about our connection to the process. Everything that comes alive seems to be in trade for something that dies, cell for cell. There might be some comfort in the recognition . . . that we all go down together, in the best of company.

LENGTH: 1,072 WORDS

9   Lewis Thomas
Death in the Open

SCORING: Reading time: _____	Rate from chart: _____ W.P.M.

RETENTION	number right _____ × 3 equals _____ points
INFERENCES	number right _____ × 5 equals _____ points
APPLICATION	number right _____ × 5 equals _____ points
VOCABULARY	number right _____ × 2 equals _____ points

(Total points: 100) **total** _____ points

RETENTION   Based on the selection, which of the following statements are True (T), False (F), or Not answerable (N)?

1. _____ Birds never die in flight.

2. _____ No birth can replace a life that has died.

3. _____ One seldom sees wild animals dead on the highway.

4. _____ Elephants never die in an open place.

5. _____ Some creatures seem to escape death.

6. _____ We tend to think of death as something we can avoid.

7. _____ We do not expect to see death openly anywhere.

8. _____ Insect populations fluctuate with the weather.

9. _____ In another fifty years, world population will have doubled.

10. _____ The insects that hover in the earth's atmosphere die visibly.

INFERENCES

1. _____ Which of the following inferences is most reasonable?
   a. Births equal deaths in the United States today.
   b. Most life forms have a shorter life span than that of human beings.
   c. Death takes most animals by surprise.

2. _____ Which of the following inferences is most unreasonable?
   a. Mutation, the change of a cell structure, is a kind of death.
   b. Human beings do not even try to be like other animals in their response to death.
   c. The sight of a dead animal is probably more startling than the unexpected sight of a live one.

3. _____ Which of the following conclusions most probably states the main idea of the selection?
   a. Dying is an inevitable part of the process of life.
   b. It is the nature of all animals to ignore death.
   c. Most animals, including humans, fear death.

APPLICATION   Choose the best answer for each question.

1. _____ Thomas warns that if animal life did not die and renew itself:
   a. humans would become bored.
   b. animals would not have enough to eat.
   c. the planet would become lifeless.
   d. the world would become overpopulated.

2. _____ Elephants probably scatter the bones of their dead because they:
   a. want to get rid of the stench.
   b. have a single elephant burial ground.
   c. do not value life as much as we do.
   d. want to conceal the fact of the deaths.

3. _____ Thomas points out that while we mourn the death of a loved one, we:
   a. forget his past failures.
   b. dispense with ceremony.
   c. remember that the future will be better.
   d. forget the billions of others who must also die.

4. _____ The insects hovering over a state the size of Pennsylvania would number in the:
   a. thousands.
   b. millions.
   c. billions.
   d. trillions.

5. _____ The author's response to death would probably be:
   a. anger at the loss of a loved one.
   b. acceptance of it as part of the scheme of things.
   c. guilt at all he has not done.
   d. inconsolable grief.

6. _____ A twenty-first-century human being will probably:
   a. understand his place in the life cycle.
   b. be able to live forever.
   c. ignore other animal life.
   d. look back with envy at the past.

7. _____ If a person saw the death process openly going on around him,
   he might:
   a. commit suicide.
   b. be unable to forget about death.
   c. become resigned to it.
   d. write obituaries.

VOCABULARY   Choose the best definition for each italic vocabulary entry.

1. _____ the *impropriety* of such visible death
   a. improbability
   b. obviousness
   c. incorrectness
   d. surprise

2. _____ vanish totally into their own *progeny*
   a. children
   b. destiny
   c. problem
   d. genius

3. _____ the *transient* tissue of a developing animal
   a. living
   b. swimming
   c. clear
   d. temporary

4. _____ *stipulated* by the certainty of the death of all birds
   a. freckled
   b. angered
   c. surprised
   d. required

5. _____ A dead bird is an *incongruity*.
   a. something upsetting
   b. an inconsistency
   c. an annoyance
   d. something gruesome

6. _____ the largest, most *conspicuous* ones
   a. visible
   b. awesome
   c. conscientious
   d. special

7. _____ some *inexplicably* suitable location
   a. totally
   b. curiously
   c. mysteriously
   d. unlikely

8. _____ in a *ponderous* ceremony
   a. piny
   b. disorderly
   c. weighty
   d. fearful

9. _____ the *obituary* pages
   a. editorial
   b. current events
   c. death
   d. comic

10. _____ we take to be *anomalies*
    a. secrets
    b. exceptions
    c. names
    d. assortments

10

LOREN EISELEY

The Brown Wasps

Loren Eiseley is another of those scientists who are able to use their knowledge of the natural world as a starting place for thoughts on the nature of life and what it means to be a human being. In this essay, he meditates on time and memory, using keen observations of birds and animals to make his point.

There is a corner in the waiting room of one of the great Eastern stations where women never sit. It is always in the shadow and overhung by rows of lockers. It is, however, always frequented—not so much by genuine travelers as by the dying. It is here that a certain element of the abandoned poor seeks a refuge out of the weather, clinging for a few hours longer to the city that has fathered them. In a precisely similar manner I have seen, on a sunny day in midwinter, a few old brown wasps creep slowly over an abandoned wasp nest in a thicket. Numbed and forgetful and frost-blackened, the hum of the spring hive still resounded faintly in their sodden tissues. Then the temperature would fall and they would drop away into the white oblivion of the snow. Here in the station it is in no way different save that the city is busy in its snows. But the old ones cling to their seats as though these were symbolic and could not be given up. Now and then they sleep, their gray old heads resting with painful awkwardness on the backs of the benches.

Also they are not at rest. For an hour they may sleep in the gasping exhaustion of the ill-nourished and aged who have to walk in the night. Then a policeman comes by on his round and nudges them upright.

"You can't sleep here," he growls.

A strange ritual then begins. An old man is difficult to waken. After a muttered conversation the policeman presses a coin into his hand and passes fiercely along the benches prodding and gesturing toward the door. In his wake, like birds rising and settling behind the passage of a farmer through a cornfield, the men totter up, move a few paces and subside once more upon the benches.

One man, after a slight, apologetic lurch, does not move at all. Tubercularly thin, he sleeps on steadily. The policeman does not look back. To him, too, this has become a ritual. He will not have to notice it again officially for another hour.

Once in a while one of the sleepers will not awake. Like the brown wasps, he will have had his wish to die in the great droning center of the hive rather than in some lonely room. It is not so bad here with the shuffle of footsteps and the knowledge that there are others who share the bad luck of the world. There are also the whistles and the sounds of everyone, everyone in the world, starting on journeys. Amidst so many journeys somebody is bound to come out all right. Somebody.

Maybe it was on a like thought that the brown wasps fell away from the old paper nest in the thicket. You hold till the last, even if it is only to a public seat in a railroad station. You want your place in the hive more than you want a room or a place where the aged can be eased gently out of the way. It is the place that matters, the place at the heart of things. It is life that you want, that bruises your gray old head with the hard chairs; a man has a right to his place.

But sometimes the place is lost in the years behind us. Or sometimes it is a thing of air, a kind of vaporous distortion above a heap of rubble. We cling to a time and place because without them man is lost, not only man but life. This is why the voices, real or unreal, which speak from the floating trumpets at spiritualist seances are so unnerving. They are voices out of nowhere whose only reality lies in their ability to stir the memory of a living person with some fragment of the past. Before the medium's cabinet both the dead and the living revolve endlessly about an episode, a place, an event that has already been engulfed by time.

This feeling runs deep in life; it brings stray cats running over endless miles, and birds homing from the ends of the earth. It is as though all living creatures, and particularly the more intelligent, can survive only by fixing or transforming a bit of time into space or by securing a bit of space with its objects immortalized and made permanent in time. For example, I once saw, on a flower pot in my own living room, the efforts of a field mouse to build a remembered field. I have lived to see this episode repeated in a thousand guises, and since I have spent a large portion of my life in the shade of a nonexistent tree, I think I am entitled to speak for the field mouse.

One day as I cut across the field which at that time extended on one side of our suburban shopping center, I found a giant slug feeding from a runnel of pink ice cream in an abandoned Dixie cup. I could see his eyes telescope and protrude in a kind of dim, uncertain ecstasy as his dark body bunched and elongated in the curve of the cup. Then, as I stood there at the edge of the concrete, contemplating the slug, I began to realize it was like standing on a shore where a different type of life creeps up and fumbles tentatively among the rocks and sea wrack. It knows its place and will only creep so far until something changes. Little by little as I stood there I began to see more of this shore that surrounds the place of man.

I looked with sudden care and attention at things I had been running over thoughtlessly for years. I even waded out a short way into the grass and the wildrose thickets to see more. A huge black-belted bee went droning by and there were some indistinct scurryings in the underbrush.

Then I came to a sign which informed me that this field was to be the site of a new Wanamaker suburban store. Thousands of obscure lives were about to perish, the spores of puffballs would go smoking off to new fields, and the bodies of little white-footed mice would be crunched under the inexorable wheels of the bulldozers. Life disappears or modifies its appearances so fast that everything takes on an aspect of illusion—a momentary fizzing and boiling with smoke rings, like pouring dissident chemicals into a retort. Here man was advancing, but in a few years his plaster and bricks would be disappearing once more into the insatiable maw of the clover. Being of an archaeological cast of mind, I thought of this fact with an obscure sense of satisfaction and waded back through the rose thickets to the concrete parking lot. As I did so, a mouse scurried ahead of me, frightened of my steps if not of that ominous Wanamaker sign. I saw him vanish in the general direction of my apartment house, his little body quivering with fear in the great open sun on the blazing concrete. Blinded and confused, he was running straight away from his field. In another week scores would follow him.

I forgot the episode then and went home to the quiet of my living room. It was not until a week later, letting myself into the apartment, that I realized I had a visitor. I am fond of plants and had several ferns standing on the floor in pots to avoid the noon glare by the south window.

As I snapped on the light and glanced carelessly around the room, I saw a little heap of earth on the carpet and a scrabble of pebbles that had been kicked merrily over the edge of one of the flower pots. To my astonishment I discovered a full-fledged burrow delving downward among the fern roots. I waited silently. The creature who had made the burrow did not appear. I remembered the wild field then, and the flight of the mice. No house mouse, no *Mus domesticus*, had kicked up this little heap of earth or sought refuge under a fern root in a flower pot. I thought of the desperate little creature I had seen fleeing from the wild-rose thicket. Through intricacies of pipes and attics, he, or one of his fellows, had climbed to this high green solitary room. I could visualize what had occurred. He had an image in his head, a world of seed pods and quiet, of green sheltering leaves in the dim light among the weed stems. It was the only world he knew and it was gone.

Somehow in his flight he had found his way to this room with drawn shades where no one would come till nightfall. And here he had smelled green leaves and run quickly up the flower pot to dabble his paws in common earth. He had even struggled half the afternoon to carry his burrow deeper and had failed. I examined the hole, but no whiskered twitching face appeared. He was gone. I gathered up the earth and refilled the burrow. I did not expect to find traces of him again.

Yet for three nights thereafter I came home to the darkened room and my ferns to find the dirt kicked gaily about the rug and the burrow reopened, though I was never able to catch the field mouse within it. I dropped a little food about the mouth of the burrow, but it was never touched. I looked under beds or sat reading with one ear cocked for rustlings in the ferns. It was all in vain; I never saw him. Probably he ended in a trap in some other tenant's room.

But before he disappeared I had come to look hopefully for his evening burrow. About my ferns there had begun to linger the insubstantial vapor of an autumn field, the distilled essence, as it were, of a mouse brain in exile from its home. It was a small dream, like our dreams, carried a long and weary journey along pipes and through spider webs, past holes over which loomed the shadows of waiting cats, and finally, desperately, into this room where he had played in the shuttered daylight for an hour among the green ferns on the floor. Every day these invisible dreams pass us on the street, or rise from beneath our feet, or look out upon us from beneath a bush.

Some years ago the old elevated railway in Philadelphia was torn down and replaced by a subway system. This ancient El with its barnlike stations containing nut-vending machines and scattered food scraps had, for generations, been the favorite feeding ground of flocks of pigeons, generally one flock to a station along the route of the El. Hundreds of pigeons were dependent upon the system. They flapped in and out of its stanchions and steel work or gathered in watchful little audiences about the feet of anyone who rattled the peanut-vending machines. They even watched people who jingled change in their hands, and prospected for food under the feet of the crowds who gathered between trains. Probably very few among the waiting people who tossed a crumb to an eager pigeon realized that this El was like a food-bearing river, and that the life which haunted its banks was dependent upon the running of the trains with their human freight.

I saw the river stop.

The time came when the underground tubes were ready; the traffic was transferred to a realm unreachable by pigeons. It was like a great river subsiding suddenly into desert sands. For a day, for two days, pigeons continued to circle over the El or stand close to the red vending machines. They were patient birds, and surely this great river which had flowed through the lives of unnumbered generations was merely suffering from some momentary drought.

They listened for the familiar vibrations that had always heralded an approaching train; they flapped hopefully about the head of an occasional workman walking along the steel runways. They passed from one empty station to another, all the while growing hungrier. Finally they flew away.

I thought I had seen the last of them about the El, but there was a revival and it provided a curious instance of the memory of living things for a way of life or a locality that has long been cherished. Some weeks after the El was abandoned workmen began to tear it down. I went to work every morning by one particular station, and the time came when the demolition crews reached this spot. Acetylene torches showered passersby with sparks, pneumatic drills hammered at the base of the structure, and a blind man who, like the pigeons, had clung with his cup to a stairway leading to the change booth, was forced to give up his place.

It was then, strangely, momentarily, one morning that I witnessed the return of a little band of the familiar pigeons. I even recognized one or two members of the flock that had lived around this particular station before they were dispersed into the streets. They flew bravely in and out among the sparks and the hammers and the shouting workmen. They had returned—and they had returned because the hubbub of the wreckers had convinced them that the river was about to flow once more. For several hours they flapped in and out through the empty windows, nodding their heads and watching the fall of girders with attentive little eyes. By the following morning the station was reduced to some burned-off stanchions in the street. My bird friends had gone. It was plain, however, that they retained a memory for an insubstantial structure now compounded of air and time. Even the blind man clung to it. Someone had provided him with a chair, and he sat at the same corner staring sightlessly at an invisible stairway where, so far as he was concerned, the crowds were still ascending to the trains.

I have said my life has been passed in the shade of a nonexistent tree, so that such sights do not offend me. Prematurely I am one of the brown wasps and I often sit with them in the great droning hive of the station, dreaming sometimes of a certain tree. It was planted sixty years ago by a boy with a bucket and a toy spade in a little Nebraska town. That boy was myself. It was a cottonwood sapling and the boy remembered it because of some words spoken by his father and because everyone died or moved away who was supposed to wait and grow old under its shade. The boy was passed from hand to hand, but the tree for some intangible reason had taken root in his mind. It was under its branches that he sheltered; it was from this tree that his memories, which are my memories, led away into the world.

After sixty years the mood of the brown wasps grows heavier upon one. During a long inward struggle I thought it would do me good to go and look upon that actual tree. I found a rational excuse in which to clothe this madness. I purchased a ticket and at the end of two thousand miles I walked another mile to an address that was still the same. The house had not been altered.

I came close to the white picket fence and reluctantly, with great effort, looked down the long vista of the yard. There was nothing there to see. For sixty years that cottonwood had been growing in my mind. Season by season its seeds had been floating farther on the hot prairie winds. We had planted it lovingly there, my father and I, because he had a great hunger for soil and live things growing, and because none of these things had long been ours to protect. We had planted the little sapling and watered it faithfully, and I remembered that I had run out with my small bucket to drench its roots the day we moved away. And all the years since it had been growing in my mind, a huge tree that somehow stood for my father and the love I bore him. I took a grasp on the picket fence and forced myself to look again.

A boy with the hard bird eye of youth pedaled a tricycle slowly up beside me. "What'cha lookin' at?" he asked curiously.

"A tree," I said.

"What for?" he said.

"It isn't there," I said, to myself mostly, and began to walk away at a pace just slow enough not to seem to be running.

"What isn't there?" the boy asked. I didn't answer. It was obvious I was attached by a thread to a thing that had never been there, or certainly not for long. Something that had to be held in the air, or sustained in the mind, because it was part of my orientation in the universe and I could not survive without it. There was more than an animal's attachment to a place. There was something else, the attachment of the spirit to a grouping of events in time; it was part of our morality.

So I had come home at last, driven by a memory in the brain as surely as the field mouse who had delved long ago into my flower pot or the pigeons flying forever amidst the rattle of nut-vending machines. These, the burrow under the greenery in my living room and the red-bellied bowls of peanuts now hovering in midair in the minds of pigeons, were all part of an elusive world that existed nowhere and yet everywhere. I looked once at the real world about me while the persistent boy pedaled at my heels.

It was without meaning, though my feet took a remembered path. In sixty years the house and street had rotted out of my mind. But the tree, the tree that no longer was, that had perished in its first season, bloomed on in my individual mind, unblemished as my father's words. "We'll plant a tree here, son, and we're not going to move any more. And when you're an old, old man you can sit under it and think how we planted it here, you and me, together."

I began to outpace the boy on the tricycle.

"Do you live here, Mister?" he shouted after me suspiciously. I took a firm grasp on airy nothing—to be precise, on the bole of a great tree. "I do," I said. I spoke for myself, one field mouse, and several pigeons. We were all out of touch but somehow permanent. It was the world that had changed.

LENGTH: 3,149 WORDS

10   Loren Eiseley
The Brown Wasps

SCORING: Reading time: _____ Rate from chart: _____ W.P.M.	

RETENTION	number right _____ × 3 equals _____ points
INFERENCES	number right _____ × 5 equals _____ points
APPLICATION	number right _____ × 5 equals _____ points
VOCABULARY	number right _____ × 2 equals _____ points
	(Total points: 100) **total** _____ points

RETENTION   Based on the selection, which of the following statements are True (T), False (F), or Not answerable (N)?

1. _____ The animal that dug in Eiseley's flower pot was a house mouse.

2. _____ Eiseley's parents lived in the Nebraska house for many years.

3. _____ Eiseley planted a cottonwood tree at his Nebraska home.

4. _____ The aged poor get a few hours of uninterrupted rest in their quiet corner of the waiting room.

5. _____ The tree in Eiseley's yard represented his love for his father.

6. _____ The slug Eiseley observed loved eating fruit.

7. _____ The pigeons depended on the El for food.

8. _____ Eiseley's old house was still there when he returned years later.

9. _____ The aged poor are in the process of dying.

10. _____ The El station was so completely demolished that no sign of it was left.

INFERENCES

1. _____ Which of the following inferences is most reasonable?
   a. The mouse was frightened by what the Wanamaker sign said.
   b. The mood of the brown wasps is felt by many creatures, including human beings.
   c. Once the El station was no longer used, the pigeons forgot about it.

2. ____ Which of the following inferences is most unreasonable?
   a. Eiseley is squeamish about mice.
   b. The things that man builds are more permanent than those that nature builds.
   c. The policeman knows that the old people will probably not really move on.

3. ____ Which of the following conclusions best states the main idea of the selection?
   a. A remembered place can have an important permanent meaning.
   b. Everyone has a right to a place in the world.
   c. Adapting to change is a necessity in everyone's life.

APPLICATION   Choose the best answer for each question.

1. ____ The pigeons probably returned because they saw:
   a. the author walking along.
   b. the blind man sitting in his chair.
   c. the acetylene torches.
   d. the demolition crews working.

2. ____ Eiseley outpaces the boy as he walks because:
   a. the boy's legs are shorter than his are.
   b. the boy is part of his past.
   c. the boy belongs to the real world, the present.
   d. the boy understands him too well.

3. ____ The writer compares the aged poor and the brown wasps in order to show that they both:
   a. seek warmth.
   b. need to be gotten rid of.
   c. cling to their place in life.
   d. are capable of being aroused.

4. ____ Eiseley felt that his decision to return to look at the tree was:
   a. unreasonable.
   b. cute.
   c. practical.
   d. expensive.

5. ____ The pigeons at the El did not:
   a. eat crumbs.
   b. often change stations.
   c. respond to the sound of money.
   d. walk among the crowds of people.

6. _____ The mouse tried to build a burrow in the flower pot because:
   a. he remembered having built a similar one in a field.
   b. he liked the apartment.
   c. it was easier than digging one in a field.
   d. he preferred ferns to weeds.

7. _____ The tree in the yard:
   a. probably died in its first year.
   b. had never existed.
   c. had been long forgotten.
   d. had been cut down by the young boy.

VOCABULARY   Choose the best definition for each italic vocabulary entry.

1. _____ the white *oblivion* of the snow
   a. beauty
   b. chilliness
   c. regret
   d. forgetfulness

2. _____ A strange *ritual* then begins.
   a. missal
   b. discussion
   c. ceremony
   d. anger

3. _____ repeated in a thousand *guises*
   a. steps
   b. fields
   c. animals
   d. aspects

4. _____ like pouring *dissident* chemicals into a retort
   a. different
   b. several
   c. disagreeing
   d. heated

5. _____ the *insubstantial* vapor of an autumn field
   a. airy
   b. odorous
   c. moist
   d. earthy

6. _____ *subsiding* suddenly into desert sands
   a. breathing
   b. sinking
   c. living
   d. evaporating

7. _____ had always *heralded* an approaching train
   a. herded
   b. halted
   c. speeded up
   d. announced

8. _____ for some *intangible* reason
   a. strange
   b. understandable
   c. vague
   d. unusual

9. _____ my *orientation* in the universe
   a. acquaintance
   b. newness
   c. location
   d. friend

10. _____ an *elusive* world that existed nowhere
    a. slippery
    b. frightening
    c. exciting
    d. persistent

11

MAXINE HONG KINGSTON

No Name Woman

A Chinese-American woman, Maxine Hong Kingston reflects the immigrant experience shared by so many other Americans. She retraces her family's steps back to mainland China, trying to make the connection between the culture in which her aunt lived and died and her own life.

"You must not tell anyone," my mother said, "what I am about to tell you. In China your father had a sister who killed herself. She jumped into the family well. We say that your father has all brothers because it is as if she had never been born.

"In 1924 just a few days after our village celebrated seventeen hurry-up weddings—to make sure that every young man who went 'out on the road' would responsibly come home—your father and his brothers and your grandfather and his brothers and your aunt's new husband sailed for America, the Gold Mountain. It was your grandfather's last trip. Those lucky enough to get contracts waved good-bye from the decks. They fed and guarded the stowaways and helped them off in Cuba, New York, Bali, Hawaii. 'We'll meet in California next year,' they said. All of them sent money home.

"I remember looking at your aunt one day when she and I were dressing; I had not noticed before that she had such a protruding melon of a stomach. But I did not think, 'She's pregnant,' until she began to look like other pregnant women, her skirt pulling and the white tops of her black pants showing. She could not have been pregnant, you see, because her husband had been gone for years. No one said anything. We did not discuss it. In early summer she was ready to have the child, long after the time when it could have been possible.

"The village had also been counting. On the night the baby was to be born the villagers raided our house. Some were crying. Like a great saw, teeth strung with lights, files of people walked zigzag across our land, tearing the rice. Their lanterns doubled in the disturbed black water, which drained away through the broken bunds. As the villagers closed in, we could see that some of them, probably men and women we knew well, wore white masks. The people with long hair hung it over their faces. Women with short hair made it stand up on end. Some had tied white bands around their foreheads, arms, and legs.

"At first they threw mud and rocks at the house. Then they threw eggs and began slaughtering our stock. We could hear the animals scream their deaths— the roosters, the pigs, a last great roar from the ox. Familiar wild heads flared in our night windows; the villagers encircled us. Some of the faces stopped to peer at us, their eyes rushing like searchlights. The hands flattened against the panes, framed heads, and left red prints.

"The villagers broke in the front and the back doors at the same time, even though we had not locked the doors against them. Their knives dripped with the blood of our animals. They smeared blood on the doors and walls. One woman swung a chicken, whose throat she had slit, splattering blood in red arcs about her. We stood together in the middle of our house, in the family hall with the pictures and tables of the ancestors around us, and looked straight ahead.

"At that time the house had only two wings. When the men came back, we would build two more to enclose our courtyard and a third one to begin a second courtyard. The villagers pushed through both wings, even your grandparents' rooms, to find your aunt's, which was also mine until the men returned. From this room a new wing for one of the younger families would grow. They ripped up her clothes and shoes and broke her combs, grinding them underfoot. They tore her work from the loom. They scattered the cooking fire and rolled the new weaving in it. We could hear them in the kitchen breaking our bowls and banging the pots. They overturned the great waist-high earthenware jugs; duck eggs, pickled fruits, vegetables burst out and mixed in acrid torrents. The old woman from the next field swept a broom through the air and loosed the spirits-of-the-broom over our heads. 'Pig.' 'Ghost.' 'Pig,' they sobbed and scolded while they ruined our house.

"When they left, they took sugar and oranges to bless themselves. They cut pieces from the dead animals. Some of them took bowls that were not broken and clothes that were not torn. Afterward we swept up the rice and sewed it back up into sacks. But the smells from the spilled preserves lasted. Your aunt gave birth in the pigsty that night. The next morning when I went for the water, I found her and the baby plugging up the family well.

"Don't let your father know that I told you. He denies her. Now that you have started to menstruate, what happened to her could happen to you. Don't humiliate us. You wouldn't like to be forgotten as if you had never been born. The villagers are watchful."

Whenever she had to warn us about life, my mother told stories that ran like this one, a story to grow up on. She tested our strength to establish realities.

Those in the emigrant generations who could not reassert brute survival died young and far from home. Those of us in the first American generations have had to figure out how the invisible world the emigrants built around our childhoods fit in solid America.

The emigrants confused the gods by diverting their curses, misleading them with crooked streets and false names. They must try to confuse their offspring as well, who, I suppose, threaten them in similar ways—always trying to get things straight, always trying to name the unspeakable. The Chinese I know hide their names; sojourners take new names when their lives change and guard their real names with silence.

Chinese-Americans, when you try to understand what things in you are Chinese, how do you separate what is peculiar to childhood, to poverty, insanities, one family, your mother who marked your growing with stories, from what is Chinese? What is Chinese tradition and what is the movies?

If I want to learn what clothes my aunt wore, whether flashy or ordinary, I would have to begin, "Remember Father's drowned-in-the-well sister?" I cannot ask that. My mother has told me once and for all the useful parts. She will add nothing unless powered by Necessity, a riverbank that guides her life. She plants vegetable gardens rather than lawns; she carries the odd-shaped tomatoes home from the fields and eats food left for the gods.

Whenever we did frivolous things, we used up energy; we flew high kites. We children came up off the ground over the melting cones our parents brought home from work and the American movie on New Year's Day — *Oh, You Beautiful Doll* with Betty Grable one year, and *She Wore A Yellow Ribbon* with John Wayne another year. After the one carnival ride each, we paid in guilt; our tired father counted his change on the dark walk home.

Adultery is extravagance. Could people who hatch their own chicks and eat the embryos and the heads for delicacies and boil the feet in vinegar for party food, leaving only the gravel, eating even the gizzard lining—could such people engender a prodigal aunt? To be a woman, to have a daughter in starvation time was a waste enough. My aunt could not have been the lone romantic who gave up everything for sex. Women in the old China did not choose. Some man had commanded her to lie with him and be his secret evil. I wonder whether he masked himself when he joined the raid on her family.

Perhaps she encountered him in the fields or on the mountain where the daughters-in-law collected fuel. Or perhaps he first noticed her in the marketplace. He was not a stranger because the village housed no strangers. She had to have dealings with him other than sex. Perhaps he worked an adjoining field, or he sold her the cloth for the dress she sewed and wore. His demand must have surprised, then terrified her. She obeyed him; she always did as she was told.

When the family found a young man in the next village to be her husband, she stood tractably beside the best rooster, his proxy, and promised before they met that she would be his forever. She was lucky that he was her age and she would be the first wife, an advantage secure now. The night she first saw him, he had sex with her. Then he left for America. She had almost forgotten what he looked like. When she tried to envision him, she only saw the black and white face in the group photograph the men had had taken before leaving.

The other man was not, after all, much different from her husband. They both gave orders: she followed. "If you tell your family, I'll beat you. I'll kill you. Be here again next week." No one talked sex, ever. And she might have separated the rapes from the rest of living if only she did not have to buy her oil from him or gather wood in the same forest. I want her fear to have lasted just as long as rape lasted so that the fear could have been contained. No drawn-out fear. But women at sex hazarded birth and hence lifetimes. The fear did not stop but permeated everywhere. She told the man, "I think I'm pregnant." He organized the raid against her.

On nights when my mother and father talked about their life back home, sometimes they mentioned an "outcast table" whose business they still seemed to be settling, their voices tight. In a commensal tradition, where food is precious, the powerful older people made wrongdoers eat alone. Instead of letting them start separate new lives like the Japanese, who could become samurais and geishas, the Chinese family, faces averted but eyes glowering sideways, hung on to the offenders and fed them leftovers. My aunt must have lived in the same house as my parents and eaten at an outcast table. My mother spoke about the raid as if she had seen it, when she and my aunt, a daughter-in-law to a different household, should not have been living together at all. Daughters-in-law lived with their husbands' parents, not their own; a synonym for marriage in Chinese is "taking a daughter-in-law." Her husband's parents could have sold her, mortgaged her, stoned her. But they had sent her back to her own mother and father, a mysterious act hinting at disgraces not told me. Perhaps they had thrown her out to deflect the avengers.

She was the only daughter; her four brothers went with her father, husband, and uncles "out on the road" and for some years became western men. When the goods were divided among the family, three of the brothers took land, and the youngest, my father, chose an education. After my grandparents gave their daughter away to her husband's family, they had dispensed all the adventure and all the property. They expected her alone to keep the traditional ways, which her brothers, now among the barbarians, could fumble without detection. The heavy, deep-rooted women were to maintain the past against the flood, safe for returning. But the rare urge west had fixed upon our family, and so my aunt crossed boundaries not delineated in space. . . .

At the mirror my aunt combed individuality into her bob. A bun could have been contrived to escape into black streamers blowing in the wind or in quiet wisps about her face, but only the older women in our picture album wear buns. She brushed her hair back from her forehead, tucking the flaps behind her ears. She looped a piece of thread, knotted into a circle between her index fingers and thumbs, and ran the double strand across her forehead. When she closed her fingers as if she were making a pair of shadow geese bite, the string twisted together catching the little hairs. Then she pulled the thread away from her skin, ripping the hairs out neatly, her eyes watering from the needles of pain. Opening her fingers, she cleaned the thread, then rolled it along her hairline and the tops of her eyebrows. My mother did the same to me and my sisters and herself. I used to believe that the expression "caught by the short hairs" meant a captive held with a depilatory string. It especially hurt at the temples, but my mother said we were lucky we didn't have to have our feet bound when we were seven. Sisters used to sit on their beds and cry together, she said, as their mothers or their slave removed the bandages for a few minutes each night and let the blood gush back into their veins. I hope that the man my aunt loved appreciated a smooth brow, that he wasn't just a tits-and-ass man.

Once my aunt found a freckle on her chin, at a spot that the almanac said predestined her for unhappiness. She dug it out with a hot needle and washed the wound with peroxide.

More attention to her looks than these pullings of hairs and pickings at spots would have caused gossip among the villagers. They owned work clothes and good clothes, and they wore good clothes for feasting the new seasons. But since a woman combing her hair hexes beginnings, my aunt rarely found an occasion to look her best. Women looked like great sea snails—the corded wood, babies, and laundry they carried were the whorls on their backs. The Chinese did not admire a bent back; goddesses and warriors stood straight. Still there must have been a marvelous freeing of beauty when a worker laid down her burden and stretched and arched.

Such commonplace loveliness, however, was not enough for my aunt. She dreamed of a lover for the fifteen days of New Year's, the time for families to exchange visits, money, and food. She plied her secret comb. And sure enough she cursed the year, the family, the village, and herself.

Even as her hair lured her imminent lover, many other men looked at her. Uncles, cousins, nephews, brothers would have looked, too, had they been home between journeys. Perhaps they had already been restraining their curiosity, and they left, fearful that their glances, like a field of nesting birds, might be startled and caught. Poverty hurt, and that was their first reason for leaving. But another, final reason for leaving the crowded house was the never-said.

She may have been unusually beloved, the precious only daughter, spoiled and mirror gazing because of the affection the family lavished on her. When her husband left, they welcomed the chance to take her back from the in-laws; she could live like the little daughter for just a while longer. There are stories that my grandfather was different from other people, "crazy ever since the little Jap bayoneted him in the head." He used to put his naked penis on the dinner table, laughing. And one day he brought home a baby girl, wrapped up inside his brown western-style greatcoat. He had traded one of his sons, probably my father, the youngest, for her. My grandmother made him trade back. When he finally got a daughter of his own, he doted on her. They must have all loved her, except perhaps my father, the only brother who never went back to China, having once been traded for a girl. . . .

In the village structure, spirits shimmered among the live creatures, balanced and held in equilibrium by time and land. But one human being flaring up into violence could open up a black hole, a maelstrom that pulled in the sky. The frightened villagers, who depended on one another to maintain the real, went to my aunt to show her a personal, physical representation of the break she had made in the "roundness." Misallying couples snapped off the future, which was to be embodied in true offspring. The villagers punished her for acting as if she could have a private life, secret and apart from them.

If my aunt had betrayed the family at a time of large grain yields and peace, when many boys were born, and wings were being built on many houses, perhaps she might have escaped such severe punishment. But the men—hungry, greedy, tired of planting in dry soil, cuckolded—had had to leave the village in order to send food-money home. There were ghost plagues, bandit plagues, wars with the Japanese, floods. My Chinese brother and sister had died of an unknown sickness. Adultery, perhaps only a mistake during good times, became a crime when the village needed food.

The round moon cakes and round doorways, the round tables of graduated size that fit one roundness into another, round windows and rice bowls—these talismans had lost their power to warn this family of the law: a family must be whole, faithfully keeping the descent line by having sons to feed the old and the dead, who in turn look after the family. The villagers came to show my aunt and her lover-in-hiding a broken house. The villagers were speeding up the circling of events because she was too shortsighted to see that her infidelity had already harmed the village, that waves of consequences would return unpredictably, sometimes in disguise, as now, to hurt her. This roundness had to be made coin-sized so that she would see its circumference: punish her at the birth of her baby. Awaken her to the inexorable. People who refused fatalism because they could invest small resources insisted on culpability. Deny accidents and wrest fault from the stars.

After the villagers left, their lanterns now scattering in various directions toward home, the family broke their silence and cursed her. "Aiaa, we're going to die. Death is coming. Death is coming. Look what you've done. You've killed us. Ghost! Dead ghost! Ghost! You've never been born." She ran out into the fields, far enough from the house so that she could no longer hear their voices, and pressed herself against the earth, her own land no more. When she felt the birth coming, she thought that she had been hurt. Her body seized together. "They've hurt me too much," she thought. "This is gall, and it will kill me." With forehead and knees against the earth, her body convulsed and then relaxed. She turned on her back, lay on the ground. The black well of sky and stars went out and out and out forever; her body and her complexity seemed to disappear. She was one of the stars, a bright dot in blackness, without home, without a companion, in eternal cold and silence. An agoraphobia rose in her, speeding higher and higher, bigger and bigger; she would not be able to contain it; there would be no end to fear.

Flayed, unprotected against space, she felt pain return, focusing her body. This pain chilled her—a cold, steady kind of surface pain. Inside, spasmodically, the other pain, the pain of the child, heated her. For hours she lay on the ground, alternately body and space. Sometimes a vision of normal comfort obliterated reality: she saw the family in the evening gambling at the dinner table, the young people massaging their elders' backs. She saw them congratulating one another, high joy on the mornings the rice shoots came up. When these pictures burst, the stars drew yet further apart. Black space opened.

She got to her feet to fight better and remembered that old-fashioned women gave birth in their pigsties to fool the jealous, pain-dealing gods, who do not snatch piglets. Before the next spasms could stop her, she ran to the pigsty, each step a rushing out into emptiness. She climbed over the fence and knelt in the dirt. It was good to have a fence enclosing her, a tribal person alone.

Laboring, this woman who had carried her child as a foreign growth that sickened her every day, expelled it at last. She reached down to touch the hot, wet, moving mass, surely smaller than anything human, and could feel that it was human after all—fingers, toes, nails, nose. She pulled it up on to her belly, and it lay curled there, butt in the air, feet precisely tucked one under the other. She opened her loose shirt and buttoned the child inside. After resting, it squirmed and thrashed and she pushed it up to her breast. It turned its head this way and that until it found her nipple. There, it made little snuffling noises. She clenched her teeth at its preciousness, lovely as a young calf, a piglet, a little dog.

She may have gone to the pigsty as a last act of responsibility: she would protect this child as she had protected its father. It would look after her soul, leaving supplies on her grave. But how would this tiny child without family find her grave when there would be no marker for her anywhere, neither in the earth nor the family hall? No one would give her a family hall name. She had taken the child with her into the wastes. At its birth the two of them had felt the same raw pain of separation, a wound that only the family pressing tight could close. A child with no descent line would not soften her life but only trail after her, ghostlike, begging her to give it purpose. At dawn the villagers on their way to the fields would stand around the fence and look.

Full of milk, the little ghost slept. When it awoke, she hardened her breasts against the milk that crying loosens. Toward morning she picked up the baby and walked to the well.

Carrying the baby to the well shows loving. Otherwise abandon it. Turn its face into the mud. Mothers who love their children take them along. It was probably a girl; there is some hope of forgiveness for boys.

"Don't tell anyone you had an aunt. Your father does not want to hear her name. She has never been born." I have believed that sex was unspeakable and words so strong and fathers so frail that "aunt" would do my father mysterious harm. I have thought that my family, having settled among immigrants who had also been their neighbors in the ancestral land, needed to clean their name, and a wrong word would incite the kinspeople even here. But there is more to this silence: they want me to participate in her punishment. And I have.

In the twenty years since I heard this story I have not asked for details nor said my aunt's name; I do not know it. People who can comfort the dead can also chase after them to hurt them further—a reverse ancestor worship. The real punishment was not the raid swiftly inflicted by the villagers, but the family's deliberately forgetting her. Her betrayal so maddened them, they saw to it that she should suffer forever, even after death. Always hungry, always needing, she would have to beg food from other ghosts, snatch and steal it from those whose living descendants give them gifts. She would have to fight the ghosts massed at crossroads for the buns a few thoughtful citizens leave to decoy her away from village and home so that the ancestral spirits could feast unharassed. At peace, they could act like gods, not ghosts, their descent lines providing them with paper suits and dresses, spirit money, paper houses, paper automobiles, chicken, meat, and rice into eternity—essences delivered up in smoke and flames, steam and incense rising from each rice bowl. In an attempt to make the Chinese care for people outside the family, Chairman Mao encourages us now to give our paper replicas to the spirits of outstanding soldiers and workers, no matter whose ancestors they may be. My aunt remains forever hungry. Goods are not distributed evenly among the dead.

My aunt haunts me—her ghost drawn to me because now, after fifty years of neglect, I alone devote pages of paper to her, though not origamied into houses and clothes. I do not think she always means me well. I am telling on her, and she was a spite suicide, drowning herself in the drinking water. The Chinese are always very frightened of the drowned one, whose weeping ghost, wet hair hanging and skin bloated, waits silently by the water to pull down a substitute.

LENGTH: 3,272 WORDS

11 Maxine Hong Kingston
No Name Woman

SCORING: Reading time: _____ Rate from chart: _____ W.P.M.

RETENTION	number right _____ × 3 equals _____ points
INFERENCES	number right _____ × 5 equals _____ points
APPLICATION	number right _____ × 5 equals _____ points
VOCABULARY	number right _____ × 2 equals _____ points

(Total points: 100) **total** _____ points

RETENTION   Based on the selection, which of the following statements are True (T), False (F), or Not answerable (N)?

1. _____ After marriage, a Chinese man goes to live in the house of his wife's parents.

2. _____ Kingston believes that her aunt was raped by the man whose child she carried.

3. _____ Kingston's family knew some of the people who attacked their house.

4. _____ Kingston's aunt killed herself in order to save her child's life.

5. _____ The aunt had fallen in love with her husband when they were both children.

6. _____ The aunt gave birth in a pigsty.

7. _____ The men who sailed to America all had work contracts.

8. _____ The Chinese government now forbids giving paper replicas of food and money to those who have died.

9. _____ The men left the village so that they could send money for food back to their families.

10. _____ The author has never returned to her native China.

1. _____ Which of the following inferences is most reasonable?
   a. The Chinese feared their gods more than they loved them.
   b. China was a relatively rich country during this time.
   c. The Chinese invented the idea of romantic love.

2. _____ Which of the following inferences is most unreasonable?
   a. The Chinese men in the story intended to return to China after they had earned some money.
   b. Adultery was considered even worse during hard times in China.
   c. Daughters are preferable to sons because they can help around the house during hard times.

3. _____ Which of the following conclusions is most probable?
   a. For the Chinese, to be born and to live without a name is one of life's greatest curses.
   b. An unwanted pregnancy can cause hardship, not only to a family, but to an entire village.
   c. The author feels haunted by the memory of her aunt.

APPLICATION   Choose the best answer for each question.

1. _____ The author's mother would probably not:
   a. have a daughter.
   b. plant a flower garden.
   c. tell about her sister-in-law.
   d. hatch her own chickens.

2. _____ The real crime in adultery for the Chinese was that it:
   a. robbed a couple of true offspring.
   b. ended up costing money.
   c. was against their religion.
   d. brought about a divorce.

3. _____ For the author, the most important reason for her family's wanting her to keep silent about her aunt was that:
   a. they wanted her to help punish the aunt by forgetting her.
   b. silence will be most comforting to the aunt's ghost.
   c. they wanted to clear her aunt's name.
   d. silence would remind the townspeople of the family's shame.

4. _____ The author thinks of her aunt's pregnancy as:
   a. a sign of her unusual beauty.
   b. a pledge of her admirer's love.
   c. a breaking with traditional rules.
   d. something that makes her different from her brothers.

5. _____ The author and her siblings felt guilty after the carnival ride because they:
   a. really wanted to go to the movies.
   b. had eaten too much ice cream.
   c. should have been spending more time with their mother.
   d. realized that they had spent money frivolously.

6. _____ The author's aunt would probably suffer most after death because she would be:
   a. guilty about wronging her family.
   b. unequal to the other ghosts.
   c. separated from her child.
   d. longing for her husband.

7. _____ The author's mother tells her the story of her aunt in order to:
   a. entertain her on a dull afternoon.
   b. humiliate her.
   c. warn her about life.
   d. divert the curses of the gods.

VOCABULARY   Choose the best definition for each italic vocabulary entry.

1. _____ a *protruding* melon of a stomach
   a. warm
   b. noticeable
   c. bulging
   d. aching

2. _____ drained away through the broken *bunds*
   a. embankments
   b. holes
   c. tubs
   d. wells

3. _____ a *prodigal* aunt
   a. abandoned
   b. huge
   c. ungrateful
   d. wasteful

4. _____ the best rooster, his *proxy*
   a. property
   b. substitute
   c. pride
   d. beloved

5. _____ a *commensal* tradition
   a. consenting
   b. eating together
   c. communicating well
   d. strictly disciplined

6. _____ a *maelstrom* that pulled in the sky
   a. fire
   b. whirlpool
   c. lightning bolt
   d. godlike being

7. _____ These *talismans* had lost their power.
   a. signs
   b. architectural details
   c. prayers
   d. lucky pieces

8. _____ She stood *tractably* beside the rooster.
   a. foolishly
   b. in a heavy manner
   c. in a well-behaved manner
   d. awkwardly

9. _____ A vision of normal comfort *obliterated* reality.
   a. enhanced
   b. changed
   c. threatened
   d. wiped out

10. _____ The ancestral spirits could feast *unharassed*.
    a. carefree
    b. displeased
    c. at length
    d. harnessed

12

EDITH HAMILTON

The Religion of the Greeks

When we think of Greek religion at all,
we think of Greek mythology, which we
associate with gods such as Zeus and Hera,
who lived on Mount Olympus and engaged
in the same sort of misbehaviors as the
people who worshiped them. Edith Hamilton
tells us of the real Greek religion, one which
she argues is more ethical and more spiritual
than most of us suspect.

What the Greeks did for religion is in general not highly esteemed. Their achievement in that field is usually described as unimportant, without any real significance. It has even been called paltry and trivial. The reason people think of it in this way is that Greek religion has got confused with Greek mythology. The Greek gods are certainly Homer's Olympians, and the jovial company of the *Iliad* who sit at the banqueting board in Olympus making heaven shake with their shouts of inextinguishable laughter are not a religious gathering. Their morality, even, is more than questionable and also their dignity. They deceive each other; they are shifty and tricky in their dealings with mortals; they act sometimes like rebellious subjects and sometimes like naughty children and are kept in order only by Father Zeus' threats. In Homer's pages they are delightful reading, but not in the very least edifying.

If Homer is really the Greek Bible and these stories of his are accepted as the Greek idea of spiritual truth, the only possible conclusion is that in the enormously important sphere of religion the Greeks were naïve, not to say childish, and quite indifferent to ethical conduct. Because Homer is far and away the best known of the Greeks, this really is the prevailing idea, absurd as it must appear in face of the Greek achievement. There is no truth whatever in it. Religion in Greece shows one of the greatest of what Schopenhauer calls the "singular swing to elevation" in the history of the human spirit. It marks a great stage on the long road that leads up from savagery, from senseless and horrible rites, toward a world still so very dim and far away that its outline can hardly be seen; a world in which no individual shall be sacrificed for an end, but in which each will be willing to sacrifice himself for the end of working for the good of others in the spirit of love with the God who is love.

It would be impossible to compress Greek religion into the compass of a single chapter, but it is perhaps possible to give an idea of the special Greek stamp which marked it out from the others. Greek religion was developed not by priests nor by prophets nor by saints nor by any set of men who were held to be removed from the ordinary run of life because of a superior degree of holiness; it was developed by poets and artists and philosophers, all of them people who instinctively leave thought and imagination free, and all of them, in Greece, men of practical affairs. The Greeks had no authoritative Sacred Book, no creed, no ten commandments, no dogmas. The very idea of orthodoxy was unknown to them. They had no theologians to draw up sacrosanct definitions of the external and infinite. They never tried to define it; only to express or suggest it. St. Paul was speaking as a Greek when he said the invisible must be understood by the visible. That is the basis of all great art, and in Greece great artists strove to make the visible express the invisible. They, not theologians, defined it for the Greeks. Phidias' statue of Zeus at Olympia was his definition of Zeus, the greatest ever achieved in terms of beauty. Phidias said, so Dion Chrysostom reports, that pure thought and spirit cannot be portrayed, but the artist has in the human body a true vessel of thought and spirit. So he made his statue of God, the sight of which drew the beholder away from himself to the contemplation of the divine. "I think," Dion Chrysostom writes, "that if a man heavy of heart, who had drunk often of the cup of adversity and sorrow should stand before it, he would remember no longer the bitter hardships of his life. Your work, O Phidias, is

> Grief's cure,
> Bringing forgetfulness of every care."

"The Zeus of Phidias," said the Roman Quintilian, "has added to our conception of religion."

That was one way the Greeks worked out their theology. Another way was the poet's, as when Æschylus used his power to suggest what is beyond categorical statement:

> God—the pathways of his purpose
> Are hard to find.
> And yet it shines out through the gloom,
> In the dark chance of human life.

Effortless and calm
He works his perfect will.

Words that define God clamp down walls before the mind, but words like these open out vistas. The door swings wide for a moment.

Socrates' way was the same. Nothing to him was important except finding the truth, the reality in all that is, which in another aspect is God. He spent his life in the search for it, but he never tried to put what he had seen into hard and fast statements. "To find the Father and Maker of all is hard," he said, "and having found him it is impossible to utter him."

The way of Greek religion could not but be different from the ways of religions dependent not upon each man's seeking the truth for himself, as an artist or a poet must seek it, but upon an absolute authority to which each man must submit himself. In Greece there was no dominating church or creed, but there was a dominating ideal which everyone would want to pursue if he caught sight of it. Different men saw it differently. It was one thing to the artist, another to the warrior. "Excellence" is the nearest equivalent we have to the word they commonly used for it, but it meant more than that. It was the utmost perfection possible, the very best and highest a man could attain to, which when perceived always has a compelling authority. A man must strive to attain it. We needs must love the highest when we see it. "No one," Socrates said, "is willingly deprived of the good." To win it required all that a man could give. Simonides wrote:

Not seen in visible presence by the eyes of men
Is Excellence, save his from whom in utmost toil
Heart-racking sweat comes, at his manhood's height.

Hesiod had already said the same:

Before the gates of Excellence the high gods have placed sweat.
Long is the road thereto and steep and rough at the first.
But when the height is won, then is there ease,
Though grievously hard in the winning.

Aristotle summed up the search and struggle: "Excellence much labored for by the race of men." The long and steep and rough road to it was the road Greek religion took.

In the very earliest Greek records we have, a high stage has been reached. All things Greek begin for us with Homer, and in the *Iliad* and the *Odyssey* the Greeks have left far behind not only the bestialities of primitive worship, but the terrible and degrading rites the terror-stricken world around them was practicing. In Homer, magic has been abolished. It is practically nonexistent in the *Iliad* and the *Odyssey*. The enormous spiritual advance this shows—and intellectual, no less—is hard for us to realize. Before Greece all religion was magical. Magic was of supreme importance. It was mankind's sole defense against fearful powers leagued against mankind. Myriads of malignant spirits were bent on bringing every kind of evil to it. They were omnipresent. A Chaldean inscription runs:

> They lie in wait. They twine around the rafters. They take their way from house to house and the door cannot stop them. They separate the bride from the embraces of the bridegroom; they snatch the child from between his father's knees.

Life was possible only because, fearful as they were, they could be appeased or weakened by magical means. These were often terrible as well as senseless. The human mind played no part at all in the whole business. It was enslaved by terror. A magical universe was so terrifying because it was so irrational, and therefore completely incalculable. There was no dependable relation anywhere between cause and effect. It will readily be seen what it did to the human intellect to live in such an atmosphere, and what it did to the human character, too. Fear is of all the emotions the most brutalizing.

In this terror-haunted world a strange thing came to pass. In one little country the terror was banished. For untold ages it had dominated mankind and stunted its growth. The Greeks dismissed it. They changed a world that was full of fear into a world full of beauty. We have not the least idea when or how this extraordinary change came about. We know only that in Homer men are free and fearless. There are no fearful powers to be propitiated in fearful ways. Very humanlike gods inhabit a very delightful heaven. Strange and terrifying unrealities — shapes made up of bird and beast and human joined together by artists who thought only the unhuman could be divine—have no place in Greece. The universe has become rational. An early Greek philosopher wrote: "All things were in confusion until Mind came and set them in order." That mind was Greek, and the first exponent of it we know about was Homer. In the *Iliad* and the *Odyssey* mankind has been delivered from the terror of the unhuman supreme over the human.

LENGTH: 1,562 WORDS

12 Edith Hamilton
The Religion of the Greeks

<table>
<tr><td colspan="2">SCORING: Reading time: _____ Rate from chart: _____ W.P.M.</td></tr>
<tr><td>RETENTION</td><td>number right _____ × 3 equals _____ points</td></tr>
<tr><td>INFERENCES</td><td>number right _____ × 5 equals _____ points</td></tr>
<tr><td>APPLICATION</td><td>number right _____ × 5 equals _____ points</td></tr>
<tr><td>VOCABULARY</td><td>number right _____ × 2 equals _____ points</td></tr>
<tr><td colspan="2">(Total points: 100) total _____ points</td></tr>
</table>

RETENTION   Based on the selection, which of the following statements are True (T), False (F), or Not answerable (N)?

1. _____ The Greek religion was developed by artists, not by theologians.

2. _____ Greek religion had no single leader or set of rules.

3. _____ Earlier religions were based on magic.

4. _____ The Greeks were childish when it came to religion.

5. _____ Perfection was the ideal goal of the Greeks.

6. _____ The Greeks tried hard to define God.

7. _____ The Greek religion influenced Indian philosophy.

8. _____ Greek religion is full of awe and fear.

9. _____ Phidias' statue of Zeus was considered a great source of inspiration for lovers.

10. _____ Greek mythology is not Greek religion.

INFERENCES

1. _____ Which of the following inferences is most reasonable?
   a. The rules of Greek religion were very strict.
   b. The Greeks would probably not have statues in their temples.
   c. A religious Greek would have lived an ordinary, practical life.

2. _____ Which of the following inferences is most unreasonable?
   a. Early Christian saints like St. Paul were influenced by Greek religious thought.
   b. The early Chaldeans probably made sacrifices to their gods.
   c. If it hadn't been for Greek mythology, religion would not be what it is today.

3. _____ Which of the following conclusions best states the main idea of the selection?
   a. The Greeks developed a new and spiritually advanced idea of religion.
   b. Most religions are based on myth.
   c. Greek art, both writing and sculpture, was one of mankind's greatest achievements.

APPLICATION   Choose the best answer for each question.

1. _____ The biggest difference between the Greek religion and earlier religions was the Greek characteristic of:
   a. emotion.
   b. intellect.
   c. heart.
   d. physical pleasure.

2. _____ A Greek warrior would probably:
   a. reflect an earlier stage of religious development.
   b. have a different idea of religion from that of an artist.
   c. avoid religion completely.
   d. worship only the god of war.

3. _____ At a Greek religious gathering, one would be most likely to see:
   a. the Greek gods banqueting.
   b. incense burning.
   c. statues of the gods.
   d. human sacrifice.

4. _____ The author feels that definitions of God bring about:
   a. liberation of the mind.
   b. words and statues.
   c. a sense of clarity.
   d. limitations.

5. _____ A successful ancient Greek would probably give credit for his success to:
   a. hard work.
   b. luck.

c. the gods.

d. his ancestors.

6. _____ Earlier religions performed terrible rites because the people:

a. loved their gods.

b. needed an outlet for their cruelty.

c. thought their gods would be appeased by them.

d. had rejected weak ideas.

7. _____ The author's ultimate ideal of religion would probably be:

a. that of a nonbeliever.

b. associated with love for fellow human beings.

c. exactly like that of the ancient Greeks.

d. influenced by Greek mythology.

VOCABULARY   Choose the best definition for each italic vocabulary entry.

1. _____ It has even been called *paltry* and trivial.

a. ugly

b. evil

c. worthless

d. demanding

2. _____ not in the very least *edifying*

a. soothing

b. pleasing

c. enlightening

d. modern

3. _____ The very idea of *orthodoxy* was unknown to them.

a. religion

b. immorality

c. strict rules

d. ethical behavior

4. _____ the *contemplation* of the divine

a. consideration

b. contempt

c. deliverance

d. domination

5. _____ the *bestialities* of primitive worship (behaviors that are . . .)

a. exaggerated

b. most wise

c. beautiful

d. animal-like

6. _____ myriads of *malignant* spirits
   a. flying
   b. fearful
   c. thoughtful
   d. harmful

7. _____ They were *omnipresent*.
   a. physical
   b. everywhere
   c. gift giving
   d. all powerful

8. _____ therefore completely *incalculable* (not able to be . . .)
   a. sensed
   b. multiplied and divided
   c. rationally understood
   d. consoled

9. _____ powers to be *propitiated*
   a. encouraged
   b. calmed
   c. adored
   d. altered

10. _____ the first *exponent* of it
    a. demonstrator
    b. joiner
    c. sensor
    d. critic

Readings in Science and Sociology

13

JIM CARRIER

Glaciers Melting into History

In Glacier National Park, Montana,
students of glaciers have a chance to examine
them under a wide variety of conditions. Like
other natural and geological events, glaciers
grow, change, and reveal something of their
background and development. To people
like Paul Carrara and Cliff Martinka, they
begin to take on the qualities of personality,
endearing themselves in special ways. Not
only do students of glaciers worry about
them, they even root for them the way others
might root for a team or a sports star.

When Paul Carrara stopped talking, you could hear the glacier
dying. Dripping from sculptured corners, twice as fast as a human pulse, adding
to rivulets already alive with motion.

Deep in the crevasses, out of sight, the water ran faster, rolling rocks along
blue ice, sending out echoes of winters past.

At the front edge, the white marbled monolith broke off occasionally, turning
icebergs into cold gray soup. It was the only sign of the glacier moving, that and
the sound: a deep groan from nowhere in particular. A death moan from
Grinnell Glacier.

Carrara watched as two kids danced from piece to floating piece, until they
fell into the icy drink. "This is a sick glacier," he said. "A bad year for the ice."

Since 1850, Grinnell Glacier has been dripping away its life, shrinking back
toward the shadow cast by the Garden Wall, where the sun never touches the
winter's snow. It is this snow, year after year, that feeds this glacier, that becomes
the glacier, packing itself into airless, blue cold, hard as rock and 200 feet thick,
but flowing, like plastic.

Climbing toward Grinnell, as he does to study its history for the U.S. Geological Survey, Carrara adds gloves and layers of clothing, whooping and hollering to alert the bears, passing the early signs of autumn in Glacier National Park: yellowing dogbane, the red berries of mountain ash, fireweed seed fuzz—and goldenrod, the universal sign that summer is over. It is like a time-lapse walk into winter.

Even in summer, the glacier is a reminder of winter. Walking onto it is like walking into a cooler. Grizzlies often ramble across it to cool off. Grinnell is not high by mountain standards, about 9,000 feet. But it is near the Canadian border, where winter comes first to the Rockies.

It snows so much at Glacier, even in summer, that the park's senior scientist, Cliff Martinka, doesn't consider it a place of seasons. "There's snow-free periods," he says. Periods when the yellow glacier lillies rush to flower and the Columbian ground squirrels break their endless hibernation for four months of eating and breeding.

By mid-September, the first "winter" storm comes in from the Pacific, rising against the Continental Divide, dumping snow, the first of a series of Pacific storms that will close the Going-to-the-Sun road in October and pile up to 70 feet of snow in wind-blown places. On the divide, 150 inches of moisture is not unusual.

Ironically, Martinka says, all that water is tied up much of the year in snow and ice, making the park a desert of sorts.

In about 75 places in the park, by Carrara's count, winter's store becomes a glacier. And its slow release through the year keeps the creeks high, the waterfalls gushing, the irrigation ditches running on the plains of eastern Montana.

Glaciers once covered the park; only the tips of the mountains showed through the ice. With Carrara's help, you can see the line near the top of the canyons where the ice scraped the rocks smooth. It made the park what it is today: deep U-shaped valleys, lakes dammed by terminal moraines, matterhorn peaks, and loose soil that drains water through hidden cavities.

The last great Ice Age was 10,000 to 20,000 years ago. By 1850, the end of a period known as the Little Ice Age, about 150 glaciers remained in the park, most of them less than a square mile in size. The warm climate since then, especially during the Dust Bowl days, ate them alive.

Along Grinnell's melting edge, Carrara points to layers of winters, where rocks and dust are caught, forming dark lines in the ice, yielding information about the glacier and the climate, just as rings in a tree do. Bugs are trapped in there. Even air is trapped, Carrara says; holding clues to how pure the atmosphere was before the Industrial Revolution, or atomic testing or the greenhouse effect.

By counting rings on trees that grew back when the glaciers receded, checking soil samples for volcanic ash, and other sleuthing, including radiocarbon dating, Carrara is able to write a rough history of glaciers.

At Logan Pass, Carrara climbed over a moraine of loose gravel, much like bulldozed tailings, to look down at a cavity that in the 1930s was Clements Glacier. "He's dead," Carrara says. "But at one time he was healthy and respectable."

Behind the moraine, lichens and algae, the beginnings of life, are fastening themselves to the bedrock once hidden by ice. Carrara ran the toe of his sneaker across scratch marks in the rock. The track of a glacier. As it slid forward, carrying rocks, it ground out dust as sandpaper would do, dust that turns glacier runoff milky, that gives high mountain lakes a turquoise color, that gave the Milk River its name. It is a sure sign that a glacier is alive.

Carrara, who has been climbing glaciers since 1969, believes the bigger glaciers in the park will never disappear. There is too much new snow each year, the remaining glaciers are shaded much of the time, and it just doesn't get warm enough.

He estimates that to kill Jackson Glacier, for example, the average summer temperature would have to increase several degrees, a change that would affect the North American climate profoundly. A couple of glaciers in the park actually are growing.

Carrara believes it is only a matter of time before the glaciers return—in a big way. "I kinda root for them to get bigger, and they will," he says.

"They'll be another time when they'll be down on the plains of Montana. It may be 10,000 or 20,000 years. But they'll be back."

LENGTH: 919 WORDS

13 Jim Carrier
Glaciers Melting into History

SCORING: Reading time: _____ Rate from chart: _____ W.P.M.

RETENTION	number right _____ × 2 equals _____ points		
MAIN IDEAS	number right _____ × 4 equals _____ points		
APPLICATION	number right _____ × 4 equals _____ points		
VOCABULARY	number right _____ × 2 equals _____ points		

(Total points: 100) **total** _____ points

RETENTION   Based on the selection, which of the following statements are True (T), False (F), or Not answerable (N)?

1. _____ The last great ice age ended in 1850.

2. _____ Columbian ground squirrels hibernate for only four months, then breed.

3. _____ The track of a glacier is the scratch marks in the bedrock.

4. _____ Glacier National Park has only dying glaciers.

5. _____ Even though there is an immense amount of moisture in the glaciers, the park is something of a desert.

6. _____ Winter begins in the park in mid-September.

7. _____ The Continental Divide goes through the largest glacier.

8. _____ The dripping that Carrara heard was the melting glacier.

9. _____ Like bedrock, Grinnell Glacier is soundless.

10. _____ Goldenrod is the universal sign of summer's beginning.

11. _____ Grinnell, at 9,000 feet, is relatively high by mountain standards.

12. _____ There are about 150 glaciers in the park.

13. _____ Carrara is sure this is the end of the glaciers.

14. _____ Grinnell Glacier may be as much as 200 feet thick.

15. _____ In places, snow will drift to seventy feet in the park.

1. _____ Which of the following best states the main idea of this selection?
   a. Glaciers are melting because we are in a warming trend.
   b. We are not paying enough attention to our glaciers.
   c. Glaciers are among our most important geological resources.

2. _____ If the main idea of this selection is true, which of the following is most likely to happen?
   a. If we are not careful, our glaciers will melt into nothing.
   b. A period of intense cooling will bring the glaciers back.
   c. Glaciers can be analyzed to tell us a great deal about geology.

APPLICATION   Choose the best answer for each question.

1. _____ Martinka does not think of the park as a place of seasons because:
   a. there are no true flowers blooming there.
   b. only animals could survive in those conditions.
   c. the snow piles up even in summer.
   d. the latitude is so high that sometimes the sun does not set.

2. _____ The layers in the glaciers can:
   a. be as much as five inches thick.
   b. give clues as to past atmospheric conditions.
   c. be artistically arranged.
   d. melt at twice the rate of a heartbeat.

3. _____ The deep U-shaped valleys in the park:
   a. were there from the beginning.
   b. make the place unapproachable by car.
   c. give the place an unearthly cast.
   d. were made by the glaciers.

4. _____ Grinnell Glacier was described as being plastic:
   a. instead of being like a rock.
   b. because it flows and moves.
   c. since it can adapt to many shapes.
   d. until the little ice age.

5. _____ The runoff of a glacier is milky because:
   a. some glaciers have a white or a blue cast to them.
   b. the glacier melts too quickly.
   c. algae settles in early in its formation.
   d. ground-up rock-dust is suspended in the water.

6. _____ Because of the snow and shade, Carrara:
   a. feels the bigger glaciers will not melt.

b. can never be fully warm when in the park.

c. has recommended establishing a new base camp.

d. fears his job may eventually become unnecessary.

7. _____ Carrara described Grinnell as a sick glacier because:
   a. it dripped the way a stuffy nose drips.
   b. the park was neglecting its maintenance seriously.
   c. he regarded it almost as a living thing.
   d. a drip beat of 100 per minute means trouble.

8. _____ The breaking off of icebergs at the front of Grinnell:
   a. was a sign of the movement of the glacier.
   b. was welcomed by the frolicking kids.
   c. would have been dangerous if it happened in the ocean.
   d. gave the grizzlies an annual treat.

VOCABULARY   Choose the best definition for each italic vocabulary entry.

1. _____ The glacier dripped from *sculptured* corners.
   a. beautiful
   b. man-made
   c. shaped
   d. cast

2. _____ The drips added to *rivulets* already alive with motion.
   a. small streams
   b. gorges
   c. fastening places
   d. drainages

3. _____ The waters sent out *echoes* of winters past.
   a. sounds
   b. noises
   c. reminders
   d. patterns

4. _____ hollering to *alert* the bears
   a. scare
   b. spot
   c. seize
   d. warn

5. _____ The Columbian ground squirrels break their *hibernation*.
   a. winter sleep
   b. summer torpor
   c. habitual patterns
   d. social interrelationship

6. _____ A white *monolith* broke off occasionally.
   a. polar bear
   b. floe
   c. large block
   d. jutting corner

7. _____ lakes dammed by *terminal* moraines
   a. frightening
   b. buslike
   c. ending
   d. lost

8. _____ lakes dammed by terminal *moraines*
   a. masses of rocks
   b. wooden planks
   c. mountain ranges
   d. happenstances

9. _____ draining water through hidden *cavities*
   a. open spaces
   b. declivities
   c. gullies
   d. spots

10. _____ The dark lines in the ice *yield* information.
    a. interpret
    b. give up
    c. supply
    d. manipulate

11. _____ examining trees that grew back when glaciers *receded*
    a. moved
    b. extended their base
    c. drew back
    d. flowed forward

12. _____ Checking soil and other *sleuthing* yields clues.
    a. samples
    b. investigation
    c. sieving
    d. poking

13. _____ loose gravel much like bulldozed *tailings*
    a. waste
    b. products
    c. hills
    d. landscapes

14. _____ change the climate *profoundly*
    a. insignificantly
    b. pro forma
    c. radically
    d. proportionately

15. _____ Grizzlies *ramble* across the glacier.
    a. gambol
    b. roam aimlessly
    c. stroll purposively
    d. walk

14

ANNIE DILLARD

Learning to See

Annie Dillard has become well known for
her sensitive and thoughtful meditations on
some of the simple things in life, such as the
way the sun looks, and the way the air feels.
She has been observing nature for years and
her observations have been nourishing her
readers for as long as she has been writing.
This short piece is typical of the care with
which she reflects about her subject, and it is
curiously appropriate to the way she works:
it considers the effect of sight on those from
whom it had been withheld.

I chanced on a wonderful book called *Space and Sight*, by Marius
Von Senden. When Western surgeons discovered how to perform safe cataract
operations, they ranged across Europe and America operating on dozens of men
and women of all ages who had been blinded by cataracts since birth. Von
Senden collected accounts of such cases; the histories are fascinating. Many
doctors had tested their patients' sense perceptions and ideas of space both
before and after the operations. The vast majority of patients, of both sexes and
all ages, had, in Von Senden's opinion, no idea of space whatsoever. Form,
distance, and size were so many meaningless symbols. A patient "had no idea of
depth, confusing it with roundness." Before the operation a doctor would give a
blind patient a cube and a sphere; the patient would tongue it or feel it with his
hands, and name it correctly. After the operation the doctor would show the
same objects to the patient without letting him touch them; now he had no clue
whatsoever to what he was seeing. One patient called lemonade "square"
because it pricked on his tongue as a square shape pricked on the touch of his
hands. Of another postoperative patient the doctor writes, "I have found in her
no notion of size, for example, not even within the narrow limits which she
might have encompassed with the aid of touch. Thus when I asked her to show

me how big her mother was, she did not stretch out her hands, but set her two index fingers a few inches apart."

For the newly sighted, vision is pure sensation unencumbered by meaning. When a newly sighted girl saw photographs and paintings, she asked, " 'Why do they put those dark marks all over them?' 'Those aren't dark marks,' her mother explained, 'those are shadows. That is one of the ways the eye knows that things have shape. If it were not for shadows, many things would look flat.' 'Well, that's how things do look,' Joan answered. 'Everything looks flat with dark patches.' "

In general the newly sighted see the world as a dazzle of "color-patches." They are pleased by the sensation of color, and learn quickly to name the colors, but the rest of seeing is tormentingly difficult. Soon after his operation a patient "generally bumps into one of these colour-patches and observes them to be substantial, since they resist him as tactual objects do. In walking about it also strikes him—or can if he pays attention—that he is continually passing in between the colours he sees, that he can go past a visual object, that a part of it then steadily disappears from view; and that in spite of this, however he twists and turns—whether entering the room from the door, for example, or returning back to it—he always has a visual space in front of him. Thus he gradually comes to realize that there is also a space behind him, which he does not see."

The mental effort involved in these reasonings proves overwhelming for many patients. It oppresses them to realize, if they ever do at all, the tremendous size of the world, which they had previously conceived of as something touchingly manageable. It oppresses them to realize that they have been visible to people all along, perhaps unattractively so, without their knowledge or consent. A disheartening number of them refuse to use their new vision, continuing to go over objects with their tongues, and lapsing into apathy and despair.

On the other hand, many newly sighted people speak well of the world, and teach us how dull our own vision is. To one patient, a human hand, unrecognized, is "something bright and then holes." Shown a bunch of grapes, a boy calls out, "It is dark, blue and shiny. . . . It isn't smooth, it has bumps and hollows." A little girl visits a garden. "She is greatly astonished, and can scarcely be persuaded to answer, stands speechless in front of the tree, which she only names on taking hold of it, and then as 'the tree with the lights in it.' " Another patient, a twenty-two-year-old girl, was dazzled by the world's brightness and kept her eyes shut for two weeks. When at the end of that time she opened her eyes again, she did not recognize any objects, but "the more she now directed her gaze upon everything about her, the more it could be seen how an expression of gratification and astonishment overspread her features; she repeatedly exclaimed: 'Oh God! How beautiful!' "

I saw color-patches for weeks after I read this wonderful book. It was summer; the peaches were ripe in the valley orchards. When I woke in the morning, color-patches wrapped round my eyes, intricately, leaving not one unfilled spot. All day long I walked among shifting color-patches that parted before me like the Red Sea and closed again in silence, transfigured, wherever I looked back. Some patches swelled and loomed, while others vanished utterly, and dark marks flitted at random over the whole dazzling sweep. But I couldn't sustain the illusion of flatness. I've been around for too long. Form is condemned to an eternal danse macabre [dance of death] with meaning: I couldn't unpeach the peaches. Nor can I remember ever having seen without understanding; the color-patches of infancy are lost. My brain then must have been smooth as any balloon. I'm told I reached for the moon; many babies do. But the color-patches of infancy swelled as meaning filled them; they arrayed themselves in solemn ranks down distance which unrolled and stretched before me like a plain. The moon rocketed away. I live now in a world of shadows that shape and distance color, a world where space makes a kind of terrible sense. . . . The fluttering patch I saw in my nursery window—silver and green and shape-shifting blue—is gone; a row of Lombardy poplars takes its place, mute, across the distant lawn. That humming oblong creature pale as light that stole along the walls of my room at night, stretching exhilaratingly around the corners, is gone, too, gone the night I ate of the bittersweet fruit, put two and two together and puckered forever my brain. Martin Buber tells this tale: "Rabbi Mendel once boasted to his teacher Rabbi Elimelekh that evenings he saw the angel who rolls away the light before the darkness, and mornings the angel who rolls away the darkness before the light. 'Yes,' said Rabbi Elimelekh, 'in my youth I saw that too. Later on you don't see these things anymore.'"

Why didn't someone hand those newly sighted people paints and brushes from the start, when they still didn't know what anything was? Then maybe we all could see color-patches too, the world unraveled from reason, Eden before Adam gave names. The scales would drop from my eyes; I'd see trees like men walking; I'd run down the road against all orders, hallooing and leaping.

LENGTH: 1,175 WORDS

14   Annie Dillard
Learning to See

SCORING: Reading time: _____ Rate from chart: _____ W.P.M.

RETENTION	number right _____ × 2 equals _____ points	
MAIN IDEAS	number right _____ × 4 equals _____ points	
APPLICATION	number right _____ × 4 equals _____ points	
VOCABULARY	number right _____ × 2 equals _____ points	

(Total points: 100) **total** _____ points

RETENTION   Based on the selection, which of the following statements are True (T), False (F), or Not answerable (N)?

1. _____   When she was young, Dillard remembered, she had once seen without understanding.

2. _____   The young woman who kept her eyes shut for two weeks finally gave up in despair.

3. _____   The formerly blind were oppressed by the thought that people had been able to see them without their knowing it.

4. _____   Some newly sighted people show us that our vision is dull.

5. _____   Western surgeons discovered how to cure cataracts in the mid-nineteenth century.

6. _____   One patient is reported to have thought a lemon was square.

7. _____   Depth and roundness are the same thing.

8. _____   Learning colors is fairly easy for many newly sighted.

9. _____   The size of the world is difficult for the newly sighted to accept.

10. _____   Shadows help us interpret the depth of things.

11. _____   When she tried, Dillard could keep the world flat.

12. _____   In Dillard's world, space makes sense.

13. _____   Part of the experiment was to hand newly sighted people paints and brushes.

14. _____ An understanding of space depended on the patient's sex and age.

15. _____ Reaching for the moon is rather odd behavior for babies.

MAIN IDEAS

1. _____ Which of the following best states the main idea of this selection?
   a. Medicine can work wonders in the field of vision restoration, but it cannot guarantee happiness.
   b. Psychological guidance is essential if a thorough success is to be achieved in medical breakthroughs related to vision.
   c. Making visual sense of the world is not done automatically, but requires intellectual effort.

2. _____ If the main idea of this selection is true, which of the following is most likely to happen?
   a. More psychiatrists will be involved in medical experiments.
   b. We will begin to understand more about what goes into acts of spatial interpretation.
   c. Training sessions will include a better theoretical understanding of basic phenomena.

APPLICATION   Choose the best answer for each question.

1. _____ The idea of testing patients before and after the cataract operation:
   a. was standard medical procedure at the time.
   b. surprised even the most demanding doctors.
   c. was an isolated event.
   d. seems to have been carried out widely.

2. _____ After Dillard read the book about eye surgery:
   a. she feared her own eyes would need it.
   b. much of the time she went around with her eyes shut.
   c. she tried to see the way the newly sighted did.
   d. all her friends were expected to read it too.

3. _____ The humming oblong creature Dillard imagined seeing in her youth:
   a. was a result of childhood cataracts.
   b. was similar to what a rabbi called an angel.
   c. disappeared when she grew to understand the shape of things.
   d. was a comfort to her when she slept in her crib.

4. _____ Many of the newly sighted refused to use their sight because:
   a. the world of vision is too confusing and demanding.

b. no one told them what to expect of the visual world.

c. things are simply too big for them to accept.

d. they were disappointed in the fact that things are not as they wish them to be.

5. _____ For the newly sighted, vision is pure sensation:

   a. without a clear sense of importance or significance.

   b. which may be too intense for enjoyment.

   c. until they begin to touch and tongue objects.

   d. unless they are also deaf.

6. _____ One thing the newly sighted seem to lack is:

   a. appreciation for the operation.

   b. the need to ask questions.

   c. a sense of size.

   d. adequate preparation for their experience.

7. _____ The experience of the newly sighted passing in between color-patches is described as if the patient were:

   a. demented.

   b. out of touch with reality.

   c. swimming through a continuous field of colors.

   d. hostile or removed.

8. _____ Making sense of visual space involves:

   a. intense mental effort.

   b. the collaboration of several systems.

   c. knowing colors and their names, then understanding the absence of color.

   d. reassurance and the hopefulness that resists defeat.

VOCABULARY   Choose the best definition for each italic vocabulary entry.

1. _____ I *chanced* on a wonderful book.

   a. gambled

   b. bought for very little

   c. found accidentally

   d. discovered eventually

2. _____ Surgeons *ranged* across Europe and America.

   a. spread

   b. rode

   c. saw

   d. migrated to

3. _____ A doctor would produce a cube and a *sphere*.
   a. globe
   b. weapon
   c. space
   d. tool

4. _____ There were several *postoperative* patients.
   a. cured
   b. prepared to have an operation
   c. having completed an operation
   d. generally uncooperative

5. _____ the limits that she might have *encompassed* with the aid of touch
   a. included
   b. pointed the way to
   c. agreed upon
   d. ultimately accepted

6. _____ a sensation *unencumbered* by meaning
   a. not weighted down
   b. not including
   c. denied the advantage of
   d. not aroused

7. _____ to see the world as a *dazzle* of color patches
   a. buzz
   b. meaningless jumble
   c. startling sensation
   d. collection

8. _____ The rest of seeing is *tormentingly* difficult.
   a. unbearably
   b. amusingly
   c. painfully
   d. annoyingly

9. _____ The patient observes these color-patches to be *substantial*.
   a. solid
   b. pleasurable
   c. valuable
   d. really big

10. _____ They resist him as *tactual* objects do.
    a. strategic
    b. touchable
    c. previous
    d. smaller

11. _____ They *conceived* the world as touchingly manageable.
    a. saw
    b. imagined
    c. knew
    d. suspected

12. _____ A *disheartening* number of them refuse to see.
    a. large
    b. decent
    c. uncertain
    d. depressing

13. _____ Some lapse into *apathy* and despair.
    a. blindness
    b. a state of uncaring
    c. a form of mental disease
    d. alarm

14. _____ On her face was an expression of *gratification*.
    a. joy
    b. despair
    c. satisfaction
    d. fascination

15. _____ As I walked through the shifting color-patches, the world was *transfigured* for me.
    a. changed into something better
    b. thoroughly reorganized
    c. sustained as never before
    d. reproduced

15

ELLIOT LIEBOW

Tally's Corner

Twenty years ago, sociologist Elliot Liebow
developed an unusual closeness with an
inner-city streetcorner man, Tally Jackson.
Liebow learned a great deal about black city
culture as it develops on the streetcorner, and
he worked to understand the problems and
the attitudes that prevail there. What Liebow
learned twenty years ago is to some extent
still true. The relationship between a man
and the job he has will mean one thing
for the middle-class society in general, but
it means quite a different thing for the
undereducated black streetcorner man.

Bernard assesses the objective job situation dispassionately over a
cup of coffee, sometimes poking at the coffee with his spoon, sometimes staring
at it as if, like a crystal ball, it holds tomorrow's secrets. He is twenty-seven years
old. He and the woman with whom he lives have a baby son, and she has another
child by another man. Bernard does odd jobs—mostly painting—but here it is
the end of January, and his last job was with the Post Office during the Christmas
mail rush. He would like postal work as a steady job, he says. It pays well (about
$2.00 an hour) but he has twice failed the Post Office examination (he graduated
from a Washington high school) and has given up the idea as an impractical one.
He is supposed to see a man tonight about a job as a parking attendant for a
large apartment house. The man told him to bring his birth certificate and
driver's license, but his license was suspended because of a backlog of unpaid
traffic fines. A friend promised to lend him some money this evening. If he gets it,
he will pay the fines tomorrow morning and have his license reinstated. He
hopes the man with the job will wait till tomorrow night.

A "security job" is what he really wants, he said. He would like to save up
money for a taxicab. (But having twice failed the postal examination and having

a bad driving record as well, it is highly doubtful that he could meet the qualifications or pass the written test.) That would be "a good life." He can always get a job in a restaurant or as a clerk in a drugstore but they don't pay enough, he said. He needs to take home at least $50 to $55 a week. He thinks he can get that much driving a truck somewhere . . . Sometimes he wishes he had stayed in the army . . . A security job, that's what he wants most of all, a real security job . . .

When we look at what the men bring to the job rather than at what the job offers the men, it is essential to keep in mind that we are not looking at men who come to the job fresh, just out of school perhaps, and newly prepared to undertake the task of making a living, or from another job where they earned a living and are prepared to do the same on this job. Each man comes to the job with a long job history characterized by his not being able to support himself and his family. Each man carries this knowledge, born of his experience, with him. He comes to the job flat and stale, wearied by the sameness of it all, convinced of his own incompetence, terrified of responsibility—of being tested still again and found wanting. Possible exceptions are the younger men not yet, or just, married. They suspect all this but have yet to have it confirmed by repeated personal experience over time. But those who are or have been married know it well. It is the experience of the individual and the group of their fathers and probably their sons. Convinced of their inadequacies, not only do they not seek out those few better-paying jobs which test their resources, but they actively avoid them, gravitating in a mass to the menial, routine jobs which offer no challenge—and therefore pose no threat—to the already diminished images they have of themselves.

Thus Richard does not follow through on the real estate agent's offer. He is afraid to do on his own—minor plastering, replacing broken windows, other minor repairs and painting—exactly what he had been doing for months on a piecework basis under someone else (and which provided him with a solid base from which to derive a cost estimate).

Richard once offered an important clue to what may have gone on in his mind when the job offer was made. We were in the Carry-out, at a time when he was looking for work. He was talking about the kind of jobs available to him.

> I graduated from high school [Baltimore] but I don't know any-thing. I'm dumb. Most of the time I don't even say I graduated, 'cause then somebody asks me a question and I can't answer it, and they think I was lying about graduating. . . . They graduated me but I didn't know anything. I had lousy grades but I guess they wanted to get rid of me.
>
> I was at Margaret's house the other night and her little sister asked me to help her with her homework. She showed me some fractions and I knew right away I couldn't do them. I was ashamed so I told her I had to go to the bathroom.

And so it must have been, surely, with the real estate agent's offer. Convinced that "I'm dumb . . . I don't know anything," he "knew right away" he couldn't do it, despite the fact that he had been doing just this sort of work all along.

Thus, the man's low self-esteem generates a fear of being tested and prevents him from accepting a job with responsibilities or, once on a job, from staying with it if responsibilities are thrust on him, even if the wages are commensurately higher. Richard refuses such a job, Leroy leaves one, and another man, given more responsibility and more pay, knows he will fail and proceeds to do so, proving he was right about himself all along. The self-fulfilling prophecy is everywhere at work. In a hallway, Stanton, Tonk and Boley are passing a bottle around. Stanton recalls the time he was in the service. Everything was fine until he attained the rank of corporal. He worried about everything he did then. Was he doing the right thing? Was he doing it well? When would they discover their mistake and take his stripes (and extra pay) away? When he finally lost his stripes, everything was all right again.

Lethargy, disinterest and general apathy on the job, so often reported by employers, has its streetcorner counterpart. The men do not ordinarily talk about their jobs or ask one another about them. Although most of the men know who is or is not working at any given time, they may or may not know what particular job an individual man has. There is no overt interest in job specifics as they relate to this or that person, in large part perhaps because the specifics are not especially relevant. To know that a man is working is to know approximately how much he makes and to know as much as one needs or wants to know about how he makes it. After all, how much difference does it make to know whether a man is pushing a mop and pulling trash in an apartment house, a restaurant, or an office building, or delivering groceries, drugs, or liquor, or, if he's a laborer, whether he's pushing a wheelbarrow, mixing mortar, or digging a hole. So much does one job look like every other that there is little to choose between them. In large part, the job market consists of a narrow range of nondescript chores calling for nondistinctive, undifferentiated, unskilled labor. "A job is a job."

A crucial factor in the streetcorner man's lack of job commitment is the overall value he places on the job. *For his part, the streetcorner man puts no lower value on the job than does the larger society around him.* He knows the social value of the job by the amount of money the employer is willing to pay him for doing it. In a real sense, every pay day, he counts in dollars and cents the value placed on the job by society at large. He is no more (and frequently less) ready to quit and look for another job than his employer is ready to fire him and look for another man. Neither the streetcorner man who performs these jobs nor the society which requires him to perform them assesses the job as one "worth doing and worth doing well." Both employee and employer are contemptuous of the job. The employee shows his contempt by his reluctance to accept it or keep it, the employer by paying less than is required to support a family. Nor does the low-wage job offer prestige, respect, interesting work, opportunity for learning or advancement, or any other compensation. With few exceptions, jobs filled by the streetcorner men are at the bottom of the employment ladder in every respect, from wage level to prestige. Typically, they are hard, dirty, uninteresting and underpaid. The rest of society (whatever its ideal values regarding the dignity of labor) holds the job of the dishwasher or janitor or unskilled laborer in low esteem if not outright contempt. So does the streetcorner man. He cannot do otherwise. He cannot draw from a job those social values which other people do not put into it.

Only occasionally does spontaneous conversation touch on these matters directly. Talk about jobs is usually limited to isolated statements of intention, such as "I think I'll get me another gig [job]," "I'm going to look for a construction job when the weather breaks," or "I'm going to quit. I can't take no more of his shit." Job assessments typically consist of nothing more than a noncommittal shrug and "It's O.K." or "It's a job."

One reason for the relative absence of talk about one's job is, as suggested earlier, that the sameness of job experiences does not bear reiteration. Another and more important reason is the emptiness of the job experience itself. The man sees middle-class occupations as a primary source of prestige, pride and self-respect; his own job affords him none of these. To think about his job is to see himself as others see him, to remind him of just where he stands in this society. And because society's criteria for placement are generally the same as his own, to talk about his job can trigger a flush of shame and a deep, almost physical ache to change places with someone, almost anyone, else. The desire to be a person in his own right, to be noticed by the world he lives in, is shared by each of the men on the streetcorner. Whether they articulate this desire (as Tally does below) or not, one can see them position themselves to catch the attention of their fellows in much the same way as plants bend or stretch to catch the sunlight.

Tally and I were in the Carry-out. It was summer, Tally's peak earning season as a cement finisher, a semiskilled job a cut or so above that of the unskilled laborer. His take-home pay during these weeks was well over a hundred dollars — "a lot of bread." But for Tally, who no longer had a family to support, bread was not enough.

> "You know that boy came in last night? That Black Moozlem? That's what I ought to be doing. I ought to be in his place."
> "What do you mean?"
> "Dressed nice, going to [night] school, got a good job."
> "He's no better off than you, Tally. You make more than he does."
> "It's not the money. [Pause] It's position, I guess. He's got position. When he finish school he gonna be a supervisor. People respect him. . . . Thinking about people with position and education gives me a feeling right here [pressing his fingers into the pit of his stomach]."

"You're educated, too. You have a skill, a trade. You're a cement finisher. You can make a building, pour a sidewalk."

"That's different. Look, can anybody do what you're doing? Can anybody just come up and do your job? Well, in one week I can teach you cement finishing. You won't be as good as me 'cause you won't have the experience but you'll be a cement finisher. That's what I mean. Anybody can do what I'm doing and that's what gives me this feeling. [Long pause] Suppose I like this girl. I go over to her house and I meet her father. He starts talking about operating on somebody and sewing them up and about surgery. I know he's a doctor 'cause of the way he talks. Then she starts talking about what she did. Maybe she's a boss or a supervisor. Maybe she's a lawyer and her father says to me, 'And what do you do, Mr. Jackson?' [Pause] You remember at the courthouse, Lonny's trial? You and the lawyer was talking in the hall? You remember? I just stood there listening. I didn't say a word. You know why? 'Cause I didn't even know what you was talking about. That's happened to me a lot."

"Hell, you're nothing special. That happens to everybody. Nobody knows everything. One man is a doctor, so he talks about surgery. Another man is a teacher, so he talks about books. But doctors and teachers don't know anything about concrete. You're a cement finisher and that's your specialty."

"Maybe so, but when was the last time you saw anybody standing around talking about concrete?"

The streetcorner man wants to be a person in his own right, to be noticed, to be taken account of, but in this respect, as well as in meeting his money needs, his job fails him. The job and the man are even. The job fails the man and the man fails the job.

Furthermore, the man does not have any reasonable expectation that, however bad it is, his job will lead to better things. Menial jobs are not, by and large, the starting point of a track system which leads to even better jobs for those who are able and willing to do them. The busboy or dishwasher in a restaurant is not on a job track which, if negotiated skillfully, leads to chef or manager of the restaurant. The busboy or dishwasher who works hard becomes, simply, a hard-working busboy or dishwasher. Neither hard work nor perseverance can conceivably carry the janitor to a sit-down job in the office building he cleans up. And it is the apprentice who becomes the journeyman electrician, plumber, steam fitter or bricklayer, not the common unskilled Negro laborer.

Thus, the job is not a stepping stone to something better. It is a dead end. It promises to deliver no more tomorrow, next month or next year than it does today.

LENGTH: 2,897 WORDS

15 Elliot Liebow
Tally's Corner

SCORING: Reading time: _____ Rate from chart: _____ W.P.M.

RETENTION   number right _____ × 2 equals _____ points

MAIN IDEAS   number right _____ × 4 equals _____ points

APPLICATION   number right _____ × 4 equals _____ points

VOCABULARY   number right _____ × 2 equals _____ points

(Total points: 100) **total** _____ points

RETENTION   Based on the selection, which of the following statements are True (T), False (F), or Not answerable (N)?

1. _____ Talking about jobs can cause a streetcorner man to virtually ache to change places with someone else.

2. _____ Actually, streetcorner men have no desire to be noticed by the world they live in.

3. _____ Menial jobs are usually the starting point that leads to better jobs.

4. _____ Richard admitted that he graduated from high school, but that he doesn't know anything.

5. _____ The streetcorner man devalues his job even more than the society does.

6. _____ Thinking about his job reminds the streetcorner man just where he stands in his society.

7. _____ Examinations play little or no part in the world of work for the streetcorner men after they leave school.

8. _____ Restaurant and clerk jobs pay enough for a streetcorner man to live on.

9. _____ Hard work and perseverance can carry the janitor upward to a better job.

10. _____ The streetcorner man, like society in general, knows that the social value of a job is measured by what he gets paid.

11. _____ Low prestige jobs are held in contempt by both employer and employee.

12. _____ The streetcorner man usually talks a lot about his job, praising it or condemning it.

13. _____ When Stanton lost his corporal's stripes he actually felt better.

14. _____ The streetcorner man sees middle-class jobs as possessing prestige.

15. _____ Liebow discovered that streetcorner men never look for work.

MAIN IDEAS

1. _____ Which of the following best states the main idea of this selection?
   a. Streetcorner men have the same values as the rest of society.
   b. Streetcorner men dislike work.
   c. Low self-esteem produces failure after failure.

2. _____ If the main idea of this selection is true, which of the following is most likely to happen?
   a. If Richard gets a job with a bit of responsibility, he will fail at it.
   b. Most streetcorner men will turn a job offer down without looking into it.
   c. Streetcorner men often want to be surgeons.

APPLICATION   Choose the best answer for each question.

1. _____ As far as the streetcorner man is concerned:
   a. the social value of a job is established by someone else.
   b. there is no social value to any job.
   c. social values are distinct from jobs.
   d. the social value of a job is impossible to determine.

2. _____ Most of the men Liebow got to know came to a job:
   a. almost entirely by luck.
   b. through references from social agencies.
   c. with a history of past failures.
   d. with great enthusiasm at first.

3. _____ Because of a lack of success in the past, streetcorner men:
   a. shied away from reporters.
   b. would not talk with Liebow at first.
   c. never let on what they were doing.
   d. were terrified of responsibility.

4. _____ Because they were convinced of their inadequacies:
   a. they would halt conversations abruptly.
   b. they would actually avoid better-paying jobs.
   c. no one could comfort them or tell them different.
   d. social agencies had essentially written them off.

5. _____ The jobs available to streetcorner men:
   a. generally lack variety, interest, and challenges.
   b. are really much better than they realize.
   c. would be much the same as those available to anyone.
   d. made Liebow wonder what the problem was.

6. _____ Tally's observations about Liebow's conversation with a lawyer demonstrate that:
   a. Liebow has had some training in the law.
   b. Tally has a sense of the value of professional work.
   c. Tally likes neither lawyers nor professors.
   d. Tally gets into a lot of trouble.

7. _____ When Tally complained about his work:
   a. Liebow agreed with him.
   b. there was nothing Liebow could say in return.
   c. Liebow pretended he did not hear.
   d. Liebow tried to reassure him that his work was important.

8. _____ Tally admired the young black Muslim because:
   a. Tally did not belong to a religion.
   b. Tally's family had left him.
   c. of the man's position in life.
   d. the young man was already earning a good wage.

VOCABULARY   Choose the best definition for each italic vocabulary entry.

1. _____ *Spontaneous* conversation touches on these matters.
   a. unplanned
   b. noisy
   c. sudden
   d. agitated

2. _____ Talk about jobs is limited to *isolated* statements of intention.
   a. insulated
   b. infrequent
   c. intentional
   d. integrated

3. _____ Job *assessments* typically consist of shrugs.
   a. comments
   b. discussions
   c. descriptions
   d. evaluations

4. _____ The sameness of the job experience does not bear *reiteration*.
   a. restitution
   b. discussion
   c. restatement
   d. rehearing

5. _____ even if wages are *commensurately* higher for a given job
   a. proportionately
   b. unusually
   c. immediately
   d. normally

6. _____ Everything was fine until he *attained* the rank of corporal.
   a. earned
   b. was given
   c. reached
   d. retained

7. _____ *gravitating* in a mass to the low-paying jobs
   a. moving toward
   b. falling
   c. struggling
   d. drawn

8. _____ a base from which to *derive* a cost estimate
   a. find
   b. get
   c. sustain
   d. produce

9. _____ a narrow range of *nondescript* chores
   a. boring
   b. tiresome
   c. annoying
   d. similar

10. _____ They are *contemptuous* of the job.
    a. hold in disregard
    b. be suspicious of
    c. thoughtful about
    d. worn out with

11. _____ Bernard assesses the job *dispassionately* over a cup of coffee.
   a. without emotion
   b. indistinctly
   c. creditably
   d. disdainfully

12. _____ *Menial* jobs are all that are available.
   a. minimal
   b. disinterest
   c. social
   d. servile

13. _____ Society's *criteria* for placement are the same as his.
   a. measurement
   b. attitude
   c. standards of judgment
   d. establishment of value

14. _____ whether they *articulate* this desire or not
   a. put into action
   b. classify
   c. touch upon
   d. express

15. _____ The apprentice becomes the *journeyman* electrician.
   a. professional
   b. regular
   c. qualified worker
   d. inexperienced employee

16

MARTIN LUTHER KING, JR.

I Have a Dream

This speech was given before the nation at one of our most critical periods, a time when black Americans were struggling for their basic human rights. Martin Luther King, Jr., came to Washington, D.C., with 200,000 followers on the hundredth anniversary of President Lincoln's Emancipation Proclamation freeing the slaves on August 28, 1863. Until that time, it was the largest number of people ever to journey to Washington to plead a cause. King was assassinated in 1968, but his dreams have continued to inspire Americans everywhere. His birthday is now a national holiday.

I am happy to join with you today in what will go down in history as the greatest demonstration for freedom in the history of our nation.

Five score years ago, a great American, in whose symbolic shadow we stand today, signed the Emancipation Proclamation. This momentous decree came as a great beacon light of hope to millions of Negro slaves who had been seared in the flames of withering injustice. It came as a joyous daybreak to end the long night of their captivity.

But one hundred years later, the Negro still is not free; one hundred years later, the life of the Negro is still sadly crippled by the manacles of segregation and the chains of discrimination; one hundred years later, the Negro lives on a lonely island of poverty in the midst of a vast ocean of material prosperity; one hundred years later, the Negro is still languished in the corners of American society and finds himself in exile in his own land.

So we've come here today to dramatize a shameful condition. In a sense we've come to our nation's capital to cash a check. When the architects of our republic wrote the magnificent words of the Constitution and the Declaration of Independence, they were signing a promissory note to which every American was to fall heir. This note was the promise that all men, yes, black men as well as white men, would be guaranteed the unalienable rights of life, liberty, and the pursuit of happiness.

It is obvious today that America has defaulted on this promissory note insofar as her citizens of color are concerned. Instead of honoring this sacred obligation, America has given the Negro people a bad check; a check which has come back marked "insufficient funds." But we refuse to believe that the bank of justice is bankrupt. We refuse to believe that there are insufficient funds in the great vaults of opportunity of this nation. And so we've come to cash this check, a check that will give us upon demand the riches of freedom and the security of justice.

We have also come to this hallowed spot to remind America of the fierce urgency of now. This is no time to engage in the luxury of cooling off or to take the tranquilizing drug of gradualism. Now is the time to make real the promises of democracy; now is the time to rise from the dark and desolate valley of segregation to the sunlit path of racial justice; now is the time to lift our nation from the quicksands of racial injustice to the solid rock of brotherhood; now is the time to make justice a reality for all of God's children. It would be fatal for the nation to overlook the urgency of the moment. This sweltering summer of the Negro's legitimate discontent will not pass until there is an invigorating autumn of freedom and equality.

Nineteen sixty-three is not an end, but a beginning. And those who hope that the Negro needed to blow off steam and will now be content, will have a rude awakening if the nation returns to business as usual. There will be neither rest nor tranquility in America until the Negro is granted his citizenship rights. The whirlwinds of revolt will continue to shake the foundations of our nation until the bright day of justice emerges.

But there is something that I must say to my people, who stand on the worn threshold which leads into the palace of justice. In the process of gaining our rightful place, we must not be guilty of wrongful deeds. Let us not seek to satisfy our thirst for freedom by drinking from the cup of bitterness and hatred. We must forever conduct our struggle on the high plain of dignity and discipline. We must not allow our creative protests to degenerate into physical violence. Again and again we must rise to the majestic heights of meeting physical force with soul force. The marvelous new militancy, which has engulfed the Negro community, must not lead us to a distrust of all white people. For many of our white brothers, as evidenced by their presence here today, have come to realize that their destiny is tied up with our destiny. And they have come to realize that their freedom is inextricably bound to our freedom. We cannot walk alone. And as we walk, we must make the pledge that we shall always march ahead. We cannot turn back.

There are those who are asking the devotees of Civil Rights, "When will you be satisfied?" We can never be satisfied as long as the Negro is the victim of the unspeakable horrors of police brutality; we can never be satisfied as long as our bodies, heavy with the fatigue of travel, cannot gain lodging in the motels of the highways and the hotels of the cities; we cannot be satisfied as long as the Negro's basic mobility is from a smaller ghetto to a larger one; we can never be satisfied as long as our children are stripped of their selfhood and robbed of their dignity by signs stating "For White Only"; we cannot be satisfied as long as the Negro in Mississippi cannot vote and a Negro in New York believes he has nothing for which to vote. No! No, we are not satisfied, and we will not be satisfied until "justice rolls down like waters and righteousness like a mighty stream."

I am not unmindful that some of you have come here out of great trials and tribulations. Some of you have come fresh from narrow jail cells. Some of you have come from areas where your quest for freedom left you battered by the storms of persecution and staggered by the winds of police brutality. You have been the veterans of creative suffering. Continue to work with the faith that unearned suffering is redemptive. Go back to Mississippi. Go back to Alabama. Go back to South Carolina. Go back to Georgia. Go back to Louisiana. Go back to the slums and ghettos of our Northern cities, knowing that somehow this situation can and will be changed. Let us not wallow in the valley of despair.

I say to you today, my friends, so even though we face the difficulties of today and tomorrow, I still have a dream. It is a dream deeply rooted in the American dream. I have a dream that one day this nation will rise up and live out the true meaning of its creed, "We hold these truths to be self-evident, that all men are created equal." I have a dream that one day on the red hills of Georgia, sons of former slaves and the sons of former slave owners will be able to sit down together at the table of brotherhood. I have a dream that one day even the state of Mississippi, a state sweltering with the heat of injustice, sweltering with the heat of oppression, will be transformed into an oasis of freedom and justice. I have a dream that my four little children will one day live in a nation where they will not be judged by the color of their skin, but by the content of their character.

I have a dream today!

I have a dream that one day down in Alabama—with its vicious racists, with its Governor having his lips dripping with the words of interposition and nullification—one day right there in Alabama, little black boys and black girls will be able to join hands with little white boys and white girls as sisters and brothers.

I have a dream today!

I have a dream that one day every valley shall be exalted, every hill and mountain shall be made low. The rough places will be plain and the crooked places will be made straight, "and the glory of the Lord shall be revealed, and all flesh shall see it together."

This is our hope. This is the faith that I go back to the South with. With this faith we will be able to hew out of the mountain of despair, a stone of hope. With this faith we will be able to transform the jangling discords of our nation into a beautiful symphony of brotherhood. With this faith we will be able to work together, to pray together, to struggle together, to go to jail together, to stand up for freedom together, knowing that we will be free one day. And this will be the day. This will be the day when all of God's children will be able to sing with new meaning, "My country 'tis of thee, sweet land of liberty, of thee I sing. Land where my father died, land of the pilgrim's pride, from every mountainside, let freedom ring." And if America is to be a great nation, this must become true.

So let freedom ring from the prodigious hilltops of New Hampshire; let freedom ring from the mighty mountains of New York; let freedom ring from the heightening Alleghenies of Pennsylvania; let freedom ring from the snow-capped Rockies of Colorado; let freedom ring from the curvaceous slopes of California. But not only that. Let freedom ring from Stone Mountain of Georgia; let freedom ring from Lookout Mountain of Tennessee; let freedom ring from every hill and mole hill of Mississippi. "From every mountainside, let freedom ring."

And when this happens, and when we allow freedom to ring, when we let it ring from every village and every hamlet, from every state and every city, we will be able to speed up that day when all of God's children, black men and white men, Jews and Gentiles, Protestants and Catholics, will be able to join hands and sing in the words of the old Negro spiritual: "Free at last. Free at last. Thank God Almighty, we are free at last."

LENGTH: 1,630 WORDS

16 Martin Luther King, Jr. I Have a Dream

SCORING: Reading time: _____ Rate from chart: _____ W.P.M.

RETENTION	number right _____ × 2 equals _____ points	
MAIN IDEAS	number right _____ × 4 equals _____ points	
APPLICATION	number right _____ × 4 equals _____ points	
VOCABULARY	number right _____ × 2 equals _____ points	

(Total points: 100) **total** _____ points

RETENTION   Based on the selection, which of the following statements are True (T), False (F), or Not answerable (N)?

1. _____ Not all white Americans realized their destiny was tied to that of black Americans.

2. _____ One complaint of blacks was that motels were not open to them.

3. _____ There had been no recent social disturbances before King's speech.

4. _____ King is negatively critical of the terminology of the Constitution and the Declaration of Independence.

5. _____ Even though blacks were freed by law, King felt they were not free in fact.

6. _____ King felt that his presence, and that of his followers, dramatized the inequities of society.

7. _____ The check he wanted to cash for freedom and justice was real.

8. _____ Ironically, because slavery was legal, King could not call it unjust.

9. _____ One question people asked of King was "When will you be satisfied?"

10. _____ Segregation and discrimination are similar to forms of imprisonment.

11. _____ King expresses a moment of personal despair in this speech.

12. _____ The president had tried to block the gathering at which King spoke.

13. _____ The governor of Alabama had been a leader in desegregation and ending racial discrimination.

14. _____ After this speech, King expected to return to the South.

15. _____ King expressed approval of the Emancipation Proclamation.

MAIN IDEAS

1. _____ Which of the following best states the main idea of this selection?
    a. It is time for America to make good on earlier promises.
    b. Injustice causes very hard feelings on the part of the oppressed.
    c. Segregation and discrimination were totally unimagined consequences of the Emancipation Proclamation.

2. _____ If the main idea of this selection is true, which of the following would King most likely have believed?
    a. No people are whole until they are free.
    b. Instead of being freed, the original slaves should have been returned to their homeland.
    c. Some whites have denied blacks the opportunities which were supposed to be theirs in the first place.

APPLICATION   Choose the best answer for each question.

1. _____ King specifically rejected gradualism because:
    a. it lulled people into thinking things were all right.
    b. he had not personally invented the idea.
    c. no one had ever seriously proposed it.
    d. in other countries gradualism had been a failure.

2. _____ King wanted freedom for black Americans, but:
    a. he wanted others to desire it, too.
    b. he knew it was really impossible.
    c. his own views centered on the freedom of his children.
    d. one of his primary hopes was to achieve it nonviolently.

3. _____ The people who came out of jail cells to be at the rally were probably:
    a. protestors for civil rights.
    b. hoping King would look into their cases.
    c. in Washington to look up a good lawyer.
    d. less interested in justice than in freedom.

4. _____ In celebrating the regions of America, King expresses a:
    a. good knowledge of geography.
    b. willingness to travel.
    c. sense of insouciance.
    d. sincere affection for America.

5. _____ When he says he dreams that America will live out the true meaning of its creed, he affirms that:
 a. the creed is good; the failure to practice it is bad.
 b. the creed needs interpretation in light of today.
 c. no one ever expected the creed to be put into action.
 d. there is much more reason to hope than to fear.

6. _____ Justice is a sacred obligation probably because:
 a. God declared it so in the Old Testament.
 b. King regards justice as God given.
 c. the president had said so.
 d. white America had long agreed it was.

7. _____ Blacks in New York apparently do not vote because:
 a. whites will not let them.
 b. it is dangerous just to go out of the apartment.
 c. voting will never change their circumstances.
 d. they feel they have nothing to vote for.

8. _____ The American Constitution:
 a. was not a legal document.
 b. made a promise to every American.
 c. originally made the slaves free.
 d. is the basis for King's speech.

VOCABULARY   Choose the best definition for each italic vocabulary entry.

1. _____ *Five score* years ago, a great American stood here.
 a. quite a long time
 b. fifty
 c. one hundred
 d. five decades

2. _____ The *momentous* decree came as a beacon light.
 a. timely
 b. gigantic
 c. significant
 d. exhilarating

3. _____ The Negro is crippled by the *manacles* of segregation.
 a. chains
 b. prisons
 c. leg irons
 d. handcuffs

4. _____ The Negro is still *languished* in the corners of the nation.
   a. wasting away
   b. hiding
   c. resting
   d. struggling

5. _____ when the *architects* of our republic wrote the Constitution
   a. designers
   b. builders
   c. founders
   d. patrons

6. _____ All men would be guaranteed *unalienable* rights.
   a. good
   b. unbelievable
   c. permanent, inseparable
   d. fundamental, basic

7. _____ America has *defaulted* on this promissory note.
   a. gone back on
   b. not used good faith
   c. failed
   d. defeated

8. _____ the time to rise from the dark and *desolate* valley of segregation
   a. unsoulful
   b. painful
   c. depressing
   d. lonely

9. _____ the *invigorating* autumn of freedom and equality
   a. vitalizing
   b. belated
   c. unexpected
   d. thrilling

10. _____ The freedom is *inextricably* bound with our freedom.
    a. permanently
    b. once and for all
    c. not capable of being separated
    d. felicitously and unsuspectingly

11. _____ continue to believe that unearned suffering is *redemptive*
    a. sacred
    b. godlike
    c. saving
    d. freeing

12. _____ The governor's lips are dripping with the words of *interposition* and nullification.
    a. judgment
    b. interference
    c. interaction
    d. anger

13. _____ I have a dream that every valley shall be *exalted*.
    a. raised high
    b. flattened out
    c. inhabited
    d. traveled through

14. _____ We wish to *hew* out of the mountain of despair a stone of hope.
    a. cry
    b. carve
    c. find
    d. make

15. _____ Let freedom ring from the *prodigious* hilltops of New Hampshire.
    a. tiny
    b. wondrous
    c. lucky
    d. inconspicuous

17

BANESH HOFFMANN

My Friend, Albert Einstein

Banesh Hoffmann met Albert Einstein, the scientist whose theories made the atomic bomb possible, while they worked in Princeton. Einstein was already a renowned genius of modern physics, and Hoffmann hardly knew what to expect. What he discovered was that Einstein was both friendly and human. He revealed himself through his simplicity and his personal charm. Hoffmann recalls him now, with great admiration for his genius and for his humility.

He was one of the greatest scientists the world has ever known, yet if I had to convey the essence of Albert Einstein in a single word, I would choose *simplicity*. Perhaps an anecdote will help. Once, caught in a downpour, he took off his hat and held it under his coat. Asked why, he explained, with admirable logic, that the rain would damage the hat, but his hair would be none the worse for its wetting. This knack for going instinctively to the heart of a matter was the secret of his major scientific discoveries—this and his extraordinary feeling for beauty.

I first met Albert Einstein in 1935, at the famous Institute for Advanced Study in Princeton, N.J. He had been among the first to be invited to the Institute, and was offered *carte blanche* as to salary. To the director's dismay, Einstein asked for an impossible sum: it was far too *small*. The director had to plead with him to accept a larger salary.

I was in awe of Einstein, and hesitated before approaching him about some ideas I had been working on. When I finally knocked on his door, a gentle voice

Excerpted from "My Friend, Albert Einstein" by Banesh Hoffmann, *Reader's Digest,* January 1968. Reprinted with permission.

said, "Come"—with a rising inflection that made the single word both a welcome and a question. I entered his office and found him seated at a table, calculating and smoking his pipe. Dressed in ill-fitting clothes, his hair characteristically awry, he smiled a warm welcome. His utter naturalness at once set me at ease.

As I began to explain my ideas, he asked me to write the equations on the blackboard so he could see how they developed. Then came the staggering—and altogether endearing—request: "Please go slowly. I do not understand things quickly." This from Einstein! He said it gently, and I laughed. From then on, all vestiges of fear were gone.

Einstein was born in 1879 in the German city of Ulm. He had been no infant prodigy; indeed, he was so late in learning to speak that his parents feared he was a dullard. In school, though his teachers saw no special talent in him, the signs were already there. He taught himself calculus, for example, and his teachers seemed a little afraid of him because he asked questions they could not answer. At the age of 16, he asked himself whether a light wave would seem stationary if one ran abreast of it. From that innocent question would arise, ten years later, his theory of relativity.

Einstein failed his entrance examinations at the Swiss Federal Polytechnic School, in Zurich, but was admitted a year later. There he went beyond his regular work to study the masterworks of physics on his own. Rejected when he applied for academic positions, he ultimately found work, in 1902, as a patent examiner in Berne, and there in 1905 his genius burst into fabulous flower.

Among the extraordinary things he produced in that memorable year were his theory of relativity, with its famous offshoot, $E = mc^2$ (energy equals mass times the speed of light squared), and his quantum theory of light. These two theories were not only revolutionary, but seemingly contradictory: the former was intimately linked to the theory that light consists of waves, while the latter said it consists somehow of particles. Yet this unknown young man boldly proposed both at once—and he was right in both cases, though how he could have been is far too complex a story to tell here.

Collaborating with Einstein was an unforgettable experience. In 1937, the Polish physicist Leopold Infeld and I asked if we could work with him. He was pleased with the proposal, since he had an idea about gravitation waiting to be worked out in detail. Thus we got to know not merely the man and the friend, but also the professional.

The intensity and depth of his concentration were fantastic. When battling a recalcitrant problem, he worried it as an animal worries its prey. Often, when we found ourselves up against a seemingly insuperable difficulty, he would stand up, put his pipe on the table, and say in his quaint English, "I will a little tink" (he could not pronounce "th"). Then he would pace up and down, twirling a lock of his long, graying hair around his forefinger.

A dreamy, faraway and yet inward look would come over his face. There was no appearance of concentration, no furrowing of the brow—only a placid inner communion. The minutes would pass, and then suddenly Einstein would stop pacing as his face relaxed into a gentle smile. He had found the solution to the problem. Sometimes it was so simple that Infeld and I could have kicked ourselves for not having thought of it. But the magic had been performed invisibly in the depths of Einstein's mind, by a process we could not fathom.

Although Einstein felt no need for religious ritual and belonged to no formal religious group, he was the most deeply religious man I have known. He once said to me, "Ideas come from God," and one could hear the capital "G" in the reverence with which he pronounced the word. On the marble fireplace in the mathematics building at Princeton University is carved, in the original German, what one might call his scientific credo: "God is subtle, but he is not malicious." By this Einstein meant that scientists could expect to find their task difficult, but not hopeless: the Universe was a Universe of law, and God was not confusing us with deliberate paradoxes and contradictions.

Einstein was an accomplished amateur musician. We used to play duets, he on the violin, I at the piano. One day he surprised me by saying Mozart was the greatest composer of all. Beethoven "created" his music, but the music of Mozart was of such purity and beauty one felt he had merely "found" it—that it had always existed as part of the inner beauty of the Universe, waiting to be revealed.

It was this very Mozartean simplicity that most characterized Einstein's methods. His 1905 theory of relativity, for example, was built on just two simple assumptions. One is the so-called principle of relativity, which means, roughly speaking, that we cannot tell whether we are at rest or moving smoothly. The other assumption is that the speed of light is the same no matter what the speed of the object that produces it. You can see how reasonable this is if you think of agitating a stick in a lake to create waves. Whether you wiggle the stick from a stationary pier, or from a rushing speedboat, the waves, once generated, are on their own, and their speed has nothing to do with that of the stick.

Each of these assumptions, by itself, was so plausible as to seem primitively obvious. But together they were in such violent conflict that a lesser man would have dropped one or the other and fled in panic. Einstein daringly kept both— and by so doing he revolutionized physics. For he demonstrated they could, after all, exist peacefully side by side, provided we gave up cherished beliefs about the nature of time.

Science is like a house of cards, with concepts like time and space at the lowest level. Tampering with time brought most of the house tumbling down, and it was this that made Einstein's work so important—and controversial. At a conference in Princeton in honor of his 70th birthday, one of the speakers, a Nobel Prize-winner, tried to convey the magical quality of Einstein's achievement. Words failed him, and with a shrug of helplessness he pointed to his wristwatch, and said in tones of awed amazement, "It all came from this."

His very ineloquence made this the most eloquent tribute I have heard to Einstein's genius.

We think of Einstein as one concerned only with the deepest aspects of science. But he saw scientific principles in everyday things to which most of us would give barely a second thought. He once asked me if I had ever wondered why a man's feet will sink into either dry or completely submerged sand, while sand that is merely damp provides a firm surface. When I could not answer, he offered a simple explanation.

It depends, he pointed out, on *surface tension*, the elastic-skin effect of a liquid surface. This is what holds a drop together, or causes two small raindrops on a windowpane to pull into one big drop the moment their surfaces touch.

When sand is damp, Einstein explained, there are tiny amounts of water between grains. The surface tensions of these tiny amounts of water pull all the grains together, and friction then makes them hard to budge. When the sand is dry, there is obviously no water between grains. If the sand is fully immersed, there is water between grains, but no water *surface* to pull them together.

This is not as important as relativity; yet there is no telling what seeming trifle will lead an Einstein to a major discovery. And the puzzle of the sand does give us an inkling of the power and elegance of his mind.

Einstein's work, performed quietly with pencil and paper, seemed remote from the turmoil of everyday life: But his ideas were so revolutionary they caused violent controversy and irrational anger. Indeed, in order to be able to award him a belated Nobel Prize, the selection committee had to avoid mentioning relativity, and pretend the prize was awarded primarily for his work on the quantum theory.

Political events upset the serenity of his life even more. When the Nazis came to power in Germany, his theories were officially declared false because they had been formulated by a Jew. His property was confiscated, and it is said a price was put on his head.

When scientists in the United States, fearful that the Nazis might develop an atomic bomb, sought to alert American authorities to the danger, they were scarcely heeded. In desperation, they drafted a letter which Einstein signed and sent directly to President Roosevelt. It was this act that led to the fateful decision to go all-out on the production of an atomic bomb—an endeavor in which Einstein took no active part. When he heard of the agony and destruction that his $E = mc^2$ had wrought, he was dismayed beyond measure, and from then on there was a look of ineffable sadness in his eyes.

There was something elusively whimsical about Einstein. It is illustrated by my favorite anecdote about him. In his first year in Princeton, on Christmas Eve, so the story goes, some children sang carols outside his house. Having finished, they knocked on his door and explained they were collecting money to buy Christmas presents. Einstein listened, then said, "Wait a moment." He put on his scarf and overcoat, and took his violin from its case. Then, joining the children as they went from door to door, he accompanied their singing of "Silent Night" on his violin.

How shall I sum up what it meant to have known Einstein and his works? Like the Nobel Prize-winner who pointed helplessly at his watch, I can find no adequate words. It was akin to the revelation of great art that lets one see what was formerly hidden. And when, for example, I walk on the sand of a lonely beach, I am reminded of his ceaseless search for cosmic simplicity—and the scene takes on a deeper, sadder beauty.

LENGTH: 1,931 WORDS

17　Banesh Hoffmann
My Friend, Albert Einstein

SCORING: Reading time: _____ Rate from chart: _____ W.P.M.

RETENTION	number right _____ × 2 equals _____ points
MAIN IDEAS	number right _____ × 4 equals _____ points
APPLICATION	number right _____ × 4 equals _____ points
VOCABULARY	number right _____ × 2 equals _____ points

(Total points: 100) **total** _____ points

RETENTION　Based on the selection, which of the following statements are True (T), False (F), or Not answerable (N)?

1. _____ Apparently Hoffmann could not follow the mathematical language of Einstein.

2. _____ Hoffmann was hesitant about first meeting Einstein.

3. _____ Einstein failed the entrance exams for the polytechnic school that he eventually attended.

4. _____ Gravitational theories were of no interest to Einstein.

5. _____ Einstein was interested in Mozart and Beethoven.

6. _____ The theory of relativity relates to the question of whether we are moving or not.

7. _____ Einstein was able at times to make contradictory theories work together.

8. _____ Einstein saw no scientific principles in everyday life.

9. _____ The Nazis refused to believe Einstein's theories because he was a Jew.

10. _____ Einstein took a personal interest in helping America develop the atomic bomb.

11. _____ Although he deserved it, Einstein never won the Nobel Prize.

12. _____ Surface tension relates more to sand than it does to water.

13. _____ Einstein's work with time is what makes his theories so controversial.

14. _____ Hoffmann was surprised to see that Einstein rarely appeared to concentrate on a problem.

15. _____ Einstein's parents actually wondered whether he was a normal child.

MAIN IDEAS

1. _____ Which of the following best states the main idea of this selection?
   a. Einstein's problems were not only scientific, but often political.
   b. One of the secrets of making a scientific breakthrough is to seek out apparently conflicting theoretical views.
   c. Einstein surprisingly combined brilliance and personal simplicity.

2. _____ If the main idea of this selection is true, which of the following is most probable?
   a. The next theoretical breakthrough will combine theories of time and of place.
   b. Politics and science may combine in ways that will continue to surprise us.
   c. Those who did not know his reputation would have been surprised to know he was a genius.

APPLICATION   Choose the best answer for each question.

1. _____ Hoffmann's first shock on meeting him came when Einstein:
   a. spoke in a creaky little voice.
   b. revealed that he had an accent.
   c. refused to shake his hand.
   d. asked him to go slowly.

2. _____ Although he belonged to no religion, Einstein expressed a religious belief through:
   a. his manner of referring to God.
   b. his personal piety.
   c. writings and other documents.
   d. the kind of music that he preferred.

3. _____ The fact that Einstein taught himself calculus and conducted independent research in physics suggests that:
   a. he was interested in science.
   b. he was an obedient, quiet student.
   c. the school may not have been advanced enough for him.
   d. infant prodigies are not always successful in later life.

4. _____ Hoffmann thought that any seeming trifle might lead Einstein to a major discovery because:
   a. trifles, like Newton's apple, have always led to discoveries.
   b. no one understood trifles the way Einstein did.
   c. Einstein was such a keen observer of the details of life.
   d. Princeton had interesting parties at the Institute.

5. _____ Apparently, some theories can make scientists:
   a. cautious.
   b. irrational.
   c. fiddle.
   d. pause.

6. _____ Mozart and Einstein have in common:
   a. the fact that they played the violin.
   b. powers of deep concentration.
   c. an approach to style that is reassuring.
   d. a simplicity of the sense of discovery.

7. _____ The waves caused by a moving stick in the water will not be affected by the speed of the stick because:
   a. once the wave has begun, the stick is unimportant.
   b. as far as the water is concerned, the stick is not moving.
   c. the water reacts against, not concurs with, the stick.
   d. there will be other forces operating upon them.

8. _____ Hoffmann's story about Einstein's putting his hat under his coat during a downpour demonstrates:
   a. why he had asked for such a low salary at Princeton.
   b. how irrelevant clothing was to Einstein.
   c. the simplicity and clarity of Einstein's thought.
   d. that Einstein never quite got used to American ways.

VOCABULARY   Choose the best definition for each italic vocabulary entry.

1. _____ if I had to convey the *essence* of Einstein in one word
   a. reasonableness
   b. simplicity
   c. basic nature
   d. most truthful sort

2. _____ the knack of going *instinctively* to the heart of a matter
   a. without hesitation
   b. suddenly
   c. naturally
   d. responsibly

3. _____ He was offered *carte blanche* as to salary.
   a. a two-tiered system
   b. a blank check
   c. an open account
   d. a credit card

4. _____ A rising *inflection* made the word a welcome and a question.
   a. tone of voice
   b. change
   c. emotional quality
   d. German accent

5. _____ From then on, all *vestiges* of fear were gone.
   a. signs
   b. kinds
   c. remains
   d. qualities

6. _____ He was by no means an infant *prodigy*.
   a. talker
   b. wonder
   c. thinker
   d. performer

7. _____ From that *innocent* question came the theory of relativity.
   a. foolish
   b. good
   c. simple
   d. unsuspecting

8. _____ He worried a *recalcitrant* problem as an animal worries prey.
   a. stubborn
   b. unanticipated
   c. physical
   d. monstrous

9. _____ when finding himself against a seemingly *insuperable* difficulty
   a. weak
   b. overwhelming
   c. not able to be overcome
   d. striking

10. _____ There was no furrowing the brow, only a *placid* inner communication.
   a. pleasing
   b. peaceful

c. disturbing
d. mysterious

11. _____ God is subtle, but he is not *malicious*.
a. well intentioned
b. problematic
c. bad
d. spiteful

12. _____ The waves once *generated* are on their own.
a. seen
b. begun
c. formed
d. there

13. _____ if we give up *cherished* beliefs about time
a. ancient
b. well held
c. valuable
d. held dear

14. _____ His *ineloquence* made an eloquent tribute.
a. silence
b. refusal to be fair
c. incapacities
d. intelligence

15. _____ There was a look of *ineffable* sadness in his eyes.
a. incoherent
b. inescapable
c. unexpressible
d. intolerable

18

ALBERT EINSTEIN

$E = mc^2$

As you might expect, listening closely
to the man whose theories made it possible
to develop the atomic bomb is a challenging
experience. Albert Einstein has become the
symbol of genius in the twentieth century,
and his work is not always easy to read.
This discussion of the relationship of the
mass of an atom and the energy it contains
is remarkable. Carefully, Einstein reviews
theories of nineteenth-century physics and
shows how they were modified and absorbed
by contemporary theories. He then goes on to
explain why the separation of an atom will
release huge quantities of energy.

In order to understand the law of the equivalence of mass and energy, we must go back to two conservation or "balance" principles which, independent of each other, held a high place in pre-relativity physics. These were the principle of the conservation of energy and the principle of the conservation of mass. The first of these, advanced by Leibnitz as long ago as the seventeenth century, was developed in the nineteenth century essentially as a corollary of a principle of mechanics.

Consider, for example, a pendulum whose mass swings back and forth between the points A and B. At these points the mass m is higher by the amount h than it is at C, the lowest point of the path [see drawing on p. 166]. At C, on the other hand, the lifting height has disappeared and instead of it the mass has a velocity v. It is as though the lifting height could be converted entirely into velocity, and vice versa. The exact relation would be expressed as $mgh = \frac{m}{2} v^2$, with g representing the acceleration of gravity. What is interesting here is that this relation is independent of both the length of the pendulum and the form of the path through which the mass moves.

From *Out of My Later Years* by Albert Einstein. Reprinted with permission of Philosophical Library Publishers.

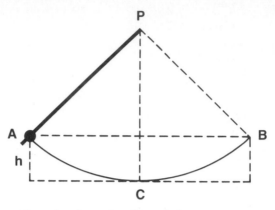

Drawing from Dr. Einstein's manuscript.

The significance is that something remains constant throughout the process, and that something is energy. At A and at B it is an energy of position, or "potential" energy; at C it is an energy of motion, or "kinetic" energy. If this concept is correct, then the sum $mgh + m \frac{v^2}{2}$ must have the same value for any position of the pendulum, if h is understood to represent the height above C, and v the velocity at that point in the pendulum's path. And such is found to be actually the case. The generalization of this principle gives us the law of the conservation of mechanical energy. But what happens when friction stops the pendulum?

The answer to that was found in the study of heat phenomena. This study, based on the assumption that heat is an indestructible substance which flows from a warmer to a colder object, seemed to give us a principle of the "conservation of heat." On the other hand, from time immemorial it has been known that heat could be produced by friction, as in the fire-making drills of the Indians. The physicists were for long unable to account for this kind of heat "production." Their difficulties were overcome only when it was successfully established that, for any given amount of heat produced by friction, an exactly proportional amount of energy had to be expended. Thus did we arrive at a principle of the "equivalence of work and heat." With our pendulum, for example, mechanical energy is gradually converted by friction into heat.

In such fashion the principles of the conservation of mechanical and thermal energies were merged into one. The physicists were thereupon persuaded that the conservation principle could be further extended to take in chemical and electromagnetic processes—in short, could be applied to all fields. It appeared that in our physical system there was a sum total of energies that remained constant through all changes that might occur.

Now for the principle of the conservation of mass. Mass is defined by the resistance that a body opposes to its acceleration (inert mass). It is also measured by the weight of the body (heavy mass). That these two radically different definitions lead to the same value for the mass of a body is, in itself, an astonishing fact. According to the principle—namely, that masses remain unchanged under any physical or chemical changes—the mass appeared to be the essential (because unvarying) quality of matter. Heating, melting, vaporization, or combining into chemical compounds would not change the total mass.

Physicists accepted this principle up to a few decades ago. But it proved inadequate in the face of the special theory of relativity. It was therefore merged with the energy principle—just as, about 60 years before, the principle of the conservation of mechanical energy had been combined with the principle of the conservation of heat. We might say that the principle of the conservation of energy, having previously swallowed up that of the conservation of heat, now proceeded to swallow that of the conservation of mass—and holds the field alone.

It is customary to express the equivalence of mass and energy (though somewhat inexactly) by the formula $E = mc^2$, in which c represents the velocity of light, about 186,000 miles per second. E is the energy that is contained in a stationary body; m is its mass. The energy that belongs to the mass m is equal to this mass, multiplied by the square of the enormous speed of light—which is to say, a vast amount of energy for every unit of mass.

But if every gram of material contains this tremendous energy, why did it go so long unnoticed? The answer is simple enough: so long as none of the energy is given off externally, it cannot be observed. It is as though a man who is fabulously rich should never spend or give away a cent; no one could tell how rich he was.

Now we can reverse the relation and say that an increase of E in the amount of energy must be accompanied by an increase of $\frac{E}{c^2}$ in the mass. I can easily supply energy to the mass—for instance, if I heat it by 10 degrees. So why not measure the mass increase, or weight increase, connected with this change? The trouble here is that in the mass increase the enormous factor c^2 occurs in the denominator of the fraction. In such a case the increase is too small to be measured directly; even with the most sensitive balance.

For a mass increase to be measurable, the change of energy per mass unit must be enormously large. We know of only one sphere in which such amounts of energy per mass unit are released: namely, radioactive disintegration. Schematically, the process goes like this: An atom of the mass M splits into two atoms of the mass M′ and M″, which separate with tremendous kinetic energy. If we imagine these two masses as brought to rest—that is, if we take this energy of motion from them—then, considered together, they are essentially poorer in energy than was the original atom. According to the equivalence principle, the mass sum M′ + M″ of the disintegration products must also be somewhat smaller than the original mass M of the disintegrating atom—in contradiction to the old principle of the conservation of mass. The relative difference of the two is on the order of 1/10 of one percent.

Now, we cannot actually weigh the atoms individually. However, there are indirect methods for measuring their weights exactly. We can likewise determine the kinetic energies that are transferred to the disintegration products M' and M". Thus it has become possible to test and confirm the equivalence formula. Also, the law permits us to calculate in advance, from precisely determined atom weights, just how much energy will be released with any atom disintegration we have in mind. The law says nothing, of course, as to whether—or how—the disintegration reaction can be brought about.

What takes place can be illustrated with the help of our rich man. The atom M is a rich miser who, during his life, gives away no money (*energy*). But in his will he bequeaths his fortune to his sons M' and M", on condition that they give to the community a small amount, less than one thousandth of the whole estate (*energy or mass*). The sons together have somewhat less than the father had (*the mass sum M' + M" is somewhat smaller than the mass M of the radioactive atom*). But the part given to the community, though relatively small, is still so enormously large (*considered as kinetic energy*) that it brings with it a great threat of evil. Averting that threat has become the most urgent problem of our time.

LENGTH: 1,345 WORDS

18   Albert Einstein
$E = mc^2$

SCORING: Reading time: _____ Rate from chart: _____ W.P.M.

RETENTION	number right _____ × 2 equals _____ points	
MAIN IDEAS	number right _____ × 4 equals _____ points	
APPLICATION	number right _____ × 4 equals _____ points	
VOCABULARY	number right _____ × 2 equals _____ points	

(Total points: 100) **total** _____ points

RETENTION   Based on the selection, which of the following statements are True (T), False (F), or Not answerable (N)?

1. _____ One cannot supply energy to mass.

2. _____ Today it is possible to weigh atoms directly.

3. _____ There is no test for the confirmation of the equivalence formula.

4. _____ A central focus of this essay is on explaining the equivalence of mass and energy.

5. _____ Throughout the swing of the pendulum, energy remains constant, although mass changes.

6. _____ A pendulum can swing from point to point, but its mass cannot.

7. _____ The formula concerning the velocity of a swinging pendulum depends on the length of the pendulum.

8. _____ Prerelativity physics goes back at least to the seventeenth century.

9. _____ Einstein says, in the pendulum example, that mechanical energy is converted by friction into heat.

10. _____ There is only one satisfactory way of determining mass.

11. _____ Physicists used to think heating something did not change its mass.

12. _____ Every unit of mass has a vast amount of energy.

13. _____ Potential energy and kinetic energy are the same.

14. _____ When an atom splits, its remaining parts lose an energy of motion.

15. _____ Einstein showed that kinetic energy produces heat and light.

MAIN IDEAS

1. _____ Which of the following best states the main idea of this selection?
    a. All theories in time seem to boil down to a single theory.
    b. Conservation theories have depended on moving from one basic theory to another that absorbs it.
    c. The people who developed the atomic bomb are less interested in the theories than in the power of destruction.

2. _____ If the main idea of this selection is true, which of the following is most likely to happen?
    a. In time the theory of conservation of energy may be absorbed by a new theory.
    b. The theory of conservation of energy is ultimately a political theory.
    c. The theory of conservation of energy will soon be shown to have only one form.

APPLICATION   Choose the best answer for each question.

1. _____ The most urgent problem of our time:
    a. is learning how to avoid the potential evil of atomic energy.
    b. is coping with the residue of the fallout of the conservation of energy theory.
    c. will be to find the next theory that will clarify the relationship between energy and mass.
    d. should be connected to establishing the limits of radioactivity in the universe.

2. _____ The two parts of an atom that have been split:
    a. have less energy than the original atom.
    b. change in mass but not energy.
    c. do not reveal the nature of the energy exchange.
    d. operate exactly as they did before the transformation.

3. _____ The original principle of the "conservation of heat":
    a. was elegant and essentially simple.
    b. showed that friction was an important part of the laws of physics.
    c. depended on thinking of heat as a substance.
    d. was disproved by the Indians.

4. _____ Physicists eventually solved the "production" of heat by friction theory when they realized that:

a. friction and heat were identical.
b. heat was not produced, but released.
c. heat produced by friction equaled the amount of heat expended in producing it.
d. there was no need for a separable friction theory, since the heat theory was sufficient.

5. _____ Because mechanical energy gradually converts into heat:
   a. theories of mechanical and thermal energy merged.
   b. friction becomes a handmaid of science.
   c. a pendulum can actually warm a small room.
   d. people thought heat absorbed energy.

6. _____ Radioactive disintegration contradicts:
   a. theories that Leibnitz discovered by accident.
   b. the principle that physical and chemical changes do not alter mass.
   c. the energy principle.
   d. theories based on extensive experiments with pendulums.

7. _____ The principle of the conservation of energy:
   a. has been known since ancient days.
   b. will be replaced by the conservation of mass.
   c. does not interest Einstein on a theoretical level.
   d. is now the most basic conservation principle.

8. _____ The incredible amounts of energy contained in mass were never guessed at before because:
   a. there were no theories that could accommodate the concept.
   b. the energy of mass had never been released before.
   c. no one knew mass and energy were identical.
   d. physicists had been stuck with an antiquated theory.

VOCABULARY   Choose the best definition for each italic vocabulary entry.

1. _____ law of *equivalence* of mass and energy
   a. measurement
   b. averaging
   c. conservation
   d. sameness

2. _____ The law was developed as a *corollary* of a principle of mechanics.
   a. related concept
   b. independent point
   c. by-product
   d. cautionary point

3. _____ The mass has a *velocity* v.
   a. capacity
   b. principle
   c. speed
   d. shifting weight

4. _____ It has potential energy and *kinetic* energy.
   a. experienced
   b. related to motion
   c. fully formed
   d. loathsome

5. _____ An answer was found in the study of heat *phenomena*.
   a. surprises
   b. events
   c. strokes
   d. moments

6. _____ From time *immemorial* it has been known that friction produces heat.
   a. beyond memory
   b. memorialized by time
   c. remembered
   d. out of mind

7. _____ two *radically* different definitions
   a. basically
   b. unspecifically
   c. hopelessly
   d. dangerously

8. _____ Mass appeared to be the essential, *unvarying* quality of matter.
   a. singular
   b. unspecific
   c. most important
   d. unchanging

9. _____ When no energy is given off *externally* none can be noticed.
   a. outside itself
   b. spontaneously beyond
   c. with quickness, suddenly
   d. notoriously

10. _____ The body itself has an *inert* mass.
    a. changeless
    b. unnoticeable
    c. intimate
    d. unstable

11. _____ The change would be measured by a sensitive *balance*.
   a. weight
   b. scales
   c. position
   d. relationship

12. _____ We know of only one *sphere* in which large amounts of energy are released.
   a. area
   b. ball
   c. ovoid
   d. planet

13. _____ We must study radioactive *disintegration*.
   a. dispensation
   b. fragmentation
   c. dialysis
   d. production

14. _____ *Schematically*, the process goes like this.
   a. sometimes
   b. possibly
   c. in a simple form
   d. ultimately

15. _____ *Averting* that threat has become the most urgent problem of our time.
   a. stopping
   b. sensing
   c. eliminating
   d. avoiding

19

ELISABETH KUBLER-ROSS

On the Fear of Death

Elisabeth Kubler-Ross has the advantage
of seeing our culture through the eyes of a
person who has lived abroad and who has
seen significant changes in medicine in a short
period of time. Our attitude toward death
has been affected by modern medicine. But it
is also affected by psychological factors that
are deep-seated and personal. Kubler-Ross
wonders whether some of the medical
treatment we now give the dying may not be
an expression of childlike psychological
needs.

Epidemics have taken a great toll of lives in past generations. Death
in infancy and early childhood was frequent and there were few families who
didn't lose a member of the family at an early age. Medicine has changed greatly
in the last decades. Widespread vaccinations have practically eradicated many
illnesses, at least in western Europe and the United States. The use of chemother-
apy, especially the antibiotics, has contributed to an ever-decreasing number of
fatalities in infectious diseases. Better child care and education has effected a low
morbidity and mortality among children. The many diseases that have taken an
impressive toll among the young and middle-aged have been conquered. The
number of old people is on the rise, and with this fact come the number of people
with malignancies and chronic diseases associated more with old age.

Pediatricians have less work with acute and life-threatening situations as they
have an ever-increasing number of patients with psychosomatic disturbances
and adjustment and behavior problems. Physicians have more people in their
waiting rooms with emotional problems than they have ever had before, but
they also have more elderly patients who not only try to live with their decreased
physical abilities and limitations but who also face loneliness and isolation with
all its pains and anguish. The majority of these people are not seen by a

psychiatrist. Their needs have to be elicited and gratified by other professional people, for instance, chaplains and social workers. It is for them that I am trying to outline the changes that have taken place in the last few decades, changes that are ultimately responsible for the increased fear of death, the rising number of emotional problems, and the greater need for understanding of and coping with the problems of death and dying.

When we look back in time and study old cultures and people, we are impressed that death has always been distasteful to man and will probably always be. From a psychiatrist's point of view this is very understandable and can perhaps best be explained by our basic knowledge that, in our unconscious, death is never possible in regard to ourselves. It is inconceivable for our unconscious to imagine an actual ending of our own life here on earth, and if this life of ours has to end, the ending is always attributed to a malicious intervention from the outside by someone else. In simple terms, in our unconscious mind we can only be killed; it is inconceivable to die of a natural cause or of old age. Therefore death in itself is associated with a bad act, a frightening happening, something that in itself calls for retribution and punishment.

One is wise to remember these fundamental facts as they are essential in understanding some of the most important, otherwise unintelligible communications of our patients.

The second fact that we have to comprehend is that in our unconscious mind we cannot distinguish between a wish and a deed. We are all aware of some of our illogical dreams in which two completely opposite statements can exist side by side—very acceptable in our dreams but unthinkable and illogical in our wakening state. Just as our unconscious mind cannot differentiate between the wish to kill somebody in anger and the act of having done so, the young child is unable to make this distinction. The child who angrily wishes his mother to drop dead for not having gratified his needs will be traumatized greatly by the actual death of his mother—even if this event is not linked closely in time with his destructive wishes. He will always take part or the whole blame for the loss of his mother. He will always say to himself—rarely to others—"I did it, I am responsible, I was bad, therefore Mommy left me." It is well to remember that the child will react in the same manner if he loses a parent by divorce, separation, or desertion. Death is often seen by a child as an impermanent thing and has therefore little distinction from a divorce in which he may have an opportunity to see a parent again.

Many a parent will remember remarks of their children such as, "I will bury my doggy now and next spring when the flowers come up again, he will get up." Maybe it was the same wish that motivated the ancient Egyptians to supply their dead with food and goods to keep them happy and the old American Indians to bury their relatives with their belongings.

When we grow older and begin to realize that our omnipotence is really not so omnipotent, that our strongest wishes are not powerful enough to make the impossible possible, the fear that we have contributed to the death of a loved one diminishes—and with it the guilt. The fear remains diminished, however, only so long as it is not challenged too strongly. Its vestiges can be seen daily in hospital corridors and in people associated with the bereaved.

A husband and wife may have been fighting for years, but when the partner dies, the survivor will pull his hair, whine and cry louder and beat his chest in regret, fear and anguish, and will hence fear his own death more than before, still believing in the law of talion—an eye for an eye, a tooth for a tooth—"I am responsible for her death, I will have to die a pitiful death in retribution."

Maybe this knowledge will help us understand many of the old customs and rituals which have lasted over the centuries and whose purpose is to diminish the anger of the gods or the people as the case may be, thus decreasing the anticipated punishment. I am thinking of the ashes, the torn clothes, the veil, the *Klage Weiber* [wailing wives] of the old days—they are all means to ask you to take pity on them, the mourners, and are expressions of sorrow, grief, and shame. If someone grieves, beats his chest, tears his hair, or refuses to eat, it is an attempt at self-punishment to avoid or reduce the anticipated punishment for the blame that he takes on the death of a loved one.

This grief, shame, and guilt are not very far removed from feelings of anger and rage. The process of grief always includes some qualities of anger. Since none of us likes to admit anger at a deceased person, these emotions are often disguised or repressed and prolong the period of grief or show up in other ways. It is well to remember that it is not up to us to judge such feelings as bad or shameful but to understand their true meaning and origin as something very human. In order to illustrate this I will again use the example of the child—and the child in us. The five-year-old who loses his mother is both blaming himself for her disappearance and being angry at her for having deserted him and for no longer gratifying his needs. The dead person then turns into something the child loves and wants very much but also hates with equal intensity for this severe deprivation.

The ancient Hebrews regarded the body of a dead person as something unclean and not to be touched. The early American Indians talked about the evil spirits and shot arrows in the air to drive the spirits away. Many other cultures have rituals to take care of the "bad" dead person, and they all originate in this feeling of anger which still exists in all of us, though we dislike admitting it. The tradition of the tombstone may originate in the wish to keep the bad spirits deep down in the ground, and the pebbles that many mourners put on the grave are leftover symbols of the same wish. Though we call the firing of guns at military funerals a last salute, it is the same symbolic ritual as the Indian used when he shot his spears and arrows into the skies.

I give these examples to emphasize that man has not basically changed. Death is still a fearful, frightening happening, and the fear of death is a universal fear even if we think we have mastered it on many levels.

What has changed is our way of coping and dealing with death and dying and our dying patients.

Having been raised in a country in Europe where science is not so advanced, where modern techniques have just started to find their way into medicine, and where people still live as they did in this country half a century ago, I may have had an opportunity to study a part of the evolution of mankind in a shorter period.

I remember as a child the death of a farmer. He fell from a tree and was not expected to live. He asked simply to die at home, a wish that was granted without question. He called his daughters into the bedroom and spoke with each one of them alone for a few moments. He arranged his affairs quietly, though he was in great pain, and distributed his belongings and his land, none of which was to be split until his wife should follow him in death. He also asked each of his children to share in the work, duties, and tasks that he had carried on until the time of the accident. He asked his friends to visit him once more, to bid goodbye to them. Although I was a small child at the time, he did not exclude me or my siblings. We were allowed to share in the preparations of the family just as we were permitted to grieve with them until he died. When he did die, he was left at home, in his own beloved home which he had built, and among his friends and neighbors who went to take a last look at him where he lay in the midst of flowers in the place he had lived in and loved so much. In that country today there is still no make-believe slumber room, no embalming, no false makeup to pretend sleep. Only the signs of very disfiguring illnesses are covered up with bandages and only infectious cases are removed from the home prior to the burial.

Why do I describe such "old-fashioned" customs? I think they are an indication of our acceptance of a fatal outcome, and they help the dying patient as well as his family to accept the loss of a loved one. If a patient is allowed to terminate his life in the familiar and beloved environment, it requires less adjustment for him. His own family knows him well enough to replace a sedative with a glass of his favorite wine; or the smell of a home-cooked soup may give him the appetite to sip a few spoons of fluid which, I think, is still more enjoyable than an infusion. I will not minimize the need for sedatives and infusions and realize full well from my own experience as a country doctor that they are sometimes life-saving and often unavoidable. But I also know that patience and familiar people and foods could replace many a bottle of intravenous fluids given for the simple reason that it fulfills the physiological need without involving too many people and/or individual nursing care.

The fact that children are allowed to stay at home where a fatality has struck and are included in the talk, discussions, and fears gives them the feeling that they are not alone in their grief and gives them the comfort of shared responsibility and shared mourning. It prepares them gradually and helps them view death as part of life, an experience which may help them grow and mature.

This is in great contrast to a society in which death is viewed as taboo, discussion of it is regarded as morbid, and children are excluded with the presumption and pretext that it would be "too much" for them. They are then sent off to relatives, often accompanied by some unconvincing lies of "Mother has gone on a long trip" or other unbelievable stories. The child senses that something is wrong, and his distrust in adults will only multiply if other relatives add new variations of the story, avoid his questions or suspicions, shower him with gifts as a meager substitute for a loss he is not permitted to deal with. Sooner or later the child will become aware of the changed family situation and, depending on the age and personality of the child, will have an unresolved grief and regard this incident as a frightening, mysterious, in any case very traumatic experience with untrustworthy grownups, which he has no way to cope with.

It is equally unwise to tell a little child who lost her brother that God loved little boys so much that he took little Johnny to heaven. When this little girl grew up to be a woman she never solved her anger at God, which resulted in a psychotic depression when she lost her own little son three decades later.

We would think that our great emancipation, our knowledge of science and of man, has given us better ways and means to prepare ourselves and our families for this inevitable happening. Instead the days are gone when a man was allowed to die in peace and dignity in his own home.

The more we are making advancements in science, the more we seem to fear and deny the reality of death. How is this possible?

We use euphemisms, we make the dead look as if they were asleep, we ship the children off to protect them from the anxiety and turmoil around the house if the patient is fortunate enough to die at home, we don't allow children to visit their dying parents in the hospitals, we have long and controversial discussions about whether patients should be told the truth—a question that rarely arises when the dying person is tended by the family physician who has known him from delivery to death and who knows the weaknesses and strengths of each member of the family.

I think there are many reasons for this flight away from facing death calmly. One of the most important facts is that dying nowadays is more gruesome in many ways, namely, more lonely, mechanical, and dehumanized; at times it is even difficult to determine technically when the time of death has occurred.

Dying becomes lonely and impersonal because the patient is often taken out of his familiar environment and rushed to an emergency room. Whoever has been very sick and has required rest and comfort especially may recall his experience of being put on a stretcher and enduring the noise of the ambulance siren and hectic rush until the hospital gates open. Only those who have lived through this may appreciate the discomfort and cold necessity of such transportation which is only the beginning of a long ordeal—hard to endure when you are well, difficult to express in words when noise, light, pumps, and voices are all too much to put up with. It may well be that we might consider more the patient under the sheets and blankets and perhaps stop our well-meant efficiency and rush in order to hold the patient's hand, to smile, or to listen to a question. I include the trip to the hospital as the first episode in dying, as it is for many. I am putting it exaggeratedly in contrast to the sick man who is left at home—not to say that lives should not be saved if they can be saved by a hospitalization but to keep the focus on the patient's experience, his needs and his reactions.

When a patient is severely ill, he is often treated like a person with no right to an opinion. It is often someone else who makes the decision if and when and where a patient should be hospitalized. It would take so little to remember that the sick person too has feelings, has wishes and opinions, and has—most important of all—the right to be heard.

Well, our presumed patient has now reached the emergency room. He will be surrounded by busy nurses, orderlies, interns, residents, a lab technician perhaps who will take some blood, an electrocardiogram technician who takes the cardiogram. He may be moved to X-ray and he will overhear opinions of his condition and discussions and questions to members of the family. He slowly but surely is beginning to be treated like a thing. He is no longer a person. Decisions are made often without his opinion. If he tries to rebel he will be sedated and after hours of waiting and wondering whether he has the strength, he will be wheeled into the operating room or intensive treatment unit and become an object of great concern and great financial investment.

He may cry for rest, peace, and dignity, but he will get infusions, transfusions, a heart machine, or tracheotomy if necessary. He may want one single person to stop for one single minute so that he can ask one single question—but he will get a dozen people around the clock, all busily preoccupied with his heart rate, pulse, electrocardiogram or pulmonary functions, his secretions or excretions but not with him as a human being. He may wish to fight it all but it is going to be a useless fight since all this is done in the fight for his life, and if they can save his life they can consider the person afterwards. Those who consider the person first may lose precious time to save his life! At least this seems to be the rationale or justification behind all this—or is it? Is the reason for this increasingly mechanical, depersonalized approach our own defensiveness? Is this approach our own way to cope with and repress the anxieties that a terminally or critically ill patient evokes in us? Is our concentration on equipment, on blood pressure, our desperate attempt to deny the impending death which is so frightening and discomforting to us that we displace all our knowledge onto machines, since they are less close to us than the suffering face of another human being which would remind us once more of our lack of omnipotence, our own limits and failures, and last but not least perhaps our own mortality?

Maybe the question has to be raised: Are we becoming less human or more human? . . . it is clear that whatever the answer may be, the patient is suffering more—not physically, perhaps, but emotionally. And his needs have not changed over the centuries, only our ability to gratify them.

LENGTH: 3,140 WORDS

19 Elisabeth Kubler-Ross
On the Fear of Death

SCORING: Reading time: _____ Rate from chart: _____ W.P.M.

RETENTION	number right _____ × 2 equals _____ points	
MAIN IDEAS	number right _____ × 4 equals _____ points	
APPLICATION	number right _____ × 4 equals _____ points	
VOCABULARY	number right _____ × 2 equals _____ points	

(Total points: 100) **total** _____ points

RETENTION   Based on the selection, which of the following statements are True (T), False (F), or Not answerable (N)?

1. _____ We are becoming less human.

2. _____ The patient is suffering more emotionally today than formerly.

3. _____ Death is distasteful in all cultures.

4. _____ Our unconscious mind can easily distinguish between a deed and a wish.

5. _____ The vast majority of patients with emotional problems see a psychiatrist.

6. _____ Children do not always see death as a permanent thing.

7. _____ A husband and wife who quarrel are less likely to suffer guilt at the partner's death.

8. _____ A tombstone may be a symbolic expression of distaste.

9. _____ Kubler-Ross gives these examples to show how man has basically changed.

10. _____ Wherever Kubler-Ross was raised, it was a medically advanced society.

11. _____ Permitting children to stay at home where there is a death gives them a valuable sense of responsibility.

12. _____ The more we advance in science, the less we fear death.

13. _____ Kubler-Ross feels death is more gruesome today than it used to be.

14. _____ The dying patient today is often denied the right to be heard.

15. _____ Those who are severely ill are often treated as people with no right to an opinion.

MAIN IDEAS

1. _____ Which of the following best states the main idea of this selection?
   a. Everyone has a serious psychological problem with death.
   b. Modern medicine seems to treat dying patients as things.
   c. Death is a natural part of life and must be treated as such.

2. _____ If the main idea of this selection is true, which of the following is most likely to happen?
   a. Kubler-Ross will stay at home when she knows she is dying.
   b. Kubler-Ross will urge her own patients to choose hospital care as early as possible in a serious illness.
   c. Psychiatric help will focus especially on the question of accepting death gracefully.

APPLICATION   Choose the best answer for each question.

1. _____ The reason that people do not die of epidemics today is:
   a. still one of the basic mysteries of modern medicine.
   b. accounted for by patterns of modern life.
   c. due to sanitation procedures that demand good engineering.
   d. because modern medicine has eradicated so many illnesses.

2. _____ Because of certain patterns of psychological guilt:
   a. no one will look at a dead person today.
   b. death is associated with a bad act demanding punishment.
   c. we tend to make the dead look as good as possible in the coffin.
   d. some people refuse to believe they are dying.

3. _____ Kubler-Ross perceives a major change in society is:
   a. the increased fear of death.
   b. a sense of guilt that is unresolvable.
   c. a growing fear of modern medicine.
   d. society's tendency to give people numbers instead of names.

4. _____ The result of lying to a child about death is:
   a. a deferral of the ultimate impact of loss.
   b. the development of a sense of distrust of adults.
   c. a fear of the hustle and bustle that is associated with ambulances.
   d. what makes people so edgy about death in later life.

5. _____ Kubler-Ross sees some of the ancient rituals designed to appease angry gods as associated with:
   a. our childlike behavior in the face of death.
   b. the mechanization of modern medicine.
   c. a sense of being stifled by the ultimate fear of death.
   d. a sense of guilt and fear of retribution in face of death.

6. _____ If a mother dies after her child wishes her dead, the child:
   a. will both love and hate the mother.
   b. will not be told about the mother's death.
   c. will feel responsible for her death.
   d. cannot differentiate between death and a dream.

7. _____ A young person's feelings over the death of a parent are complicated because shame and guilt are mixed with:
   a. relief and fear.
   b. independence and horror.
   c. anger and rage.
   d. pain and irritation.

8. _____ Kubler-Ross recommends home care for the dying:
   a. unless there is a clear need for blood transfusion.
   b. in order to more fully humanize the process.
   c. after having seen some painful cases in her native country.
   d. for patients who do not have a country doctor.

VOCABULARY   Choose the best definition for each italic vocabulary entry.

1. _____ Widespread vaccinations have *eradicated* many illnesses.
   a. deleted
   b. wiped out
   c. fought
   d. treated

2. _____ Better child care has *effected* lower mortality in children.
   a. helped
   b. assisted
   c. struck
   d. resulted in

3. _____ People's needs have to be *elicited* by professionals.
   a. diagnosed
   b. sensed
   c. cured
   d. drawn forth

4. _____ Death is *attributed* to some malicious intervention.
   a. set upon
   b. aimed by
   c. blamed on
   d. assigned

5. _____ a happening that calls for *retribution* and punishment
   a. deserved punishment
   b. restitution
   c. reluctance
   d. desperation

6. _____ The child who wishes his mother dead will be *traumatized* greatly if she dies.
   a. deeply shocked
   b. personally blamed
   c. thoroughly confused
   d. hurt on the head

7. _____ As we grow older we realize our *omnipotence* is not so omnipotent.
   a. personal consciousness
   b. human potential
   c. complete awareness
   d. total powers

8. _____ Guilt is frequent among the *bereaved* long after death.
   a. physicians
   b. mourners at the graveside
   c. family of the deceased
   d. people at the funeral

9. _____ These emotions are often disguised or *repressed*.
   a. hidden
   b. held back
   c. denied
   d. oppressed

10. _____ The child hates with equal intensity because of this *deprivation*.
    a. poverty
    b. loss
    c. skill
    d. emotional state

11. _____ to be allowed to terminate in a beloved *environment*
    a. surroundings
    b. home
    c. family
    d. nature

12. _____ He did not exclude me or my *siblings*
   a. friends and relations
   b. peers
   c. brothers and sisters
   d. parents

13. _____ a society in which death is viewed as a *taboo*
   a. something one cannot talk about
   b. a fear
   c. an ultimate end
   d. a social finality

14. _____ shower him with gifts as a *meager* substitute for loss
   a. inappropriate
   b. poor
   c. inadequate
   d. unhappy

15. _____ We use *euphemisms* and make the dead look as if they are asleep.
   a. makeups
   b. old sayings
   c. surgical methods
   d. inoffensive words

Readings in Business, Science, and Language Studies

20

CAROLINE SUTTON

How Did They Discover Radium?

Marie Curie is well known as the
co-discoverer of radium, the element that has
made possible the use, among other things, of
nuclear energy for both peaceful and wartime
purposes. Caroline Sutton describes the years
of sacrifice and hard work that went into that
discovery, leading tragically to Curie's early
death from exposure to radioactivity.

The story of the search for radium is a romantic and stirring one.
Behind it is a woman who was passionately curious, daring in her convictions,
and determined to work in an age hardly encouraging to professional aspirations among those of her sex. From a dilapidated shed, described by one German
chemist at the time as a "cross between a stable and a potato-cellar," came a
discovery that would throw light on the structure of the atom, open new doors
in medicine, and save lives in future generations.

Marie Sklodowska came to Paris and the Sorbonne in 1891 as a reticent Polish
woman of 24. Taking a solitary room in the Latin Quarter, she began her studies
in mathematics and physics. By 1897 she had two university degrees and a
fellowship, as well as a husband and a newborn daughter. In the physicist Pierre
Curie, Marie had found both an adviser and a lover, someone as serious as she,
who shared her interests and became drawn into her quest.

In that year Marie was casting about for an appropriate subject of study for
her doctorate. The scientific world was in an uproar over Wilhelm Röntgen's
discovery of X rays in 1895, and this was an obvious field. But Marie looked
further, and an accidental discovery by Henri Becquerel sparked her interest. In
1896 Becquerel was studying uranium salts. He had wrapped some photographic plates in a black cloth and covered them with a sheet of aluminum,

followed by crystals of a uranium compound. He planned to study the effects of the sun on the crystals, but since it was cloudy that day and on the two succeeding days he left the plates in a drawer. On removing them he was stunned to see that the plates were fogged where the crystals had covered them—that is, the uranium had produced an impression on the plate similar to that which light would make. Becquerel was the first to see evidence of the spontaneous emission of rays, what Marie Curie would later name radioactivity.

The intriguing question, of course, was where did this energy come from? What was the source of energy that allowed the rays to penetrate not only paper, but metal? An ambitious Marie Curie undertook to find out. Through her husband and the School of Physics and Chemistry, Marie obtained a small room in which to work, a glassed-in storeroom housing lumber and machines, on the ground floor of the school. It was damp, ill equipped, even lacking adequate electricity. But Marie set to work, first to determine the power of ionization of uranium—that is, its capacity to make the air conduct electricity. She used an electrometer called a piezoelectric quartz, which Pierre and Jacques Curie had devised some years before. Realizing that a crystal will be slightly deformed by an electric charge applied to it, the brothers developed an instrument that amplified this deformation; thus they could measure small electric currents. Marie's experiment using the piezoelectric quartz was quite simple. She placed the substance to be tested in a chamber of ionization consisting of a lower plate, which was charged, and another plate opposite to it, which was attached to the electrometer. She tried to make an electric current pass through the air between the plates, and if this occurred, the electrometer would detect it. Within several weeks she found that uranium's ionizing capacity was an innate characteristic, which neither resulted from a chemical reaction nor depended on external circumstances such as light, moisture, or temperature. She had shown, in fact, that the activity of uranium was an atomic property of that element, a ground-breaking find for 20th-century physics. Mme. Curie also found that the intensity of the rays was proportional to the quantity of uranium present in the compounds she examined.

If uranium had such power, why not other materials? Was it purely chance that uranium's unusual characteristic had been revealed? Marie energetically gathered materials from the School of Physics with the intent to study all known elements, whether in a pure or compound state. Before long she discovered that thorium, too, emitted rays, of an intensity comparable to those of uranium.

Fortunately, Mme. Curie did not stop with these discoveries. She wanted to test still other materials and obtained various mineral samples from the School of Physics. As might be expected, those containing thorium or uranium were radioactive; the others were not. But what came as a bewildering surprise was that the intensity of emissions by the active minerals—specifically pitchblende— was four times that of a pure oxide of uranium. Marie was sure her experiment was erroneous and repeated it scores of times. *Something* was far more radioactive than uranium or thorium, yet Marie had already tested all known elements.

On April 12, 1898, Mme. Curie's former professor, Gabriel Lippmann, made a presentation to the Académie des Sciences on her behalf. In it was expressed a "belief that these minerals may contain an element which is much more active than uranium." Curie's hypothesis, then, was the existence of a *new element*.

At this point the young scientist was overwhelmed by excitement and passion to prove her theory. Pierre, too, was intrigued enough to abandon his study of crystals to join her. Initial experiments with small amounts of pitchblende were begun. Marie and Pierre used a new method of chemical research based on radioactivity; they separated the substance into various products by traditional means of chemical analysis and then measured the radioactivity in each. As the breakdown continued, the radioactive element became increasingly concentrated. It was possible to separate it from all except one element: bismuth. By June 1898 Marie had a sample of impure bismuth sulphide that was 150 times more radioactive than uranium. Pierre placed this substance in a tube and heated it. The substance itself remained in the hotter part of the tube while a thin black powder collected apart from it. This potent powder showed an activity 330 times greater than uranium.

In the *Proceedings of the Academy* of July 1898, the Curies wrote, "If the existence of this new metal is confirmed we propose to call it *polonium*, from the name of the original country of one of us."

November brought a startling development. Upon removing bismuth and polonium from the radioactive material in pitchblende, they obtained a liquid containing barium, which was still highly radioactive. After dissolving and reprecipitating it numerous times, they had a residual substance 900 times as radioactive as uranium, yet barium itself was known *not* to be radioactive. The scientists strongly suspected the presence of a new element. They now turned to Eugène Demarçay, who operated a spectroscope, which was the means to confirm their suspicions. Demarçay dissolved a tiny sample of the Curies' barium compound in acidified water and painted it onto electrodes. He passed a spark along the electrodes and was able to photograph the spark spectrum of the substance. He found a spectral line (or linear image corresponding to a component of the radiation emitted by the substance) that did not result from any known element. As the solid was purified, furthermore, the spectral line grew more intense. On December 26, 1898, the Curies announced a new chemical element in pitchblende: radium, whose radioactivity was thought to be "enormous."

This announcement did not mark the end of Marie Curie's work. Rather, she now set herself the Herculean task of isolating the element so that chemists might *see* once and for all proof of her beloved new element. Tremendous obstacles stood in the way: an inadequate workplace, poor equipment, and a paltry budget. The government was not inclined to open its purse to the cause of science. The two were forced to make do.

It was by now apparent that the amount of radioactive element in pitchblende was so slight (actually only 0.000001 percent) that huge quantities of the mineral would be required to obtain even a negligible amount. Pitchblende ore with its valuable uranium was, furthermore, extremely expensive. The Curies learned that it originated chiefly in the St. Joachimsthal mine in Bohemia, then under the Austrian Empire. The uranium salts were extracted for the manufacture of glass, but what about the residue? The ingenious Mme. Curie offered to buy the cumbersome and useless material and, aided by Professor Eduard Suess in Vienna, her request was fulfilled, free of all costs except transportation.

Early in 1899 a huge horse-drawn wagon loaded with sacks of pitchblende, still mixed with pine needles and dirt, arrived at the School of Physics. The old studio could no longer accommodate them, and the new laboratory the Curies moved to was, if possible, worse. Marie and Pierre spent virtually four years in a tumbledown shed across the courtyard from their former studio. The skylight roof not only leaked, but had no hoods to carry off the poisonous gases from their work. When weather permitted they worked outdoors, but in rain and snow they were forced indoors, opening all the windows whatever the temperature. The shed did not even have a floor, and its furnishings consisted only of a few wooden tables, a blackboard, and an ineffectual cast-iron stove. They suffered freezing temperatures in winter, stifling heat in summer, on top of mysterious ailments they had been trying to ignore in recent years: fatigue, body pains, sore fingers—all symptoms of radiation sickness, of which the two were unwitting victims.

While Pierre studied the properties of radium, Marie became a one-woman factory. Working with batches as large as 20 kilograms, she ground the pitchblende, dissolved it, and filtered it innumerable times. She heaved the materials and stood in the courtyard day after day, month after month, stirring cauldrons of boiling liquids with a huge iron bar. She extracted barium in a chloride state, which she submitted to fractional distillation in porcelain bowls, set up along her wooden tables. Her frustrations were multiplied as airborne impurities— iron and coal dust—inevitably contaminated her rare material.

"We lived in a preoccupation as complete as that of a dream," wrote Mme. Curie. "Sometimes we returned in the evening after dinner for another survey of our domain. Our precious products for which we had no shelter, were arranged on tables and boards; from all sides we could see their slightly luminous silhouettes, and these gleamings, which seemed suspended in the darkness, stirred us with ever new emotion and enchantment."

The moments of enchantment must have been brief, however, compared with her years of tedious labor. But Mme. Curie's singular energy and sheer will prevailed: in March 1902 she had a decigram of pure radium. Demarçay's electroscope had reacted violently to the substance, from which barium at last had been removed. Mme. Curie attributed an atomic weight of 225.93 to her new substance, whose reality and individuality were now confirmed beyond doubt.

LENGTH: 1,816 WORDS

20   Caroline Sutton
How Did They Discover Radium?

SCORING: Reading time: _____	Rate from chart: _____	W.P.M.

RETENTION   number right _____ × 2 equals _____ points

MAIN POINT   number right _____ × 4 equals _____ points

INFERENCES   number right _____ × 4 equals _____ points

APPLICATION   number right _____ × 3 equals _____ points

VOCABULARY   number right _____ × 2 equals _____ points

(Total points: 100) **total** _____ points

RETENTION   Based on the selection, which of the following statements are True (T), False (F), or Not answerable (N)?

1. _____ Curie was a German scientist, although she did her work in France.

2. _____ Thorium is an element.

3. _____ A spectograph enabled the Curies to announce that they had discovered a new chemical element.

4. _____ Radium glows in the dark.

5. _____ Fortunately, the pitchblende ore Curie needed came from the South of France.

6. _____ The original presentation of Curie's findings was made, not by her, but by her former professor.

7. _____ Pierre Curie became a physicist after meeting and marrying Marie.

8. _____ The first evidence of the spontaneous emission of rays was accidentally discovered on photographic plates.

9. _____ The Curies intended to call the new metal they thought they had discovered *polonium*, after the famous Italian explorer.

10. _____ Although their original laboratory was old and decrepit, the Curies remained in it throughout their experiments.

11. _____ Increased recognition by the scientific community brought Curie money to hire assistants for her work.

12. _____ Curie used an electrometer developed by her husband and his brother in her original experiments on uranium's ionization capacity.

13. _____ Pitchblende is more radioactive than a pure oxide of uranium.

14. _____ Curie used the uranium salts found in pitchblende for her research.

15. _____ Sadly, Curie never reached her goal of isolating pure radium from mineral ore.

MAIN POINT   Which of the following statements best represents the main point of the selection? _____

1. Scientific discoveries are often made by mistake.
2. Marie and Pierre Curie's experiment illustrates the progress that can be made when scientists and government work together.
3. It isn't what you know but who you know that makes scientific advance possible.
4. Curie's search for radium was difficult and dangerous, but rewarding.
5. A husband and wife team in science can be more effective than a team whose members are unrelated.

INFERENCES   Which three of the following are the best inferences that can be drawn from this selection? _____, _____, and _____

1. Scientific discoveries are often based on the work of previous scientists.
2. Members of the scientific community are often jealous of each other's work.
3. Expensive equipment is not absolutely necessary for making scientific breakthroughs.
4. Scientific experimentation involves more moments of labor than moments of excitement.
5. A husband cannot accept a wife's success, even in the cause of scientific advancement.
6. Scientists do not have any leeway in the naming of a newly discovered element.
7. The Curie's relationship was purely friendly.
8. Once scientists have made a big discovery, the path to success is made easier for them.

APPLICATION   Choose the best answer for each question.

1. _____ If crystals of uranium salts were left in a dish overnight, they would probably:
   a. stop emitting rays after a few hours.

b. eat holes in any glass that happened to be nearby.
c. maintain radioactivity.
d. double their activity during the night.

2. _____ Curie hypothesized the existence of a new element because:
a. the pure uranium emitted such powerful rays.
b. only the thorium and the uranium emitted rays.
c. active minerals emitted more intense rays than uranium or thorium.
d. no new element had been discovered for a long time.

3. _____ If Demarçay's spectroscope were used on a new element today, it would probably:
a. make a different spectral line from that of any other known element.
b. be strongly suspicious.
c. make a more intense spectral line than any other known element.
d. not be able to be photographed properly.

4. _____ The biggest problem with working in the courtyard seemed to be that Curie:
a. was able to work only in small batches.
b. was unable to bring the materials to a complete boil.
c. had to put her distillate in porcelain bowls on wooden tables.
d. had her material contaminated by airborne impurities.

5. _____ The Curies probably tried to ignore their mysterious ailments because:
a. they didn't know any better.
b. they were so intensely involved in their work.
c. they knew that the ailments would go away.
d. they knew that body pains were an inevitable part of scientific research.

6. _____ If a characteristic of an element is an atomic property of that element, it will:
a. result from a chemical reaction.
b. depend on external circumstances such as light.
c. certainly be noticed in any experimentation.
d. be an inalienable characteristic of that element.

7. _____ One quality a chamber of ionization must have is:
a. a piezoelectric quartz crystal.
b. a source of electric current.
c. uranium.
d. a plate.

8. _____ Once a scientist suspects the existence of a new element, the first thing she must do is:
   a. name it.
   b. make a purified form of it.
   c. apply for a government grant.
   d. conduct experiments that help isolate it from other elements.

VOCABULARY   Choose the best definition for each italic vocabulary entry.

1. _____ from a *dilapidated* shed
   a. ancient
   b. tumbledown
   c. demolished
   d. unpainted

2. _____ the *spontaneous* emission of rays
   a. self-activated
   b. exuberant
   c. flowing
   d. forced

3. _____ an *innate* characteristic
   a. unusual
   b. special
   c. elaborate
   d. inborn

4. _____ dissolving and *reprecipitating* it
   a. redistilling it for liquid purity
   b. reseparating it from solution
   c. raining it down from a sieve
   d. hurrying along the scientific process

5. _____ a *paltry* budget
   a. trivial
   b. pretty
   c. substantial
   d. open-ended

6. _____ an *ineffectual* cast-iron stove
   a. embarrassing
   b. unadorned
   c. blackened
   d. unproductive

7. _____ *intrigued* enough to abandon his study of crystals
   a. exhausted
   b. interested
   c. annoyed
   d. involved

8. _____ *stifling* heat in summer
   a. prickling
   b. enlightening
   c. drying
   d. smothering

9. _____ *cauldrons* of boiling liquids
   a. hot pads
   b. quantities
   c. large pots
   d. solutions

10. _____ She submitted to fractional *distillation*.
    a. distribution
    b. excommunication
    c. extinction
    d. evaporation

11. _____ their slightly *luminous* silhouettes
    a. glowing
    b. effervescent
    c. flowing
    d. out-of-focus

12. _____ Mme. Curie *attributed* an atomic weight.
    a. assigned
    b. donated
    c. weighed
    d. characterized

13. _____ *amplified* his deformation
    a. multiplied
    b. electrified
    c. enlarged
    d. demolished

14. _____ *proportional* to the quantity of uranium
    a. opposed to
    b. in agreement with
    c. in relation to
    d. with respect to

15. _____ a *bewildering* surprise
    a. outstanding
    b. expectable
    c. frightening
    d. puzzling

21

ROBERT THOMAS

Is Corporate Executive Compensation Excessive?

To the average person, an income in the
hundreds of thousands of dollars seems like
a great deal of money, and we wonder how
anyone's work can be valuable enough to
justify that kind of income. Robert Thomas
discusses some of the reasons for the high
executive salaries paid by corporations
such as IBM, General Motors, and Procter
and Gamble.

Ralph Nader stands at the end of a long line of critics who assail the high incomes of top corporate executives.[1] Nader and his associates suggest that "in the absence of judicial limitations, excessive remuneration has become the norm."[2] They observe that the average top executive in each of the fifty largest industrial corporations earns more salary in a year than many of the corporate employees earn in a lifetime. Salaries are only part (albeit the major part) of the compensation the top executives receive. Bonuses, lavish retirements, stock options, and stock ownership combine to swell the incomes of corporate chief executives by another 50 to 75 percent of the executives' direct remunerations. Nader and his associates conclude that the top corporate executives receive "staggeringly large salaries and stock options."[3]

[1][Ralph Nader is a prominent consumer advocate.]
[2]Ralph Nader, et al., *Corporate Power in America* (New York: Norton, 1976), p. 115.
[3]Ibid., p. 118.

The Attack on Executive Income

Those who criticize the level of compensation that corporate executives receive are critical of any persons who are, or who become, rich. The top executives of our major corporations *do* become rich. *Fortune* magazine, in a survey of the chief executives of the 500 largest industrial corporations, discovered that the median income in 1976 was $209,000 a year and that when only the 100 largest corporations were considered, the median salary was $344,000 a year.[4]

Most Americans, however, do not consider becoming rich to be a crime. Indeed, the opposite is true. Achieving wealth reflects a high level of performance in providing through the market what the economy desires.

Nader and his coauthors recognize this admiration for performance and attack the level of executive compensation on other grounds. They suggest that the chief corporate executives are not entrepreneurs who risk their own capital in the search for profits, but functionaries who perform essentially the same tasks as government employees. The chief corporate executives "serve as the bureaucrats of private industry."[5]

The difference between industry and government is that the boards of directors of large corporations allegedly are more lax in discharging their responsibilities to their shareholders (by constraining excessive executive salaries) than the members of the Congress of the United States and the various elected officials of state and local governments who serve as the watchdogs for the public interest. The managements of large corporations take advantage of this laxness to request and receive excessive compensation. Moreover, this is not an isolated phenomenon confined to an occasional corporation. Nader reports that it "has become the norm."[6]

Why Executives Are Well Paid

In response, consider first who a chief corporate executive is, and examine the responsibilities a chief corporate executive must discharge. The typical top executive in each of the 500 largest industrial corporations is a white Protestant male aged sixty. He got his top position at age fifty-five; he averages between fifty-five and sixty-four hours a week on the job, takes three weeks of vacation each year, and earns a salary of $209,000 a year. He has attended graduate school, and he has worked for more than two companies during his business career. He owns less than $500,000 worth of stock in the company for which he works, and during the past decade he has seen his salary rise less rapidly, in percentage terms, than the salaries of his employees. In short, he is well prepared, experienced, hardworking, and beyond middle age.

[4]*Fortune* (May 1976), p. 172.
[5]Nader, p. 118.
[6]Ibid., p. 115.

Two things distinguish each of these 500 persons from several thousand others who have similar qualities. First, each is paid more. Second, each has been chosen as the person responsible for his company's present and future.

The Fortune 500 Company corporate executive directs a company whose sales in 1975 averaged almost $1.75 billion, whose assets totaled $1.33 billion, and which provided employment for almost 29,000 people.[7] This executive directs the firm in a manner that allows it to earn an 11.6 percent return on its total investment. Such a rate of return is not guaranteed simply because a corporation is large. The opportunities to lose money are many; the managements of 28 of the 500 largest industrial corporations managed to show a loss in the recovery year of 1975. It is possible, moreover, to lose big: Singer reported a loss of $451.9 million in that year, and Chrysler $259.5 million. A chief executive who heads a management team that can avoid such losses and constantly succeed in earning a profit is obviously very valuable to the shareholders of a corporation. He is valuable not only to his employers but also to other corporations; thus his own firm pays him handsomely to retain his services.

Many pages of our national magazines devoted to business news—*Business Week*, *Forbes*, *Fortune*—report the movements of business executives from one firm to another. These shifts are induced by substantial increases in salary, often according to one publication, of 30 percent or more.[8] Some excellently managed corporations, such as IBM, General Motors, Procter and Gamble, and Xerox, are known in industry as "executive breeders."[9] Xerox admitted in its 1976 proxy statement that its management was increasingly becoming "a target for other corporations seeking talented executives," and it proposed a new incentive plan for its executives.[10] This request for increased executive compensation was not self-serving on the part of Xerox's management; it stemmed in part from the prior move of twelve Xerox executives to a rival copier manufacturer.

The high salaries and fringe benefits that talented executives in large corporations receive stem not from laxness on the part of the boards of directors but, rather, from the boards' vigilance. Corporations must pay their executives, as well as any other employees, what they could earn by working for a rival firm, or lose them. Competition among corporations for the best people sets the level of executive compensation. If one person is to be placed in charge of a billion dollars in shareholder assets, which can easily be lost through mismanagement, even the $766,085 a year that the highest-paid corporate executive in the United States receives might not appear excessive to shareholders, especially if that salary is what it takes to get the services of the best available person.

There are many examples of corporations that are well rewarded for paying the price necessary to get the best person to remedy a bad situation. In one recent

[7]Charles G. Burck, "A Group Profile of the Fortune 500 Chief Executive," *Fortune*, May 1976, p. 173.
[8]*Business Week* (October 4, 1971), p. 62.
[9]Ibid., p. 57.
[10]Ibid., p. 57.

case, a firm that once tried to produce computers, and whose stock had sold for as high as $173 a share, fell on hard times; in 1973 it lost $119 million on sales of $177 million and had $300 million in long-term debts.[11] A new chief executive, who by 1976 had made the firm profitable once again, received $200,000 a year, performance incentives that earned him another $400,000, and stock options that made him a millionaire on paper. Clearly the compensation this executive received meets the Nader criterion for being "excessive." Yet, the Bank of America thought it was a worthwhile investment to guarantee his salary in an attempt, which proved successful, to ensure the eventual repayment of the large loans it had made to the firm. Individual shareholders also applauded the move; as a result of the executive's efforts, the value of a share has increased from $2 to over $21. In this one instance, the efforts of the new chief executive succeeded in increasing the market value of the company ten times.

A talented executive is highly paid because he is very productive. He earns for his firm additional net revenue at least equal in value to his compensation. If he did not, his firm would let him go. If his firm does not pay him what he is worth to others, it will lose him to a rival. The same holds true for any other valuable input in our economy and accounts as well for the high incomes received by talented persons in other fields.[12]

Salaries of Other Persons

Consider, for a moment, the salaries paid to entertainers. The fastest way to become a millionaire is not to become a corporate executive, but to become a big rock 'n' roll star or a superstar in professional sports. In 1973, for example, there were an estimated fifty music performers earning between $1 million and $6 million a year.[13] These thirty-five persons and fifteen groups made, annually, between three and seven times the salary paid to America's highest-paid executive. While the musicians performed, that highest-paid executive directed, and was responsible for, a company that employed 376,000 persons, had sales of over $11 billion and assets of over $10 billion, and earned almost $400 million in profits. Rock stars, moreover, earn their fortunes sooner than business executives; most start their careers as teenage idols; few have their best earning years after thirty. The average chief executive in each of the 500 largest industrial corporations does not attain that degree of success until the age of fifty-five.

Or, examine the compensation paid to the superstars in professional sports. The most interesting stories on sports pages now are not reports of games but

[11]*Forbes* (October 15, 1976), p. 78.

[12]W. Mark Crain, "Can Corporate Executives Set Their Own Wages?" in M. Bruce Johnson, ed., *The Attack on Corporate America: The Corporate Issues Sourcebook* (New York: McGraw-Hill, 1978), pp. 272–275.

[13]*Forbes* (April 15, 1973), p. 28.

stories about the fabulous salaries received by star athletes: $3 million to Julius Erving, $1.5 million each to O.J. Simpson and Pele, $500,000 to Kareem Abdul-Jabbar, $450,000 each to Tiny Archibald and Joe Namath, $400,000 to Catfish Hunter, $360,000 to Bob Lanier, $325,000 to Bill Bradley, $302,000 to Spencer Haywood, $250,000 to John Havlicek, $237,500 to Rick Barry, $230,000 to Tom Seaver, and $225,000 to Dick Allen.[14] More names from golf, hockey, and tennis could easily be added to the list. The reported incomes of these superstars are probably understated, since they exclude payments for endorsements and the like. These people, furthermore, work only part of the year, while the average chief executive has a forty-nine-week season.

When considered in the light of the compensation paid to extremely talented persons in other areas, the rewards earned by corporate executives do not appear excessive. A competitive economy ensures that highly productive persons command high rewards.

LENGTH: 1,539 WORDS

---

[14]*Fortune* (May 1976), p. 170.

21   Robert Thomas
Is Corporate Executive Compensation Excessive?

SCORING: Reading time: _____ Rate from chart: _____ W.P.M.

RETENTION	number right _____ × 2 equals _____ points	
MAIN POINT	number right _____ × 4 equals _____ points	
INFERENCES	number right _____ × 4 equals _____ points	
APPLICATION	number right _____ × 3 equals _____ points	
VOCABULARY	number right _____ × 2 equals _____ points	

(Total points: 100) **total** _____ points

RETENTION   Based on the selection, which of the following statements are True (T), False (F), or Not answerable (N)?

1. _____ The highest executive income recorded in 1976 was over $500,000.

2. _____ Fortunately, a large corporation has a built-in momentum that ensures that it will probably earn money.

3. _____ Sports stars generally earn more money than corporate executives.

4. _____ Business executives often move from one company to another because of location and vacation opportunities.

5. _____ Ralph Nader has argued in favor of high executive income.

6. _____ Sports stars work fewer weeks per year than executives do.

7. _____ Most Americans believe that becoming rich is a deserved reward for high performance.

8. _____ The level of executive compensation is set by competition.

9. _____ Rock stars reach their highest earning level after the age of thirty.

10. _____ It is the boards of directors of major corporations who request and receive large sums of money.

11. _____ A newly hired executive is responsible for his company's past and present performance.

12. _____ Computer firms are among the few companies exempt from hard times.

13. _____ An executive actually earns more in bonuses, stock options, and other compensation than he does in direct salary.

14. _____ The salary of the average executive has risen less rapidly percentage-wise than the salary of his employees.

15. _____ Sports stars earn even more than their announced salary would indicate.

MAIN POINT   Which of the following statements best represents the main point of the selection? _____

1. Corporate executives earn less than many other people in our society.
2. Corporate executive incomes are not excessive.
3. Executive incomes have been attacked by consumer advocates.
4. Corporate executives live a difficult and lonely life.
5. Most corporate executives are paid less well than one might expect.

INFERENCES   Which three of the following are the best inferences that can be drawn from this selection? _____, _____, and _____

1. Stock options and retirement benefits are an unimportant part of the overall income package for top executives.
2. Becoming the top executive of a major corporation means that one will probably become rich.
3. Boards of directors of large corporations allow increases in executive salaries without scrutiny.
4. Top executives differ from others with respect to salary and responsibility more than any other qualities.
5. Being a good manager for one company is not a very good way to get another company interested in hiring you.
6. Executive income often exceeds the profit brought about by that executive.
7. Basketball players earn higher incomes than players of other sports.
8. It is more likely that one will rise to the top of a corporation if one is a Protestant male.

APPLICATION   Choose the best answer for each question.

1. _____ The Congress of the United States is:
   a. entirely different from the board of directors of a large corporation.
   b. relatively good about not raising its salary to an extraordinary degree.
   c. the bureaucracy of private industry.
   d. involved in a search for profits.

2. _____ The average top executive has:
   a. more time, experience, and education invested than the average employee.
   b. good connections and a good family background.
   c. health problems as a result of his intense concentration on work.
   d. aspirations to become a congressman.

3. _____ As a top executive, my firm will probably not let me go if I:
   a. work hard.
   b. keep my record clean.
   c. maintain good connections with the government.
   d. earn a profit equal to the value of my compensation.

4. _____ Xerox's management proposed substantial increases in salary because:
   a. its executives were earning less than most others.
   b. its executives were more talented than others.
   c. management wanted to pay itself well.
   d. its management was being raided by rival companies.

5. _____ The Bank of America guaranteed an executive's salary because:
   a. it wanted to ensure the repayment of extensive loans it had made.
   b. it had extensive investments in company stock.
   c. the executive had once worked for the Bank of America.
   d. it would benefit from the increase in the company's market value.

6. _____ The fifty top rock stars differ from company executives in that they:
   a. earn more than the executives.
   b. work less than the executives.
   c. travel more than the average executive.
   d. are more involved in drugs than the top executives.

7. _____ Of the 500 largest industrial corporations:
   a. none lost money in 1975.
   b. none lost more than $200 million in 1975.
   c. all were listed among the Fortune 500.
   d. all were able to keep their chief executives in 1975.

8. _____ Some people argue that top executives should not be paid as well as they are because:
   a. they earn more than other employees do.
   b. they earn more than even the president of the United States does.
   c. they are bureaucratic functionaries who do not risk investing their own capital in a company.
   d. no one should earn that kind of money in a democratic country.

VOCABULARY   Choose the best definition for each italic vocabulary entry.

1. _____ Excessive *remuneration* has become the norm.
   a. reapplication
   b. pay
   c. criticism
   d. exploitation

2. _____ *albeit* the major part
   a. altogether
   b. absolutely
   c. although
   d. all things considered

3. _____ *entrepreneurs* who risk their own capital
   a. creative managers
   b. voters
   c. workers
   d. functionaries

4. _____ *allegedly* more lax in discharging their responsibilities
   a. blatantly
   b. openly
   c. clearly
   d. supposedly

5. _____ an isolated *phenomenon*
   a. surprise
   b. event
   c. prodigy
   d. island

6. _____ Two things *distinguish* each of these.
   a. make famous
   b. age
   c. differentiate
   d. anger

7. _____ These shifts are *induced*.
   a. opposed
   b. influenced
   c. forced
   d. caused

8. _____ executive *breeders*
   a. managers
   b. producers

c. stealers

d. killers

9. ____ increased executive *compensation*

    a. losses

    b. gains

    c. payment

    d. unemployment benefit

10. ____ the board's *vigilance*

    a. watchfulness

    b. reception

    c. guardianship

    d. anxiety

11. ____ to *remedy* a bad situation

    a. poison

    b. remove

    c. correct

    d. bring about

12. ____ performance *incentives*

    a. moneys

    b. rewards

    c. incomes

    d. stimuli

13. ____ *criterion* for being "excessive"

    a. criticism

    b. judgment

    c. moral

    d. test

14. ____ are probably *understated*

    a. not allowed

    b. determined

    c. played down

    d. unfinished

15. ____ They *exclude* payments for endorsements.

    a. press out

    b. leave out

    c. involve

    d. express

22

FLETCHER PRATT

How Champollion Deciphered the Rosetta Stone

Few of us stop to wonder about how we
first came to understand ancient languages
that ceased to be spoken or read long ago.
The saying "It's Greek to me" suggests
our acceptance of being puzzled by these
languages. Fletcher Pratt traces the thinking
process that one researcher followed in
decoding the Egyptian hieroglyphics.

Scientific history is filled with the strangest repetitions, as though
new ideas float into the world on some invisible medium and are caught through
senses attuned by study in many places at once. The planet Uranus was discovered twice within a month; the periodic law which forms the basis of modern
chemistry was propounded separately by two men who had never heard of each
other and were working along different lines. Similarly, at about the time that
Georg Friedrich Grotefend was painfully spelling out the names of forgotten
kings, another archaeological cryptographer was using the same methods to
work out the other great puzzle of antiquity—the Egyptian hieroglyphics.

He was Jean François Champollion, an infant prodigy, whose father had been
an archaeologist before him and had talked shop over the dinner table so
entertainingly that at the age of fifteen the boy was already publishing a learned
essay on "The Giants of the Bible" which won the applause of the bewigged
professors at the French Institute.

Champollion's problem in dealing with hieroglyphic was radically different
from the one Grotefend of Göttingen had faced. The latter had before him
various combinations of markings which were altogether meaningless except as

From *Secret and Urgent: The Story of Codes and Ciphers* (1942). Reprinted by permission of the
author's estate.

the letters of an unknown language. Champollion was trying to read verbal sense into long strings of pictures which were considered by many very good scientists to have no more than a mystic religious sense, like the work of certain savage races which draw a picture of a deer when they feel hungry, expecting the gods to send them the real article in exchange for the pictured image.

Again, Niebuhr had identified forty-two different alphabetic signs, or letters in ancient Persian; but the scientists who had already held hieroglyphic under investigation for centuries had discovered over a hundred and sixty signs—far too many to constitute any alphabet, beside which they were unmistakably conventionalized pictures. Moreover Grotefend had plunged into a new field, where all thought was independent thought; Champollion entered a domain already strewn with the wreckage of hypotheses, where it would be fatally easy to accept the errors along with the logic of some previous failure.

Particularly since the discovery of the famous Rosetta Stone. That celebrated chunk of crockery had been found by the scientists who accompanied Napoleon's expedition to Egypt, and was surrendered to the English with the remains of that expedition. It bore an inscription in Greek, together with two other inscriptions, one in hieroglyphic and one in a third form known as Egyptian Demotic, then as unreadable as hieroglyphic. No great intelligence was required to make the supposition that all three inscriptions said essentially the same thing; but some of the best brains in Europe had spent years trying to resolve the hieroglyphic into an intelligible language, and even with the aid of the Greek texts it had proved impossible. The general conclusion was that the problem was insoluble.

For everything seemed to indicate that if the hieroglyphic were a language at all (and not a series of mystical pictures) it was that extremely rare thing, a purely syllabic tongue. For example, in the place where the word *king* appeared in the Greek text, the hieroglyphic had a picture of an extraordinarily tall man with a sword in his hand. This was a logical symbol for *king*; a whole word in one picture-letter. And if this were true, many of the other symbols stood for entire words or syllables; there would be no clue from the interrelation of letters as to how the language had been pronounced, and it would be forever unreadable.

There was also another difficulty. The British scientists who first handled the Rosetta Stone had taken the obvious step of making parallel lists of Greek words and the hieroglyphics that supposedly represented them. To their dismay they discovered that Greek words which appeared more than once in the inscription were represented on these different appearances by wholly unrelated sets of hieroglyphics, and that the same hieroglyphics were sometimes used to represent different words of the Greek text. Even the names, through which Grotefend was even then breaking ancient Persian, were of no help in this case. The only personal name in the Greek text was that of King Ptolemy V; in the hieroglyphic it was represented by four symbols—too few to spell it out with letters, too many to spell it in syllables. There seemed no conclusion but that the hieroglyphics were purely symbolical; and they had been generally abandoned as such when Jean François Champollion, the boy wonder, entered the lists.

His first step was to count the total number of symbols in the Greek and hieroglyphic texts, a method which is now a commonplace of decipherment, but which Champollion seems to have been first to take in this science. The count revealed that there was something radically wrong with all previous efforts to solve hieroglyphic; for there were three times as many Egyptian as Greek letters. If the hieroglyphics were, then, either symbols for syllables or for ideas expressed as directly as the cave man's deer, the Egyptian inscription must be more than three times as long as the Greek. But the very basis of any deduction must be that the inscriptions say the same thing; and the nature of the Greek text (a hymn of praise to Ptolemy V by a corporation of priests) made it seem unreasonable that there could be any great difference. If the inscriptions were identical, then the hieroglyphics must, after all, be letter-symbols. There were too many of them for any other theory.

On the other hand an alphabet of 160 letters remained inadmissible. But since other scientists had allowed themselves to be hung up on the horns of this dilemma, Champollion neglected it and plunged ahead on the alphabetic theory, attacking the names as Grotefend had in Persian. The name of Ptolemy was neatly enclosed in an outline, preceded by the symbol the English investigators had taken to represent the word for *king*. Now "Ptolemy" is a Greek word; Champollion made the reasonable deduction that in Egyptian it would have to be spelled phonetically. If the four symbols that stood for the name on the Rosetta Stone were letters, some letters in the name must have been omitted— which? The vowels, Champollion answered himself, remembering that Hebrew, which had a considerable Egyptian heritage, also omitted the vowels. The four symbols of the name were the letters pronounced *P, T, L,* and *M.*

At this point the investigator turned to some older hieroglyphic inscriptions to check his conclusions. He had at hand a couple whose origin in the reigns of Kings Rameses and Thutmoes were proved by portraits and other evidence. The symbol he had adopted as *M* appeared in both names, and the *T* twice, in the proper places, in the second name. Thus it checked and, checking, gave him values for *R* and *S;* and with six letters to work on the scientist-cryptographer began to work through all the Egyptian inscriptions containing known names, obtaining new letter values at every step.

Very rapidly as scientific processes go—that is, in a matter of a few years—he accumulated enough data from names to provide the correct symbols for every possible consonant sound. There remained many letters of the impossibly extended alphabet for which he had no values; letters which never appeared as part of a name. Of these Champollion formed a separate list.

Returning to the Rosetta Stone inscriptions, he noted that one of these unidentified symbols appeared before every noun in the hieroglyphic text, and a few of them appeared before verbs. Now one such symbol was the picture of a tall man that had preceded King Ptolemy's name. Later, where a temple was mentioned the word was preceded by a conventionalized picture of a building, and when the sun-god Ra's name appeared there was a conventionalized solar disc. Champollion therefore reasoned that such characters were "determinatives"—special signs placed in the text by the Egyptian writers to indicate the character of the object they were talking about.

He died at the age of thirty-four without having worked out all the alphabet, and without having accounted for the remainder of the enormous surplus of letters, for even with the determinatives taken out, most of the words were far too long. It remained for later investigators to show that the Egyptians, in writing words, were never satisfied by expressing a sound in a single letter, but must repeat the same sound in three or four other ways to make certain the reader got the idea. It is as though one were to write the word "seen" as S-C-SC-EE-IE-EA-N. In a cryptological sense hieroglyphic was thus a substitution cipher with suppression of frequencies and the introduction of a prodigious number of nulls; and Champollion's great merit as a decipherer was that he held to the main issue without allowing these things to throw him off the track.

LENGTH: 1,485 WORDS

22 Fletcher Pratt
How Champollion Deciphered the Rosetta Stone

SCORING: Reading time: _____ Rate from chart: _____ W.P.M.		
RETENTION	number right ____ × 2 equals ____ points	
MAIN POINT	number right ____ × 4 equals ____ points	
INFERENCES	number right ____ × 4 equals ____ points	
APPLICATION	number right ____ × 3 equals ____ points	
VOCABULARY	number right ____ × 2 equals ____ points	
(Total points: 100) **total** ____ points		

RETENTION   Based on the selection, which of the following statements are True (T), False (F), or Not answerable (N)?

1. _____ Every noun in the hieroglyphic text was preceded by an unidentified symbol.

2. _____ There were more hieroglyphic letters than there were letters in the Greek alphabet.

3. _____ Champollion worked on deciphering hieroglyphics for forty years.

4. _____ The Rosetta Stone was inscribed in three languages.

5. _____ The personal name of only two kings appeared in the stone's inscription.

6. _____ Champollion's first published essay was severely criticized.

7. _____ Earlier scientists thought the inscriptions on the Rosetta Stone were mystical symbols.

8. _____ The hieroglyphic that stood for *king* was a tall man with a crown on his head.

9. _____ Written Hebrew does not have any vowels.

10. _____ Eventually, Champollion discovered that the Egyptians represented the same sound in a word over and over.

11. _____ The Rosetta Stone was a hymn of praise to the Egyptian god Ra.

12. _____ The Rosetta Stone presently resides in London's British Museum.

13. _____ No one had ever attempted to translate Egyptian hieroglyphics before.

14. _____ The Rosetta Stone was discovered during the Napoleonic era.

15. _____ Some of the conventionalized pictures found on the Rosetta Stone were determinatives.

MAIN POINT   Which of the following statements best represents the main point of the selection? _____

1. Two scientists are often working on the same scientific project at the same time.
2. Science depends more on careful procedure than it does on art.
3. Deciphering ancient hieroglyphics is not easy.
4. The case of Champollion indicates the futility of being a child prodigy.
5. Champollion's determined use of a careful scientific process brought him success in deciphering the Rosetta Stone.

INFERENCES   Which three of the following are the best inferences that can be drawn from this selection? _____, _____, and _____

1. Grotefend would have deciphered the Rosetta Stone if Champollion had not.
2. A purely syllabic language is not very common.
3. Grotefend was decoding ancient Persian texts.
4. Most alphabets have at least 160 signs.
5. British scientists are more skillful at translation than those from other countries.
6. There is something about scientists that makes them die young.
7. Luck is an important factor in scientific research.
8. Scientific processes such as the one described may take many, many years.

APPLICATION   Choose the best answer for each question.

1. _____ If a person stands in front of a stone with Egyptian hieroglyphics written on it, he:
   a. might be able to recognize some of the things pictured.
   b. would see the similarities to the English language.
   c. would feel the mystical religious sense with which all such objects are imbued.
   d. might be cursed with an early death.

2. _____ A further example of the coincidences described by Pratt in the introductory paragraph might be the:
   a. publication of the *New York Times* East and West Coast editions at the same time.
   b. flight of a Soviet space vehicle shortly after that of American astronauts.
   c. discovery of a new planet by amateur astronomers in England and Italy at the same time.
   d. use of television advertisements appealing to retired people by two politicians in the same campaign.

3. _____ The main reason that no one had been able to decipher the hieroglyphics before Champollion was that:
   a. no real experts had tried before.
   b. the language involved use of several symbols to represent the same sound.
   c. the Greek demotic language used on the stone was not yet fully understood.
   d. Napoleon refused to surrender the stone to British cryptographers.

4. _____ The only factor that may have made Champollion's task easier than that of Grotefend was that:
   a. the names of Egyptian kings were known, while those with which Grotefend worked were not.
   b. Grotefend had before him various combinations of seemingly meaningless markings.
   c. the hieroglyphics with which Champollion was working had over 160 signs.
   d. the field in which Grotefend was working was a new one.

5. _____ In a purely symbolic language, each symbol represents a:
   a. sound.
   b. word.
   c. letter.
   d. syllable.

6. _____ Champollion reached the conclusion that the hieroglyphics were letter-symbols because:
   a. there were three times as many hieroglyphic symbols as there were Greek letters.
   b. there were too many hieroglyphics for them to be anything else.
   c. previous scientists had reached that conclusion.
   d. the inscriptions were obviously not identical.

7. _____ Champollion concluded that the four symbols that stood for the name of Ptolemy, which has seven letters, were all:
   a. numbers.
   b. pictures.
   c. vowels.
   d. consonants.

8. _____ The most important character trait a cryptographer seems to have is:
   a. longevity.
   b. persistence.
   c. a good memory.
   d. creativity.

VOCABULARY   Choose the best definition for each italic vocabulary entry.

1. _____ some invisible *medium*
   a. mind reader
   b. substance
   c. middleman
   d. spirit

2. _____ senses *attuned* by study
   a. harmonized
   b. sharpened
   c. filled
   d. made melodious

3. _____ was *propounded* separately
   a. struck
   b. proved wrong
   c. argued
   d. suggested

4. _____ an infant *prodigy*
   a. terror
   b. trainee
   c. orphan
   d. wonder

5. _____ *radically* different from
   a. colorfully
   b. basically
   c. extremely
   d. interestingly

6. _____ the wreckage of *hypotheses*
   a. angles
   b. animals
   c. theories
   d. previously assumed knowledge

7. _____ an *intelligible* language
   a. speakable
   b. understandable
   c. smart
   d. international

8. _____ The problem was *insoluble*.
   a. unanswerable
   b. incurable
   c. undissolvable
   d. unpronounceable

9. _____ the very basis of any *deduction*
   a. conclusion
   b. removal
   c. building
   d. reason

10. _____ An alphabet of 160 letters remained *inadmissible*.
    a. mysterious
    b. serious
    c. not able to be sent
    d. not allowable

11. _____ It would have to be spelled *phonetically*.
    a. from memory
    b. falsely
    c. according to sound
    d. without using letters

12. _____ a substitution *cipher*
    a. nothing
    b. code
    c. letter
    d. symbol

13. _____ *suppression* of frequencies
    a. conquering
    b. elimination
    c. writing down
    d. expression

14. _____ a *prodigious* number
    a. false
    b. limited
    c. infinite
    d. enormous

15. _____ a number of *nulls*
    a. symbols having no value
    b. letters left over
    c. variable symbols
    d. picture letters

23

NORBERT WIENER

Why Chimpanzees Do Not Talk

Except in cartoons and fantastic stories like the famous Dr. Dolittle series, animals do not talk in a human language or in any language that is readily understood by humans. Norbert Wiener, a distinguished linguist, suggests some reasons for this phenomenon.

Let me now call the attention of the reader to something which he may not consider a problem at all—namely, the reason that chimpanzees do not talk. The behavior of chimpanzees has for a long time been a puzzle to those psychologists who have concerned themselves with these interesting beasts. The young chimpanzee is extraordinarily like a child, and clearly his equal or perhaps even his superior in intellectual matters. The animal psychologists have not been able to keep from wondering why a chimpanzee brought up in a human family and subject to the impact of human speech until the age of one or two, does not accept language as a mode of expression, and itself burst into baby talk.

Fortunately, or unfortunately, as the case may be, most chimpanzees, in fact all that have as yet been observed, persist in being good chimpanzees, and do not become quasi-human morons. Nevertheless I think that the average animal psychologist is rather longingly hoping for that chimpanzee who will disgrace his simian ancestry by adhering to more human modes of conduct. The failure so far is not a matter of sheer bulk of intelligence, for there are defective human animals whose brains would shame a chimpanzee. It just does not belong to the nature of the beast to speak, or to want to speak.

Speech is such a peculiarly human activity that it is not even approached by man's closest relatives and his most active imitators. The few sounds emitted by chimpanzees have, it is true, a great deal of emotional content, but they have not the fineness of clear and repeated accuracy of organization needed to make them into a code much more accurate than the yowlings of a cat. Moreover (and this differentiates them still more from human speech), at times they belong to the chimpanzee as an unlearned inborn manifestation, rather than as the learned behavior of a member of a given social community.

The fact that speech belongs in general to man as man, but that a particular form of speech belongs to man as a member of a particular social community, is most remarkable. In the first place, taking the whole wide range of man as we know him today, it is safe to say that there is no community of individuals, not mutilated by an auditory or a mental defect, which does not have its own mode of speech. In the second place, all modes of speech are learned, and notwithstanding the attempts of the nineteenth century to formulate a genetic evolutionistic theory of languages, there is not the slightest general reason to postulate any single native form of speech from which all the present forms are originated. It is quite clear that if left alone, babies will make attempts at speech. These attempts, however, show their own inclinations to utter something, and do not follow any existing form of language. It is almost equally clear that if a community of children were left out of contact with the language of their seniors through the critical speech-forming years, they would emerge with something, which crude as it might be, would be unmistakably a language.

Why is it then that chimpanzees cannot be forced to talk, and that human children cannot be forced not to? Why is it that the general tendencies to speak and the general visual and psychological aspects of language are so uniform over large groups of people, while the particular linguistic manifestation of these aspects is varied? At least partial understanding of these matters is essential to any comprehension of the language-based community. We merely state the fundamental facts by saying that in man, unlike the apes, the impulse to use some sort of language is overwhelming; but that the particular language used is a matter which has to be learned in each special case. It apparently is built into the brain itself, that we are to have a preoccupation with codes and with the sounds of speech, and that the preoccupation with codes can be extended from those dealing with speech to those that concern themselves with visual stimuli. However, there is not one fragment of these codes which is born into us as a pre-established ritual, like the courting dances of many of the birds, or the system by which ants recognize and exclude intruders into the nest. The gift of speech does not go back to a universal Adamite language disrupted in the Tower of Babel. It is strictly a psychological impulse, and is not the gift of speech, but the gift of the power of speech.

In other words, the block preventing young chimpanzees from learning to talk is a block which concerns the semantic and not the phonetic stage of language. *The chimpanzee has simply no built-in mechanism which leads it to translate the sounds that it hears into the basis around which to unite its own ideas or into a complex mode of behavior.* Of the first of these statements we cannot be sure because we have no direct way of observing it. The second is simply a noticeable empirical fact. It may have its limitations, but that there is such a built-in mechanism in man is perfectly clear.

We have already emphasized man's extraordinary ability to learn as a distinguishing characteristic of the species, which makes social life a phenomenon of an entirely different nature from the apparently analogous social life among the bees and ants and other social insects. The evidence concerning children who have been deprived of contact with their own race over the years normally critical in the ordinary acquisition of language, is perhaps not completely unambiguous. The "Wolf Child" stories, which have led to Kipling's imaginative *Jungle Books*, with their public-school bears and Sandhurst wolves, are almost as little to be relied on in their original stark squalidity as in the *Jungle Books* idealizations. However, what evidence there is goes to show that there is a critical period during which speech is most readily learned; and that if this period is passed over without contact with one's fellow human beings, of whatever sort they may be, the learning of language becomes limited, slow, and highly imperfect.

This is probably true of most other abilities which we consider natural skills. If a child does not walk until it is three or four years old, it may have lost all the desire to walk. Ordinary locomotion may become a harder task than driving a car for the normal adult. If a person has been blind from childhood, and the blindness has been resolved by a cataract operation or the implantation of a transparent corneal section, the vision that ensues will, for a time, certainly bring nothing but confusion to those activities which have normally been carried out in darkness. This vision may never be more than a carefully learned new attainment of doubtful value. Now, we may fairly take it that the whole of human social life in its normal manifestations centers about speech, and that if speech is not learned at the proper time, the whole social aspect of the individual will be aborted.

To sum up, the human interest in language seems to be an innate interest in coding and decoding, and this seems to be as nearly specifically human as any interest can be. *Speech is the greatest interest and most distinctive achievement of man.*

LENGTH: 1,246 WORDS

23   Norbert Wiener
Why Chimpanzees Do Not Talk

SCORING: Reading time: _____ Rate from chart: _____ W.P.M.		
RETENTION	number right _____ × 2 equals _____ points	
MAIN POINT	number right _____ × 4 equals _____ points	
INFERENCES	number right _____ × 4 equals _____ points	
APPLICATION	number right _____ × 3 equals _____ points	
VOCABULARY	number right _____ × 2 equals _____ points	
(Total points: 100) **total** _____ points		

RETENTION   Based on the selection, which of the following statements are True (T), False (F), or Not answerable (N)?

1. _____ All present forms of speech are probably derived from one original language.

2. _____ The chimpanzee has a built-in mechanism that translates sounds into an organized code.

3. _____ An interest in speech is born into human beings.

4. _____ The gift of speech is born into us as a preestablished ritual.

5. _____ A young chimpanzee is the intellectual equal of a child.

6. _____ All modes of speech are learned.

7. _____ Animal psychologists have been able to teach a chimpanzee to understand human language.

8. _____ Kipling's *Jungle Books* help us understand what life would be like for a child abandoned in the jungle at an early age.

9. _____ A person who was born blind and who gains his sight in adulthood may never be completely skillful at using his sight.

10. _____ A human child cannot be forced not to learn to talk.

11. _____ The brains of most humans are defective when compared to those of chimpanzees.

12. _____ If left alone, babies would come up with the ability to speak one of the languages known to man.

13. _____ The social life of man is remarkably like that of bees and ants.

14. _____ As a rule, chimpanzees make few sounds.

15. _____ The "Wolf Child" stories were influenced by Kipling's *Jungle Books*.

MAIN POINT   Which of the following statements best represents the main point of the selection? _____

1. Although chimpanzees are more like human beings than is any other animal, they cannot talk.
2. Unlike chimpanzees, human beings are born with the power of speech.
3. Chimpanzees do not talk because they don't need to.
4. Man's ability to speak is second only to his creative power in making him the greatest of all living creatures.
5. Human beings are merely chimpanzees whose brains evolved to a higher thinking level.

INFERENCES   Which three of the following are the best inferences that can be drawn from this selection? _____, _____, and _____

1. A chimpanzee and a child might play with a set of blocks in a very similar manner.
2. Chimpanzees probably have a strong interest in coding and decoding.
3. Wiener is more interested in humans than he is in chimpanzees.
4. There are no human beings who do not talk.
5. Inborn behaviors are more animal-like than learned behaviors.
6. Most blind persons can have their eyesight restored by an operation.
7. If an animal psychologist could spend enough time with a chimpanzee, she could get him to speak English.
8. Walking is a natural, inborn human skill.

APPLICATION   Choose the best answer for each question.

1. _____ A person who did not learn speech at the proper stage of his development would probably:
   a. never learn how to speak.
   b. not walk until he is three or four years old.
   c. have his social development impeded as well.
   d. have a hard time learning how to drive a car.

2. _____ A chimpanzee brought up alongside a human child would probably:
   a. burst into speech at the age of one or two.
   b. imitate the child in some ways.
   c. become a defective human being.
   d. never make any sound at all.

3. _____ The sounds that a chimpanzee utters are probably the result of:
   a. imitating man.
   b. a cat yowling.
   c. learning.
   d. some strong emotion.

4. _____ If a child were abandoned in the jungle and never came into contact
   with other human beings, he would probably:
   a. never talk.
   b. devise some sort of language.
   c. speak the language of the animals around him.
   d. become deaf and dumb as well.

5. _____ An example of an inborn, preestablished ritual would be:
   a. speech.
   b. nest building.
   c. a formal dinner.
   d. a dog fetching a ball.

6. _____ Man is born with:
   a. a brain smaller than a chimpanzee's.
   b. the ability to speak.
   c. the ability to learn to speak.
   d. the instinct to speak.

7. _____ The quality that makes speech different from mere sound is:
   a. the intensity of the noise that is made.
   b. the understandability of the noise by another animal.
   c. the length of the sound.
   d. the organization into a meaningful code.

8. _____ If two human languages are compared, they will probably:
   a. have some general aspects in common.
   b. be understood by the majority of people.
   c. be found to be identical.
   d. be so different as to be incomprehensible.

VOCABULARY   Choose the best definition for each italic vocabulary entry.

1. _____ become *quasi-human* morons
   a. resembling humans
   b. more than human
   c. half human
   d. less than human

2. _____ disgrace his *simian* ancestry
   a. monkey
   b. Asian
   c. animal
   d. foreign

3. _____ a *peculiarly* human activity
   a. strangely
   b. sadly
   c. especially
   d. surprisingly

4. _____ an *auditory* or a mental defect
   a. seeing
   b. hearing
   c. speaking
   d. thinking

5. _____ an *evolutionistic* theory of languages
   a. monkeylike
   b. developmental
   c. out-of-date
   d. historical

6. _____ the particular linguistic *manifestation*
   a. fear
   b. understanding
   c. tendency
   d. demonstration

7. _____ a noticeable *empirical* fact
   a. mechanical
   b. able to be extended
   c. forceful
   d. provable by direct experience

8. _____ a *preoccupation* with codes
   a. previous employment
   b. suitable observance
   c. mental absorption
   d. momentary concern

9. _____ a universal *Adamite* language
   a. pertaining to Adam
   b. atomic
   c. firm
   d. eternal

10. _____ apparently *analogous* social life
    a. unusual
    b. unethical
    c. parallel
    d. active

11. _____ the ordinary *acquisition* of language
    a. criticism
    b. curiosity about
    c. questioning
    d. learning

12. _____ not completely *unambiguous*
    a. confusing
    b. ambitious
    c. certain
    d. universal

13. _____ their original *stark* squalidity
    a. evil
    b. previous
    c. harsh
    d. dispossessed

14. _____ the "Jungle Books" *idealizations*
    a. demonstrations of value
    b. lies
    c. exaggerations of perfection
    d. moralizings

15. _____ Ordinary *locomotion* may become a harder task.
    a. movement
    b. engineering
    c. location
    d. training

24

DANIEL BOORSTIN

Advertising: The Rhetoric of Democracy

Using examples from history, including a
discussion of the development of the meaning
of the word "advertising," Daniel Boorstin
explains how democracy has shaped and
been shaped by advertising. In doing this,
he raises some questions about the effect
advertising has had on the quality of daily
life in America.

Advertising, of course, has been part of the mainstream of American
civilization, although you might not know it if you read the most respectable
surveys of American history. It has been one of the enticements to the settlement
of this New World, it has been a producer of the peopling of the United States,
and in its modern form, in its world-wide reach, it has been one of our most
characteristic products.

Never was there a more outrageous or more unscrupulous or more ill-
informed advertising campaign than that by which the promoters for the American colonies brought settlers here. Brochures published in England in the
seventeenth century, some even earlier, were full of hopeful overstatements,
half-truths, and downright lies, along with some facts which nowadays surely
would be the basis for a restraining order from the Federal Trade Commission.
Gold and silver, fountains of youth, plenty of fish, venison without limit, all
these were promised, and of course some of them were found. It would be
interesting to speculate on how long it might have taken to settle this continent if
there had not been such promotion by enterprising advertisers. How has American civilization been shaped by the fact that there was a kind of natural

selection here of those people who were willing to believe advertising?

Advertising has taken the lead in promising and exploiting the new. This was a new world, and one of the advertisements for it appears on the dollar bill on the Great Seal of the United States, which reads *novus ordo seclorum*, one of the most effective advertising slogans to come out of this country. "A new order of the centuries" — belief in novelty and in the desirability of opening novelty to everybody has been important in our lives throughout our history and especially in this century. Again and again advertising has been an agency for inducing Americans to try anything and everything—from the continent itself to a new brand of soap. As one of the more literate and poetic of the advertising copywriters, James Kenneth Frazier, a Cornell graduate, wrote in 1900 in "The Doctor's Lament":

> *This lean M.D. is Dr. Brown*
> *Who fares but ill in Spotless Town.*
> *The town is so confounded clean,*
> *It is no wonder he is lean,*
> *He's lost all patients now, you know,*
> *Because they use Sapolio.*

The same literary talent that once was used to retail Sapolio was later used to induce people to try the Edsel or the Mustang, to experiment with Lifebuoy or Body-All, to drink Pepsi-Cola or Royal Crown Cola, or to shave with a Trac II razor.

And as expansion and novelty have become essential to our economy, advertising has played an ever-larger role: in the settling of the continent, in the expansion of the economy, and in the building of an American standard of living. Advertising has expressed the optimism, the hyperbole, and the sense of community, the sense of reaching which has been so important a feature of our civilization.

Here I wish to explore the significance of advertising, not as a force in the economy or in shaping an American standard of living, but rather as a touchstone of the ways in which we Americans have learned about all sorts of things.

The problems of advertising are of course not peculiar to advertising, for they are just one aspect of the problems of democracy. They reflect the rise of what I have called Consumption Communities and Statistical Communities, and many of the special problems of advertising have arisen from our continuously energetic effort to give everybody everything.

If we consider democracy not just as a political system, but as a set of institutions which do aim to make everything available to everybody, it would not be an overstatement to describe advertising as the characteristic rhetoric of democracy. One of the tendencies of democracy, which Plato and other antidemocrats warned against a long time ago, was the danger that rhetoric would displace or at least overshadow epistemology, that is, *the temptation to allow the problem of persuasion to overshadow the problem of knowledge.* Democratic societies tend to become more concerned with what people believe than with what is true, to become more concerned with credibility than with truth. All these problems become accentuated in a large-scale democracy like ours, which possesses all the apparatus of modern industry. And the problems are accentuated still further by universal literacy, by instantaneous communication, and by the daily plague of words and images.

In the early days it was common for advertising men to define advertisements as a kind of news. The best admen, like the best journalists, were supposed to be those who were able to make their news the most interesting and readable. This was natural enough, since the verb to "advertise" originally meant, intransitively, to take note or to consider. For a person to "advertise" meant originally, in the fourteenth and fifteenth centuries, to reflect on something, to think about something. Then it came to mean, transitively, to call the attention of another to do something, to give him notice, to notify, admonish, warn or inform in a formal or impressive manner. And then, by the sixteenth century, it came to mean: to give notice of anything, to make generally known. It was not until the late eighteenth century that the word "advertising" in English came to have a specifically "advertising" connotation as we might say today, and not until the late nineteenth century that it began to have a specifically commercial connotation. By 1879 someone was saying, "Don't advertise unless you have something worth advertising." But even into the present century, newspapers continue to call themselves by the title "Advertiser"—for example, the Boston *Daily Advertiser*, which was a newspaper of long tradition and one of the most dignified papers in Boston until William Randolph Hearst took it over in 1917. Newspapers carried "Advertiser" on their mastheads, not because they sold advertisements but because they brought news.

Now, the main role of advertising in American civilization came increasingly to be that of persuading and appealing rather than that of educating and informing. By 1921, for instance, one of the more popular textbooks, Blanchard's *Essentials of Advertising*, began: "Anything employed to influence people favorably is advertising. The mission of advertising is to persuade men and women to act in a way that will be of advantage to the advertiser." This development—in a country where a shared, a rising, and a democratized standard of living was the national pride and the national hallmark—meant that advertising had become the rhetoric of democracy.

What, then, were some of the main features of modern American advertising—if we consider it as a form of rhetoric? First, and perhaps most obvious, is *repetition*. It is hard for us to realize that the use of repetition in advertising is not an ancient device but a modern one, which actually did not come into common use in American journalism until just past the middle of the nineteenth century.

The development of what came to be called "iteration copy" was a result of a struggle by a courageous man of letters and advertising pioneer, Robert Bonner, who bought the old New York *Merchant's Ledger* in 1851 and turned it into a popular journal. He then had the temerity to try to change the ways of James Gordon Bennett, who of course was one of the most successful of the American newspaper pioneers, and who was both a sensationalist and at the same time an extremely stuffy man when it came to things that he did not consider to be news. Bonner was determined to use advertisements in Bennett's wide-circulating New York *Herald* to sell his own literary product, but he found it difficult to persuade Bennett to allow him to use any but agate type in his advertising. (Agate was the smallest type used by newspapers in that day, only barely legible to the naked eye.) Bennett would not allow advertisers to use larger type, nor would he allow them to use illustrations except stock cuts, because he thought it was undignified. He said, too, that to allow a variation in the format of ads would be undemocratic. He insisted that all advertisers use the same size type so that no one would be allowed to prevail over another simply by presenting his message in a larger, more clever, or more attention-getting form.

Finally, Bonner managed to overcome Bennett's rigidity by leasing whole pages of the paper and using the tiny agate type to form larger letters across the top of the page. In this way he produced a message such as "Bring home the New York Ledger tonight." His were unimaginative messages, and when repeated all across the page they technically did not violate Bennett's agate rule. But they opened a new era and presaged a new freedom for advertisers in their use of the newspaper page. Iteration copy—the practice of presenting prosaic content in ingenious, repetitive form—became common, and nowadays of course is commonplace.

A second characteristic of American advertising which is not unrelated to this is the development of *an advertising style*. We have histories of most other kinds of style—including the style of many unread writers who are remembered today only because they have been forgotten—but we have very few accounts of the history of advertising style, which of course is one of the most important forms of our language and one of the most widely influential.

The development of advertising style was the convergence of several very respectable American traditions. One of these was the tradition of the "plain style," which the Puritans made so much of and which accounts for so much of the strength of the Puritan literature. The "plain style" was of course much influenced by the Bible and found its way into the rhetoric of American writers and speakers of great power like Abraham Lincoln. When advertising began to be self-conscious in the early years of this century, the pioneers urged copywriters not to be too clever, and especially not to be fancy. One of the pioneers of the advertising copywriters, John Powers, said, for example, "The commonplace is the proper level for writing in business; where the first virtue is plainness, 'fine writing' is not only intellectual, it is offensive." George P. Rowell, another advertising pioneer, said, "You must write your advertisement to catch damned fools—not college professors." He was a very tactful person. And he added, "And you'll catch just as many college professors as you will of any other sort."

In the 1920's, when advertising was beginning to come into its own, Claude Hopkins, whose name is known to all in the trade, said, "Brilliant writing has no place in advertising. A unique style takes attention from the subject. Any apparent effort to sell creates corresponding resistance. . . . One should be natural and simple. His language should not be conspicuous. In fishing for buyers, as in fishing for bass, one should not reveal the hook." So there developed a characteristic advertising style in which plainness, the phrase that anyone could understand, was a distinguishing mark.

At the same time, the American advertising style drew on another, and what might seem an antithetic, tradition—the tradition of hyperbole and tall talk, the language of Davy Crockett and Mike Fink. While advertising could think of itself as 99.44 percent pure, it used the language of "Toronado" and "Cutlass." As I listen to the radio in Washington, I hear a celebration of heroic qualities which would make the characteristics of Mike Fink and Davy Crockett pale, only to discover at the end of the paean that what I have been hearing is a description of the Ford dealers in the District of Columbia neighborhood. And along with the folk tradition of hyperbole and tall talk comes the rhythm of folk music. We hear that Pepsi-Cola hits the spot, that it's for the young generation— and we hear other products celebrated in music which we cannot forget and sometimes don't want to remember.

There grew somehow out of all these contradictory tendencies—combining the commonsense language of the "plain style," and the fantasy language of "tall talk"—an advertising style. This characteristic way of talking about things was especially designed to reach and catch the millions. It created a whole new world of myth. A myth, the dictionary tells us, is a notion based more on tradition or convenience than on facts; it is a received idea. Myth is not just fantasy and not just fact but exists in a limbo, in the world of the "Will to Believe," which William James has written about so eloquently and so perceptively. This is the world of the neither true nor false—of the statement that 60 percent of the physicians who expressed a choice said that our brand of aspirin would be more effective in curing a simple headache than any other leading brand.

That kind of statement exists in a penumbra. I would call this the "advertising penumbra." It is not untrue, and yet, in its connotation it is not exactly true.

Now, there is still another characteristic of advertising so obvious that we are inclined perhaps to overlook it. I call that *ubiquity*. Advertising abhors a vacuum and we discover new vacuums every day. The parable, of course, is the story of the man who thought of putting the advertisement on the other side of the cigarette package. Until then, that was wasted space and a society which aims at a democratic standard of living, at extending the benefits of consumption and all sorts of things and services to everybody, must miss no chances to reach people. The highway billboard and other outdoor advertising, bus and streetcar and subway advertising, and skywriting, radio and TV commercials— all these are of course obvious evidence that advertising abhors a vacuum.

We might reverse the old mousetrap slogan and say that anyone who can devise another place to put another mousetrap to catch a consumer will find people beating a path to his door. "Avoiding advertising will become a little harder next January," the *Wall Street Journal* reported on May 17, 1973, "when a Studio City, California, company launches a venture called Store Vision. Its product is a system of billboards that move on a track across supermarket ceilings. Some 650 supermarkets so far are set to have the system." All of which helps us understand the observation attributed to a French man of letters during his recent visit to Times Square. "What a beautiful place, if only one could not read!" Everywhere is a place to be filled, as we discover in a recent *Publishers Weekly* description of one advertising program: "The $1.95 paperback edition of Dr. Thomas A. Harris' million-copy best seller 'I'm O.K., You're O.K.' is in for full-scale promotion in July by its publisher, Avon Books. Plans range from bumper stickers to airplane streamers, from planes flying above Fire Island, the Hamptons and Malibu. In addition, the $100,000 promotion budget calls for 200,000 bookmarks, plus brochures, buttons, lipcards, floor and counter displays, and advertising in magazines and TV."

The ubiquity of advertising is of course just another effect of our uninhibited efforts to use all the media to get all sorts of information to everybody everywhere. Since the places to be filled are everywhere, the amount of advertising is not determined by the *needs* of advertising, but by the *opportunities* for advertising which become unlimited.

LENGTH: 2,608 WORDS

24   Daniel Boorstin
Advertising: The Rhetoric of Democracy

SCORING: Reading time: _____ Rate from chart: _____ W.P.M.

RETENTION	number right _____ × 2 equals _____ points
MAIN POINT	number right _____ × 4 equals _____ points
INFERENCES	number right _____ × 4 equals _____ points
APPLICATION	number right _____ × 3 equals _____ points
VOCABULARY	number right _____ × 2 equals _____ points

(Total points: 100) **total** _____ points

RETENTION   Based on the selection, which of the following statements are True (T), False (F), or Not answerable (N)?

1. _____ Historically, advertisements were a kind of news.

2. _____ Repetition is the most obvious feature of modern advertising.

3. _____ The history of advertising style has not often been written.

4. _____ The advertising used to encourage settlers to come to the American colonies was surprisingly understated.

5. _____ The dollar bill has an advertisement printed on it.

6. _____ The one quality missing from advertising slogans is that of music.

7. _____ Each advertising writer strives for a unique style.

8. _____ Painting billboards on supermarket ceilings is one of the more recent advertising notions.

9. _____ Even paperback books get full-scale promotional treatment.

10. _____ Plato criticized advertising because he was an antidemocrat who did not want the common people to know too much.

11. _____ Sapolio was a brand of soap.

12. _____ Iteration copy is used extensively in advertising today.

13. _____ The promoters for the original American colonies were aristocrats.

14. _____ A myth is just a fantasy that has been handed down for generations.

15. _____ The *New York Herald* used to be printed in the smallest type available.

MAIN POINT Which of the following statements best represents the main point of the selection? _____

1. Without advertising, America could not survive as a nation.
2. Advertising should be carefully monitored to avoid exaggeration.
3. Advertising and democracy are both words whose meanings have changed drastically.
4. Advertising has influenced and expressed American life from the beginning to the present day.
5. Advertising has certain characteristics today that it did not have 300 years ago.

INFERENCES Which three of the following are the best inferences that can be drawn from this selection? _____, _____, and _____

1. Boorstin would be in favor of controlling advertising more carefully.
2. America was settled by people who were easily swayed by advertising.
3. Without advertising, our economy would not have expanded as it has.
4. Newspapers used to be more flamboyant than they are today.
5. The "plain style" of the Puritans would not be very effective in today's world.
6. Exaggeration would not work today as it did in the seventeenth century.
7. Boorstin has done a great deal of research into advertising.
8. Advertising in any other country would be much like advertising in the United States.

APPLICATION Choose the best answer for each question.

1. _____ One statement that is not true about advertising historically is that it has been:
    a. used to encourage people to settle the New World.
    b. one of our most characteristic products to be sent abroad.
    c. written about extensively in American history surveys.
    d. a factor in building our standard of living.

2. _____ As an advertising copywriter in the early twentieth century, my main goal would have been to:
    a. make what I wrote interesting.

b. call people's attention to a subject.

c. educate and inform people.

d. persuade and appeal to people.

3. _____ Advertising has been called the rhetoric of democracy because it:

a. has been used to get out the vote.

b. was started at about the same time the United States began.

c. has been used in the United States more than in any other country.

d. was used to promote a shared, improved way of living for all citizens.

4. _____ The biggest problem with advertising is that it:

a. reflects the rise of Consumption Communities.

b. is linked with large-scale industry.

c. impacts people with too many words and images each day.

d. encourages a tendency for people to be more concerned with belief than with truth.

5. _____ If Robert Bonner, the owner of the *Merchant's Ledger*, were in advertising today, he would probably:

a. come up with a new form of advertising.

b. own the *New York Times*.

c. take out a full-page advertisement.

d. use illustrations extensively.

6. _____ The best example of what Boorstin means by the "advertising penumbra" would be:

a. "Brand X beat Brand Y two to one in nationwide taste tests."

b. "Super Sale going on for three days only."

c. "Buy two boxes; get another one free."

d. "Brand A detergent with built-in fabric softener."

7. _____ The best example of the idea that advertising abhors a vacuum would be advertising:

a. supplements in the Sunday newspaper.

b. on the inside of matchbooks.

c. on television during a prime-time program.

d. that encourages children to ask their parents for a certain toy.

8. _____ The amount of advertising in the United States is decided on the basis of:

a. need.

b. money.

c. opportunity.

d. justice.

VOCABULARY   Choose the best definition for each italic vocabulary entry.

1. _____ more *unscrupulous* advertising campaign
   a. ignorant
   b. flawed
   c. dishonest
   d. influential

2. _____ promising and *exploiting* the new
   a. discovering
   b. avoiding
   c. profiting by
   d. taking in

3. _____ Advertising has expressed the *hyperbole*.
   a. high hopes
   b. yearning
   c. exaggeration
   d. concern

4. _____ a *touchstone* of the ways
   a. hardness
   b. test
   c. shaper
   d. example

5. _____ Rhetoric would overshadow *epistemology*.
   a. theory of knowledge
   b. study of writing
   c. theory of persuasion
   d. principles of law

6. _____ what came to be called "*iteration* copy"
   a. repetition
   b. competition
   c. practical
   d. eye-catching

7. _____ He was a *sensationalist*.
   a. nudist
   b. journalist
   c. risk taker
   d. thrill seeker

8. _____ the practice of presenting *prosaic* content
   a. interesting
   b. commonplace

c. informative

d. handwritten

9. ____ *presaged* a new freedom

    a. predicted

    b. promised

    c. warned of

    d. destroyed

10. ____ what might seem an *antithetic* tradition

    a. overly clean

    b. unpatriotic

    c. opposing

    d. extraordinary

11. ____ at the end of the *paean*

    a. long talk

    b. piece of writing

    c. hymn of praise

    d. holy scripture

12. ____ Myth exists in a *limbo*.

    a. paradise

    b. final resting place

    c. lower world

    d. no man's land

13. ____ That kind of statement exists in a *penumbra*.

    a. vault

    b. umbrella

    c. nutshell

    d. shadowy area

14. ____ the *ubiquity* of advertising

    a. existence everywhere

    b. forgetfulness

    c. improper behavior

    d. ability to influence

15. ____ another effect of our *uninhibited* efforts

    a. immoral

    b. unlimited

    c. unlicensed

    d. thoughtless

25

J. R. POLE

The Language of American Presidents

As a rule, most of us pay more attention to what our president says than to how he says it. J. R. Pole analyzes the rhetorical style of presidents from Dwight Eisenhower to Jimmy Carter, using specific examples from their speeches to show how very different they are from each other.

American political speech resembles a low murmur in many dialects of a single language. Above it all, catching the occasional attention of a vast and extraordinarily heterogeneous population, the voice of the president engages with it in a dialogue unlike that of any other nation, and unlike that of any other head of government.

Events affect the language in which they are described. Since the inauguration of Woodrow Wilson in 1913, the Americans have fought four wars; they were the first people to experience the wide diffusion of the products of consumer industries and, in communications, of radio and television; and since the ending of mass immigration they have come to recognize themselves, to a degree which may have been implicit but was hardly anticipated in Wilson's time, as a nation of one law but varied cultures. All these transformations have been reflected, sometimes subtly, sometimes clearly, in the speech of political leadership. . . .

George Orwell, in his essay, "Politics and the English Language," written shortly after the Second World War, observed that the whole tendency of modern prose was away from concreteness (and also that in our time most political speech was the defense of the indefensible). Orwell's genius was for interpreting portents, and what he foresaw was perhaps to grow even worse in America than in England.

An infiltration of bureaucratic speech, deriving partly from the war, partly from the actually increasing bureaucracy and partly from an increasingly Germanic sociology, demoralized and disarmed large parts of the academic and journalistic worlds, and entered deeply into the realm of public communication. The audience was increasingly assumed to be either semiliterate or of subnormal intelligence. Tenses got out of alignment, descriptive designations were used as though they were personal titles, conditionals and subjunctives mistook each other's identity, and Orwell's perception was finding its mark in the new verbal democracy. What mattered was no longer the precise meaning (which might be a sign of overeducation) but the general idea, which could be conveyed as much by the packaging as by the content. It was perhaps a significant product of the same period that the third edition of Webster's *Dictionary of the American Language* (1961), under preparation during these years, departed from the conventional principle that each word had a correct usage, upon which others were either variants, or were incorrect, and took the novel stand that all current usage was to all intents and purposes correct usage. All words are created equal.

Not all of these trends revealed themselves at once in presidential speech, and the nation over which Dwight Eisenhower presided from 1953 to 1961 was increasingly prosperous, increasingly pleased with itself and correspondingly unself-critical. Although Eisenhower himself was not a loose thinker (and he was a sharp reader of proofs, too) he conveyed an impression of ease which almost amounted to negligence. He probably wrote very little of what passed in his name, but nearly all of his press conference answers began with "Well . . ." and many of them continued by disclaiming whatever expertise the question seemed to require. Reporters enjoyed their sense of superiority over the presidential syntax, but the nation, or large parts of it, got the impression that there was nothing much to worry about, which was no doubt exactly what their president intended. The procedure could be carried too far, however. Over the crisis of Little Rock the president gave the impression of being only dimly concerned, and he left it to others to convey his administration's guidance on the nation's one central issue of civil rights.

The contrast between Eisenhower's informal style and Truman's is striking. Eisenhower talked as though speech had been an awkwardly acquired capability; Truman was prompt, blunt and often entertaining, not so much from verbal wit as from an undisguised relish in the situation. His remarks contained few memorable phrases, and their force—which survives the passage of years—derives from their immediacy, and from a distinct sense of sharing the whole situation with the reporters, an attitude that was completely alien to his successor.

Truman's utterances, even on the more formal occasions, tended to be lacking in cadence. Eisenhower's (with rare exceptions) were lacking in the more important attribute of that emotional force which gives conviction to ordinary language. His indifference to intellectual precision became notorious, and many intellectuals resented the apparent flabbiness of the Eisenhower era—which had not been improved by such coinages as *finalize*, and from which the term *Eisenhoverian* has been derived for inelegant and unnecessary neologisms. Eisenhower was not responsible for the drift of his time, but his style reflected it with a nonchalant fidelity which encouraged loose writing and soft thinking in others; a president is closely watched, and as Stevenson as the leader of a major party showed, has it in his power to set a tone to which others must at least reply. In politics it was principally the style of Stevenson, and in more general literature the recognition of such rare stylists as Richard Hofstadter, that saved the reading public from sinking into a soapy euphoria in which the way things were said was no longer considered to matter: from which stage it is but a short step to the things themselves. . . .

After the Eisenhower era, John Kennedy made a deliberate return to conscious literary standards of public discourse, and some of his public statements begin to show signs of the strain. He liked to achieve his effects by tight constructions, which often posed alternatives in close apposition. "Ask not what your country can do for you—ask what you can do for your country" (in which *country* is the only word of more than one syllable) has become trite with quotation, but remains an obvious example—and one which had political significance from the leader of the party which had engineered America's welfare state. Kennedy knew the force of strong, short words: "But peace in space will help us naught once peace on earth is gone." ("Short words are best and old words best of all"—Churchill.) In this sentence an effect of monosyllabic austerity is modified by the archaism of *naught*. But Kennedy, who scrutinized these questions with his speech writers, knew that rhetorical eloquence is no substitute for meaning what you say. When his use of language comes to be studied the thing to be looked for in his effects is not so much rhythm (which Nixon claimed to value above everything else) as economy.

Kennedy understood exactly what, unfortunately, Richard Nixon could not afford to acknowledge. No president in recent times has contributed so much of his own to his public statements as Nixon, an admirer of Woodrow Wilson, who was also—too consciously perhaps—influenced by Churchill. The influence he would not have wished to admit was that of the TV commercial. But here is Nixon in 1952, fighting for his political life in the "Checkers" speech: "And remember, folks, Eisenhower is a great man. Folks, he is a great man. . . ." This was early Nixon, and he later eliminated such crudities, but he never eliminated, because it was part of his character, the search for applause and the repeated exhibition of a curiously piteous form of self-dramatization.

Nixon had learnt the importance of linguistic architecture, no doubt primarily from Wilson and Churchill, but the trouble was that the frame showed through the plaster. His acceptance speech in 1968 exemplified Orwell's prediction; all the visions of the future he offered his party and the American people were inflated abstractions, so devoid of specific content that they committed no one to anything—and led to considerable subsequent doubts about where he stood on civil rights. Nixon used here a simple Rooseveltian device, that of emphatic repetition. "I see a day when Americans are once again proud . . . I see a day when every child in this land . . . I see a day when life in rural America attracts . . . I see a day when [but this required an uncomfortable wrench of the neck] we can look back on massive breakthroughs. . . ." When FDR used that technique, he did it to arouse the too easily satisfied American conscience: "I see one-third of a nation, ill-clad, ill-housed, ill-nourished." And this he used again and again.

Nixon's address to the nation on the Vietnam War, on 3 November 1969, is said to have been almost entirely his own work, and correspondingly character-istic. The structure of the argument is clear, the weighing of issues is solemn, but that effect is qualified by the extraordinary bathos of his implicit appeals for personal sympathy. Less than ten months after taking office, he is already openly thinking of the next election—which, he rightly assures the voters, is less important than the search for a satisfactory peace. Is Johnson's war to become Nixon's war? That is the question that weighs on the president's too plainly revealed, although furtive, consciousness; and he gives as a *personal* reason for wanting to end the war that he has to write letters of sympathy to bereaved families.

Nixon betrayed the fact that he did not respect the people to whom he had to appeal, which may (we can at least conjecture) have derived from some pro-foundly buried lack of self-respect. He dismissed the suggestion of going on TV to use (risk?) his own popularity to fight congressional tax cutting with, "No. You can't explain economics to the American people." This dismissal of the intellectual competence of the American people was a significant departure from the expectations of Wilson, or of Roosevelt or Truman. Presidents sometimes reveal themselves among friends, and also among enemies. When Nixon took the apparently bold step of addressing the AFL-CIO convention in November 1972, he admitted to them that he had been advised not to go. "I'll tell you why I came here," he then said. "Because while some of you may be against me politically and some of you may be against my party I know from experience from the last three years that when the chips are down organized labor's for America and that's why I'm here before this convention today." This strange *non sequitur* was not only irrelevant but downright insulting. Organized labor did not require to be told that it was "for America," of which, after all, it formed a very large and indispensable part, and George Meany restored the meeting's humor and accurately reflected the theatrical nature of the performance after the president's departure by saying, "We will now go on to Act Two."

Nixon used the English language with care and not without scholarship. He could and sometimes did mount an argument of considerable power. But like his contemporary Sir Harold Wilson, he lacked the power of looking as though he was telling the truth, and perhaps for similar reasons: that too many thoughts, other than the content of the speech, were running through his scanning mechanism at the same time. Yet Nixon deserves credit for the invocation of "the great silent majority," a phrase worked into his speech of 3 November 1969 with the unobtrusive skill of a craftsman, which he is. He could also be unexpectedly witty, as when, on a formal social occasion, he overcame the awkwardness of the appointment as British ambassador of John Freeman, former editor of the *New Statesman*, who had denounced him abusively: "He's the new diplomat and I'm the new statesman."

Nixon and Johnson both suffered from a novel difficulty among American presidents: half of the country at least did not believe they were telling the truth. Neither of them could overcome this, and the strain told increasingly though in different ways. Johnson, who had no formal eloquence, liked to itemize his points after a brief general statement, and as a practical politician among professionals he could argue with considerable power. His way of expounding his decision to go on with the war on 29 September 1967 was extremely skillful. He admitted the difficulty of being sure of the right course, mentioned evidence for either view, but then invited his audience to weigh the reasons for believing that withdrawal would lead to further and greater dangers. His method was to leave the opposition with the right to their own views but to leave with them also the responsibility for the consequences of following those views: for his own part he accepted the full responsibility of going on with the war. Lyndon Johnson failed to convince the American public, and eventually recognized the loss of authority—literally reflected by the vogue word *credibility*—by his dignified decision not to seek reelection in 1968.

It is perfectly possible to tell lies in flawless English, as many presidents and prime ministers have shown, but it is much more difficult to speak persuasively on matters of great technical complexity or moral difficulty in defective English. Mr. Carter, who is by training an engineer, and who possesses possibly the most analytically competent mind to have occupied the White House in this century, talks a language that owes much to the procedures of technical exposition. He seems to eschew deliberated eloquence, and although he finds time for reading, it would be difficult to find in his pronouncements any clear sense of continuity with political literature. He often seems satisfied to be understood almost exactly as the writer of a technical manual means to be understood, and is seldom concerned to arouse sentiment which will help to convince his audience. This style clearly reflects his rapid and thorough but basically mechanical grasp of complex problems.

On occasions, however, when he does want to convey his own feelings the effect varies immensely with his audience. His inaugural address was very bad; it was suffused with images of rebirth and dreamery, it recognized with a modest, practical humility the limitations of what could be achieved, but concluded by invoking "an undiminished, ever-expanding American dream." Whatever might be the effects of an expanding dream spreading over the American people, it was not the stuff that politics are made on, or with which he was going to confront the nation or Congress. He did far better when he began his first "fireside chat" on energy by telling his audience with almost Churchillian bluntness, "Tonight I want to have an unpleasant talk with you about a problem unprecedented in our history. With the exception of preventing war, this is the greatest challenge our country will face in our lifetimes. The energy crisis has not yet overwhelmed us, but it will do if we do not act quickly." The long shadow reached down to 24 October 1978 when in his national address on inflation, Mr. Carter accepted—rather reluctantly—a wartime quotation from Winston Churchill: "What sort of people do they think we are?" In this speech, Mr. Carter took a cautious step toward mixing moral persuasion with economic analysis.

When talking to groups with whom he feels at home—"at ease," he might say, as it seems to be one of his preferred phrases—he can be transformed into an old-style Southern preacher from whom language flows with his breath. He created an astounding sensation in a meeting with the congressional black caucus in September 1978 by addressing them as no former president could ever have done, as "brothers and sisters," and his speech, which began with St. Matthew, actually developed into a call-and-response style sermon. Calling on Rosa Parks, who by refusing to stand up precipitated the great bus boycott in Montgomery, Alabama, in 1957, he quoted her own words and concluded, "Well, we've got a long way to walk in the future. We'll walk together. Our feet may be tired, but when we get through our soul will be rested."

In this setting Mr. Carter, who has too much respect for the people to talk down to them, was able to transcend the distance between himself and his audience, but most of the time he has seemed to fear any sense of distance at all. A president, however, must stand somewhere apart, as all great presidents have known instinctively. Then the language which has the power to survive its own utterance is the most likely to move those to whom it is immediately spoken.

LENGTH: 2,770 WORDS

I would like to thank Mr. James Fallows for comments on presidential speech writing and Professor Samuel P. Hays for reading a draft of this essay.

25   J. R. Pole
The Language of American Presidents

SCORING: Reading time: _____ Rate from chart: _____ W.P.M.

RETENTION	number right ____ × 2 equals ____ points	
MAIN POINT	number right ____ × 4 equals ____ points	
INFERENCES	number right ____ × 4 equals ____ points	
APPLICATION	number right ____ × 3 equals ____ points	
VOCABULARY	number right ____ × 2 equals ____ points	

(Total points: 100) **total** ____ points

RETENTION   Based on the selection, which of the following statements are True (T), False (F), or Not answerable (N)?

1. _____ Black response to Carter's addressing them as "brothers and sisters" was one of outrage.

2. _____ Half of the United States did not believe that Johnson was telling the truth in his speeches.

3. _____ Lincoln was our most eloquent president.

4. _____ Nixon's address to the American nation about the problem of the Vietnam War took place even before he took office.

5. _____ Kennedy deliberately used multisyllable words in order to confuse the people of the United States.

6. _____ The central issue facing the nation during Eisenhower's presidency was the failing economy.

7. _____ It is best for a president to maintain some distance between himself and the American voters.

8. _____ Since the inauguration of Wilson in 1913, Americans have fought in three wars.

9. _____ Surprisingly, Nixon is said not to have respected the intelligence of the American people.

10. _____ Nixon's style of speaking was influenced by television commercials.

11. _____ A person who is telling a lie will inevitably make errors in English.

12. _____ Eisenhower's style has been described as flabby.

13. _____ Orwell complained that the English language was losing abstractness and becoming too concrete.

14. _____ Stevenson's and Hofstadter's excellent styles maintained the intellectual vigor of readers during the Eisenhower years.

15. _____ Although he had been advised to go, Nixon refused to attend the AFL-CIO convention in November 1972.

MAIN POINT   Which of the following statements best represents the main point of the selection? _____

1. The speech of an American president reflects and is reflected by the times in which he lives.
2. American presidents should be extremely careful of the language that they use.
3. Since the time of Wilson, presidents have become increasingly sloppy in their speech.
4. People who choose to go into politics do so because they like to make speeches.
5. American presidents and British prime ministers have influenced each other in the way they write speeches.

INFERENCES   Which three of the following are the best inferences that can be drawn from this selection? _____, _____, and _____

1. Bureaucratic speech is undesirable.
2. Johnson was probably not very good at oratory and debate.
3. The United States is accustomed to having its economic horizons limited.
4. Rosa Parks was a timid individual who was afraid to stand up for her rights.
5. The author of this article does not like President Nixon.
6. Eisenhoverian language is desirable.
7. Emphatic repetition such as that used by Nixon in his acceptance speech bores and annoys the audience.
8. Churchill is an excellent model for presidential writers to follow.

APPLICATION   Choose the best answer for each question.

1. _____ The American people felt free of worry during Eisenhower's presidency because:
   a. there were no crises during this time.

b. Eisenhower was such a loose thinker.

c. he seemed at ease in his speeches and comfortable admitting that he didn't know things.

d. he delegated his authority to others.

2. _____ Carter's inaugural address was bad because he:

a. was not specific and down-to-earth enough.

b. spoke with a false humility.

c. said that he had unpleasant news for the nation.

d. spoke in defective English.

3. _____ An example of apposition such as that Kennedy used would be:

a. don't shoot until you see the whites of their eyes.

b. a nation that has too many poor is a poor excuse for a nation.

c. I am a Berliner.

d. naught that I have seen makes me fear for this nation.

4. _____ If all current usage is correct usage, then:

a. verb tenses will inevitably become mixed up.

b. precise meaning will be easier to grasp.

c. no one will be able to understand anyone else.

d. words in dictionaries will not have "correct" meanings.

5. _____ The greatest praise that the author has for Carter is probably for his:

a. facing the energy crisis.

b. analytically competent mind.

c. ability to get close to people.

d. respect for the American people.

6. _____ A sustained criticism of Nixon was that he:

a. used speech writers and seldom wrote speeches himself.

b. asked for too much pity and sympathy from his audience.

c. had little structure in his speeches.

d. did not support the civil rights movement.

7. _____ A lack of credibility and authority can come from:

a. seeming to be thinking of many things at the same time.

b. blunt language.

c. an attempt at moral persuasion.

d. a sense of immediacy.

8. _____ American political life is said to be unique in that:

a. events affect the way in which they are described.

b. America has a variety of cultures.

c. the president and the population engage in a dialogue.

d. America has a consumer economy.

VOCABULARY   Choose the best definition for each italic vocabulary entry.

1. _____ a vast and extraordinarily *heterogeneous* population
   a. wealthy
   b. mixed
   c. healthy
   d. competent

2. _____ which may have been *implicit* but was hardly anticipated
   a. promised
   b. an unspoken part of
   c. relied upon
   d. relatively unexpected

3. _____ an infiltration of *bureaucratic* speech
   a. having to do with furniture
   b. official
   c. coming from another language
   d. especially skillful

4. _____ superiority over the presidential *syntax*
   a. grammar
   b. morals
   c. vocabulary
   d. economy

5. _____ Utterances tended to be lacking in *cadence*.
   a. dignity
   b. meaning
   c. rhythm
   d. formality

6. _____ inelegant and unnecessary *neologisms*
   a. flaws
   b. word choices
   c. extra words
   d. new words

7. _____ sinking into a soapy *euphoria*
   a. joy
   b. water tub
   c. emotionalism
   d. foolishness

8. _____ an effect of monosyllabic *austerity*
   a. beauty
   b. frustration

    c. warmth
    d. plainness

9. _____ the extraordinary *bathos* of his appeals
    a. skillful emotionalism
    b. clean language
    c. insincere sentimentality
    d. powerful effect

10. _____ plainly revealed, although *furtive*, consciousness
    a. useless
    b. sneaky
    c. runaway
    d. clear

11. _____ It formed a very large and *indispensable* part.
    a. influential
    b. flavorful
    c. essential
    d. noisy

12. _____ He seems to *eschew* deliberated eloquence.
    a. avoid
    b. fear
    c. choose
    d. arouse

13. _____ a problem *unprecedented* in our history
    a. unauthorized
    b. new
    c. unrecognized
    d. revealed

14. _____ *precipitated* the great bus boycott
    a. rained on
    b. participated in
    c. denied
    d. hastened

15. _____ was able to *transcend* the distance
    a. change
    b. respect
    c. shorten
    d. overcome

Readings from Popular Freshman Textbooks

26

FRED R. HARRIS

A Senator's Life

Most of us are familiar with the glamour
of a senator's life. In the newspapers, we read
that it is filled with important moments and
encounters with famous people. Fred R.
Harris shows us another side of the picture
as he takes us through a day in the life of
a senator.

The senator awakes before it is light outside, dresses quickly, slips out of the house while others are still sleeping, and is soon driving in heavy traffic toward the Capitol Building. On the days when he does not have to attend a breakfast meeting with some group from his home state, as he does today, he can leave home at 8:30 A.M. and get to his office in twenty-five minutes. But at 6:45 A.M. there is heavy traffic into Washington from the suburbs. This morning he will be lucky if he arrives on time for the 7:30 breakfast.

At the Capitol, the senator parks his car in the courtyard of the Russell Building (formerly called the Old Senate Office Building) and walks briskly to a bank of elevators just inside the building's entrance. He pushes the "senators only" button, and the elevator comes at once. "Good morning, senator," a deferential young elevator operator greets him. "What floor, please?" He asks to be taken to the basement. Other people in the elevator were obviously in mid-course toward their destinations on upper floors, but the elevator goes at once to the basement. On the way, the young attendant asks the senator if he wants a trolley. He nods, and the attendant pushes a button on the elevator console, signaling the underground trolley operator that a senator is on the way.

At the basement floor, the senator exits and walks rapidly down the hall toward the subway. Senate employees and others who are arriving for work greet him cordially. "Good morning, senator." "How are you this morning, senator?"

The trolley operator is out of his seat, blocking tourists and others from sitting in the very front trolley bench, which is reserved for senators. "Good morning, senator," he says, holding back the small crowd. As soon as the senator is seated, the trolley operator bounces back into his seat and calls out, "Watch the doors, please." The trolley whirs away, perhaps leaving a number of tourists and others still waiting to get on.

Making the transit from the basement of the office building to the basement of the Capitol Building in four or five minutes, the trolley comes to rest, and the doors are opened. "Have a good day, senator," the operator says. Another attendant sees him. "Good morning, senator," he says, hurriedly pushing a button, which causes an audible ringing of bells. The senator takes an escalator up to a bank of elevators, all of which are waiting with their doors open, attendants outside. "Good morning, senator," they chorus. Tourists nudge each other, "It's a senator," they say to each other. He gets on an elevator by himself. The other people are left standing outside (unless he decides to hold the door and invite them to ride with him).

As he leaves the elevator, the senator is greeted by one of his own staff members. "They have already sat down and started breakfast. Bob is not here yet," the staff member says, referring to the other senator from the state. "You remember that this is the Farmers Union. They are really anxious for the President to lift restrictions on wheat sales to the Soviet Union. So, you will want to mention that you have cosponsored the resolution against restrictions. They will call on you first, because I've told them that you have a committee meeting you've got to get to as soon as you can."

The senator and his staff member enter the breakfast meeting, which is being held in a dining room near the Senate floor. As the senator enters, the group of about twenty farmers from his home state stands immediately and applauds him vigorously. He walks down through the aisles between each of the tables, shaking hands with everyone and speaking to them individually as the applause ends and the visitors begin to seat themselves again. At the head table, he is welcomed by the group president. The senator ignores the cold scrambled eggs and bacon. He talks with the people at the head table and with the people who come up to bring special greetings from his home state or to discuss special, individual problems. Twice he calls over his legislative aide, who is sitting in the back of the room. "Jim," he says, "you remember George, here? He's got a problem with the Soil Conservation Service. I want you to take him back over to our office after breakfast and call over there and make him an appointment to get this thing straightened out."

The president calls the meeting to order. He explains why they have come to Washington about Russian wheat sales and then asks each person present to introduce himself or herself. House members from the state then introduce themselves. The administrative assistant of the other senator rises and explains that the senator is "deeply sorry" that other business prevents him from being present. But he assures the group that the senator strongly sympathizes with the Farmers Union position. "I hope each one of you will come by the office, because I want to visit with you and see how we can be helpful," the administrative assistant concludes. The senator who is present is then introduced. He calls many of the members of the group by their first names and pledges support for their Russian wheat sales position. Then, after apologizing for having to leave, he concludes his remarks. His exit draws another standing ovation.

The senator's staff member leaves with him. Two other staff members are waiting outside. Each has a question that must be settled at once. One involves the senator's press release, which will be issued today. It opposes a proposal to add funds to the President's budget for another nuclear carrier. The other question is what to do with a group of mayors who are waiting to see the senator in his office. "Tell them to wait, and after our staff meeting, they can walk with us over to the hearings of the Governmental Affairs Committee," the senator says.

With his aides trailing behind him, the senator now retraces his earlier path. Down the elevator with the deferential attendants. Down the escalator to the waiting trolley and the deferential trolley operator. The ride back to the Russell Building. Then up the elevator with the deferential attendant to the senator's floor.

The senator walks down the hall and into the back door to his office, where his senior staff members are gathering. Some have brief questions or comments. The senator's executive secretary hands him some letters that require his attention. The senator looks at his agenda for the day. As usual, there are conflicting committee meetings. He serves on the Governmental Affairs Committee and the Finance Committee, and both are meeting simultaneously today, as usual, at ten o'clock, ten minutes from now.

As the senator steps into the reception room, the four mayors from his home state rise to greet him. "You remember Mayor Phelps, senator," a staff member prompts him, gesturing toward the nearest visitor. "Sure, how are you, Christine?" the senator says and gives her a hug. After shaking hands with the others, he leads them all down a hall, outside the building, and across the street to the Dirksen Building (formerly called the New Senate Office Building). He pushes a "senators only" button at a bank of elevators, motions his guests in with him, is whisked up to the committee room floor, and then walks down the hall to the hearing room. All along the way, the mayors have been explaining their complaints about the appropriations for revenue sharing, a program that allocates a portion of the taxes collected by the federal government to state and local governments. "Lois," the senator says to one of his staff members who has been striding along with him, "I want you to take them back to the office and go over this in detail. Find out if there isn't some way we can help."

The senator then excuses himself, goes inside the committee room, and walks up to the horseshoe-shaped table, taking a seat at the place with his nameplate in front of it. A committee staff member lays a number of papers in front of him. The committee hearing is already under way, and the director of the General Services Administration is testifying. Several senators who are present outrank the senator in seniority—they have served on the committee longer than he has— and, therefore, they would normally have the first chance to ask the witness questions or make comments. But today the senator speaks up as soon as the witness has completed the written statement. "Mr. Chairman, I apologize for interrupting at this time, out of turn, but we are having mark-up sessions in the Finance Committee on the tax bill. With the chairman's indulgence and the indulgence of the other members of the committee, I wonder if I might be permitted to ask a couple of questions of the witness out of turn, and then be excused?" The committee chairman consults briefly with the ranking minority member of the committee, the most senior member of the minority party, and then gives his consent. It is a common practice. Indeed, both the chairman and the ranking minority member of the Governmental Affairs Committee regularly engage in it themselves when they are attending other committee meetings or hearings. The senator asks the witness two questions, one of which had been written in advance for him by one of his staff members. When the questions have been answered, the senator thanks the witness, thanks the committee chairman, and excuses himself.

Outside the committee room, a staff member is waiting with a lobbyist for the Machinists Union, who wants to talk to the senator about the minimum wage bill scheduled to be voted on in the full Senate this afternoon. "Can you help us on the amendment to raise the level which the President has recommended?" the lobbyist asks. They walk together toward the elevator and then ride down to the floor where the Finance Committee is meeting. The senator is on the spot on this issue. Some personal friends and his state Chamber of Commerce office have written and called him from home. They complain that the bill would be very harmful to them because it would raise their costs of doing business. The senator is noncommittal, but he feels the pressure. "This is a really big one with our members," the lobbyist says. "I haven't wanted to cause you a lot of trouble or put a lot of pressure on you, but you know how much this means to our members in the aircraft plant in your home state," he continues, subtly applying pressure while denying the desire to do so.

The senator enters the Finance Committee meeting and quickly receives a written agenda from a committee staff member. The meeting is already in progress. One of the senator's own staff members, who has been following the meeting for him, hands him a couple of scribbled notes about the next amendments coming up for committee votes. As the senator takes his seat at the committee table, the staff member whispers an additional report in his ear.

At the head of the table is the committee chairman. To the senator's left are members of the senator's own party who are senior to him. To his right are members of the senator's party who are junior to him. Across the table, also arranged by seniority, are members of the opposing party. Committee staff members and Treasury Department and Internal Revenue Service representatives sit close to the committee members. The large audience in the front of the room is composed primarily of lobbyists for groups that would be affected by the tax bill. Discussions and voting proceed in the committee until a recess is called at noon.

The senator is scheduled to meet for lunch in the Senators Dining Room with some close friends from his home state who were very active in his last campaign. But as he leaves the Finance Committee room, his executive secretary meets him. She tells him that his wife has called to remind him that today is his daughter's birthday and that he had earlier agreed to take her to lunch at Duke Zeibert's Restaurant. "Get Jim (the senator's administrative assistant) to meet me over at the dining room," the senator says. "Tell him that I'll just barely get to sit down and visit before I'll have to leave, and he can stay on and then give them a tour of the Capitol Building. Maybe Jim can put them up in the Family Gallery in the Senate Chamber this afternoon, so they can watch the vote on the minimum wage bill."

As she walks to the trolley with him, the executive secretary shows the senator a stack of twenty-five telephone calls that must be answered. He assigns all but seven of them to be answered by various staff members and takes the rest for himself. At the Senators Dining Room, he is greeted cordially by the maitre d'. After seating his own guests, the senator is asked by other senators to come to their tables and meet their guests from home. The senator has been in the news lately and on *Meet the Press*, and it is a matter of courtesy to allow other senators to introduce him to their constituents, who are obviously impressed that their own senators know such a well-known national figure. After a brief conversation at his own table, he excuses himself and hustles out to the car that a staff member has waiting.

Duke Zeibert, the owner, greets the senator at the entrance to the popular restaurant. Famed lawyer Edward Bennett Williams, who has also just arrived, is glad to see the senator, as are a number of other people at various tables. Twice during lunch, out-of-town visitors ask the senator for his autograph. Duke takes a Polaroid picture of him with his daughter and gives it to her as a memento. After lunch, his daughter goes home in a cab, and the senator and his staff member go back to the Hill.

During the few minutes before the Finance Committee reconvenes, the senator returns some of his telephone calls. One of the calls is from the White House; a presidential aide wants to discuss the ratification of a treaty that will soon be debated and voted on in the Senate. "I haven't had too much pressure on this from home, and I believe the treaty ought to be ratified," the senator tells the aide. "You can count on me on this one."

In the Finance Committee, discussions and votes on the tax bill continue, but they are interrupted all afternoon by votes on amendments to the minimum wage bill. When the Senate is about to vote, a buzzer sounds in the committee room and a particular light flashes. The committee then takes a recess to allow senators to go over to the Senate floor.

As the senator enters the Senate chamber from the back door, a Senate staff member who works for the Senate majority party explains to him what the vote is. Not completely sure about the bill or about how he should vote, the senator talks with the manager of the bill, the senator who is handling the bill on the floor. He also discusses it with one of his seatmates, a trusted friend with similar views and outlook. By the time the senator arrives on the floor, the clerk has already called his name; so the senator rises and is recognized at the end of the roll call. He then votes in favor of this amendment. "The Chamber of Commerce is going to be on my neck," he says to his seatmate.

Before the senator can reach the Finance Committee session, a lobbyist for the Interior Department catches him in the reception room and walks with him to the elevator. "The confirmation of the new assistant secretary is coming up next Wednesday," the lobbyist tells the senator. "I will send the nominee around to see you, and, while I don't think he'll have any trouble, we would really like to have you on our side."

Discussions and debates in the committee alternate with roll calls in the Senate throughout the afternoon. When the senator leaves the committee for the Senate floor, he is usually met by staff members who have particular matters to discuss. When he can break away from committee deliberations, he gets to a telephone to try to return calls, the number of which is growing as the day wears on.

At 3:00 P.M., the senator excuses himself from the Finance Committee session to go to a press conference. He announces that he is introducing a new bill, which would establish wage-and-price controls to hold down inflation. Many reporters from the "writing press" are present, but only one network television camera is there. The senator reads a prepared statement and then answers questions. He tries not to act offended when one of the reporters asks, "Is this the kick-off for your presidential campaign?"

Toward the end of the day, during a lull in Senate voting, the senator goes to the Senate gymnasium for a sauna, a brief swim, and a massage. But the massage is cut short by a roll-call vote, and the senator, still feeling a little sweaty, has to dress quickly and rush over to the Senate floor.

The Senate session runs late. No one knows in advance exactly when it will end for the day, although the majority leader indicates that it will probably go as late as 8:30 P.M. That is a problem for the senator, because he and his wife have agreed to go to a dinner party at the home of Georgetown friends important to him especially because a couple of other senators will be there, and he will have a too-rare chance to socialize informally with them. By 8:00 P.M., the senator is already late for the dinner party. His wife has called the hosts, who are accustomed to such situations. The senator's wife brings his tuxedo to the office, where he changes. On the last several roll calls in the Senate, several senators, each with similar dinner engagements, come to the chamber in formal dress. The senator's wife and his executive secretary await him outside the Senate Chamber following the final vote for the evening. The executive secretary has brought the senator's airline ticket and itinerary for his trip to his home state tomorrow morning—a trip he makes at least two weekends a month. "Have a good evening, senator," she says as the senator and his wife rush toward their car.

That is what a senator's life is like. Although House members have similar pressures and experiences, they do not serve on as many committees and subcommittees as senators do. They do not have as many staff members, do not receive as much deferential treatment, and rarely run for President of the United States. In addition, the average House member is not as sought after by the national press and does not make as much "news" or appear as much on national television. On the other hand, House members are usually worried most of the time about whether they will have a serious opponent in the next election, which is never more than two years away.

LENGTH: 3,261 WORDS

26 Fred R. Harris
A Senator's Life

SCORING: Reading time: _____ Rate from chart: _____ W.P.M.

RETENTION	number right _____ × 2 equals _____ points	
MAIN IDEA	number right _____ × 4 equals _____ points	
INTERPRETATION	number right _____ × 3 equals _____ points	
CONCLUSION	number right _____ × 3 equals _____ points	
APPLICATION	number right _____ × 3 equals _____ points	
VOCABULARY	number right _____ × 2 equals _____ points	

(Total points: 100) **total** _____ points

RETENTION   Based on the selection, which of the following statements are True (T), False (F), or Not answerable (N)?

1. _____ The family gallery of the Senate is reserved for members of the senators' families.

2. _____ When he is not attending a breakfast meeting, the senator is due at the office at about 9:00.

3. _____ Members of the House run for office every four years.

4. _____ The senator sometimes returns phone calls personally.

5. _____ Senators are seated at committee meetings by seniority.

6. _____ The front seat of the underground trolley is reserved for senators.

7. _____ Committee meetings are delayed until all senators can attend.

8. _____ An administrative assistant cannot speak for a senator.

9. _____ Senate sessions are scheduled to end at 5:00.

10. _____ Senators customarily take strict turns in asking questions at committee meetings.

11. _____ No member of the House of Representatives has ever run for president.

12. _____ Committee meetings may be held at the same time as the Senate is in session.

13. _____ Committee meetings are carefully scheduled so that they do not conflict with one another.

14. _____ The president does not have the power to restrict wheat sales to foreign countries.

15. _____ A senator may try to work personally on behalf of an individual constituent.

MAIN IDEA   Which of the following statements best represents the main point of the selection? _____

1. A senator's work is never done.
2. Running for senator takes confidence and perseverance.
3. A senator has different responsibilities from those of a member of the House of Representatives.
4. A senator's life, while full of prestige, is also hectic and full of pressure.
5. A senator may be at the office for more than twelve hours a day.

INTERPRETATION   Which of the following is the best interpretation of a key point in this selection? _____

1. A senator may eat two breakfasts on breakfast meeting days.
2. A senator is more concerned with lobbyists than she is with mayors.
3. A senator may place family ahead of politics at times.
4. A senator places the good of the nation over that of his home state.
5. A senator sometimes has to place social dinner obligations over attendance at roll call in the Senate.

CONCLUSION   Which of the following statements is the best conclusion that can be drawn from the selection? _____

1. A person who runs for senator has to be unusually wealthy.
2. A candidate would see little difference between running for the House of Representatives and running for the Senate.
3. A person who runs for Senate should have an excellent memory for names and faces.
4. The person who applies for a job as an aide to a senator must be careful not to take any independent action.
5. Committee meetings are even more important than Senate sessions.

Choose the best answer for each question.

1. _____ The reason that trolley drivers are allowed to take off as soon as a senator is seated, leaving tourists behind, is that:
   a. they owe the senator their job.
   b. the senator would throw a fit if they didn't.
   c. the senator's time is valuable, since he is so busy.
   d. the tourists are noisy, bothersome, and ignorant.

2. _____ Aides seem to accompany the senator most of the time because:
   a. the senator needs a bodyguard against assassination attempts.
   b. they keep the senator abreast of what questions he will need to respond to.
   c. the senator needs them to send out for coffee and to perform other errands.
   d. more aides around a senator make him seem more important.

3. _____ The other senator from the state probably did not attend the breakfast meeting about Russian wheat sales because:
   a. he did not agree with the group's position on the issue.
   b. his aides were more eloquent than he was about these matters.
   c. he had another important conflicting meeting of some kind.
   d. the group had failed to invite him through an oversight.

4. _____ The senator is probably allowed to speak out of turn at the Governmental Affairs Committee meeting because:
   a. he outranks the other senators in attendance.
   b. the other senators present often have to speak out of order due to a conflict of committee meetings too.
   c. the sympathetic members of the committee understand that he is not fully prepared and want to save him embarrassment.
   d. the committee members know that the questions the senator will ask are important to the remainder of the meeting.

5. _____ The conflict that brings pressure on the senator in the Senate wage bill debate is between:
   a. the senator and his family.
   b. two opposing groups in his home state.
   c. the senator and his opponent in the other party.
   d. the senator and a lobbyist.

6. _____ The senator voted in favor of the wage bill amendment on the basis of:
   a. the pressure brought to bear on him.
   b. his conversation with the president's aide.
   c. discussions with the bill's manager and a colleague.
   d. his own experiences in earning a living.

7. ____ The senator described in this essay is probably:
   a. a potential presidential candidate.
   b. a first-term senator.
   c. at the top of the seniority list in the Senate.
   d. from a state that has little industry.

8. ____ A member of the Senate would have an easier time than a member of the House of Representatives because he:
   a. is treated with less respect.
   b. is on more committees.
   c. is more sought after by the national press.
   d. does not have to run for office as often.

9. ____ In keeping the voters of her state happy, a senator does not want to:
   a. take action on an appropriations bill.
   b. be interrupted by autograph requests.
   c. pay too much attention to the news media.
   d. neglect an opportunity to seem to be working personally on their concerns.

10. ____ The hosts at a Washington dinner party:
    a. should be careful not to invite more than one senator at a time.
    b. are concerned to create an atmosphere of formality.
    c. should expect that some of the guests will turn up late.
    d. have to be careful to include many ethnic cuisines on the menu.

VOCABULARY   Choose the best definition for each italic vocabulary entry.

1. ____ greet him *cordially*
   a. anxiously
   b. rapidly
   c. with respect
   d. warmly

2. ____ an *audible* ringing of bells
   a. able to be rung
   b. able to be heard
   c. surprising
   d. hurried

3. ____ the *deferential* attendants
   a. hard of hearing
   b. well paid
   c. respectful
   d. annoying

4. _____ Both are meeting *simultaneously*.
   a. at the same time
   b. immediately
   c. in a practice session
   d. quickly

5. _____ complaints about the *appropriations*
   a. money authorized to be spent
   b. tax bills
   c. seating allowances
   d. committee memberships

6. _____ with the chairman's *indulgence*
   a. obedience
   b. permission
   c. authority
   d. payment

7. _____ Can you help us on the *amendment*?
   a. protection
   b. refusal
   c. change
   d. authorization

8. _____ The senator is *noncommittal*.
   a. uncommunicative
   b. uncomplaining
   c. friendly
   d. neutral

9. _____ the *lobbyist* says
   a. representative of a special interest group
   b. labor organizer
   c. senior officer on the janitorial staff
   d. influence peddler

10. _____ *subtly* applying pressure
    a. unobviously
    b. angrily
    c. strongly
    d. respectfully

11. _____ before the Finance Committee *reconvenes*
    a. dismisses
    b. takes a vote
    c. holds a final discussion
    d. calls the meeting to order again

12. _____ the *ratification* of a treaty
    a. signing
    b. formal consent
    c. reading of
    d. rejection of

13. _____ the *confirmation* of the new assistant secretary
    a. religious ceremony
    b. approval
    c. vote
    d. interview

14. _____ goes to the gymnasium for a *sauna*
    a. slow walk
    b. run
    c. steam bath
    d. massage

15. _____ *itinerary* for his trip
    a. ticket
    b. money
    c. schedule
    d. destination

27

ROBERT F. MURPHY

Culture

To most of us, culture means an interest in
the arts or forms of civilization, examples of
which include oddities about such matters
as eating habits and mating rituals. Robert
F. Murphy takes us more deeply into this
subject, showing how a study of culture can
be of help in defining the very nature of what
it is to be human.

The most important single attribute of humankind is intelligence.
Other animals are capable of some learning, but we are unique in that the
overwhelming bulk of our behavior is learned. Moreover, it is through the
socialization process that this acquired behavior becomes organized into a
coherent, consistent personality. Humans are also distinctive in the possession of
language, a statement that will be roundly disputed by everybody who has seen a
television special on talking chimpanzees. It would not slight the intelligence of
the chimps, or the patience of their trainers, to say that what often passes for
language in these cases are rather elaborate sign systems. The Russian psychologist Pavlov conditioned a dog to salivate at the ringing of a bell, but he never
claimed that "ding" was the dog's word for "food." The animal experiments are,
however, too intriguing to be dismissed out of hand, though I will only become
convinced of their linguistic abilities when one chimp teaches another how
to speak.

The signal outcome of human intelligence is culture. Human cultures are
defined as distinctive life-styles characteristic of different societies. Culture
includes designs or models for behavior—norms for what is considered proper,
or moral, or even sane. These are modes for acting that are learned, rather than
biological, in origin and that are shared to at least some extent by other members
of the society. Culture is a body of knowledge and tools by which we adapt to the
physical environment; it is a set of rules by which we relate to each other; it is a

Robert F. Murphy, CULTURAL & SOCIAL ANTHROPOLOGY: *An Overture,* 2nd ed., © 1986, pp. 24–32.
Reprinted by permission of Prentice-Hall, Englewood Cliffs, New Jersey.

storehouse of knowledge, beliefs, and formulae through which we try to understand the universe and our place in it. Culture is preeminently a means of communicating with others, a tautology in the linguistic aspect of culture but equally true of manners and etiquette and the language of gesture and expression. It is culture that stabilizes the social environment and makes it possible for people to associate with each other. The sociologist Georg Simmel once said that every social encounter is an immanent disaster. Cues get mixed, signals scrambled, and people become angry, embarrassed, or reduced to inaction by the failure of scenarios to come off as planned. Interaction is not always a smooth process. Culture minimizes this uncertainty by setting the rules on how one should behave in a given situation. It is in this sense that the sociologist Talcott Parsons's definition of culture as a "set of expectations" is most instructive. Culture not only tells us how we should act, but it also tells us what we can expect of the other person. Sounds and movements become transformed into language and social conduct by making them orderly and assigning meaning to them. In a world with no natural or absolute meanings, culture makes the universe and our position within it intelligible and social interaction possible.

Culture, as the anthropologist Leslie White wrote some decades ago, consists of a system of symbols or signs endowed with general and abstract meanings. A simple sign is some visual or auditory stimulus that has a single and narrowly defined connotation. The red-and-green traffic signals designate only stop and go and nothing more. Similarly, Pavlov's dog had learned to make a simple bell-food identification and was thus responding to a sign. Symbols, on the other hand, are signs to which more general meaning has been attributed. They refer less to single objects or phenomena than to classes of objects and phenomena. Your dog Fido may come when he is called by that name or sign, but the word "dog" is a true symbol, for it generalizes a whole category of life forms under one rubric. . . .

The capacity for culture, for the coining and use of symbols, is simultaneously the capacity for abstract thought, and this is a peculiarly human attribute. One answer, then, to the question of what kind of animal human beings are would be that they are sapient and cultural, the gifts of a large brain and a highly complex central nervous system. One of the byproducts of the large brain—besides abstract thinking processes and the use of language—is self-awareness. We are not, of course, sure of whether other animals may or may not have a notion of themselves as independent entities, for they cannot tell us; but humans do indeed universally conceptualize the self and distinguish this ego from all others. This introduces a primary dichotomy between the "I" and the "Thou" that serves as a template and model for other forms of classification. The ego-other separation is important for social interaction in that we all operate with some kind of idea of what we as individuals are like, a self-image, as it is popularly called. We also have broad, generalized notions of what other people are like. The two preconceptions are conditioning factors for almost all social behavior. The contents of the images of self and other are, however, neither God-given nor idiosyncratic, for ample models are presented to us within our cultural traditions. The sociologist George Herbert Mead wrote that everybody's idea of the self is ultimately a product of how he was treated by others. Similarly, there are cultural norms and standards in every society that tell us what all humans are like and what certain classes of humans are like. Even our most closely guarded, private mental domains are invaded by society, which from the time we are at mother's breast extends threads of culture into our every sense of being.

Another product of intelligent self-awareness is that we have the knowledge of life and death. Other animals struggle just as we do to defend their bodies and prolong their lives, but it is doubtful whether any animals know that they, too, must inevitably die. This we do know from childhood and it poses a paradox. People have a sense of "life" and "being" that is directly related to a keen apprehension of death. Death is the counterpoint of life, and the zest and joy of living are accented by human transiency. Life and death create each other as categories of experience, but each one negates the other in the passage of time. Knowledge of the certainty of death and the uncertainty of its time of arrival introduces a deep note of anxiety in all human existence. Most people do not sit around in fearful brooding over their mortality, but for all it is a background motif in their thoughts and actions and a precondition of how they approach themselves and the world. It is an existential fear, one that is too pervasive to be isolated and too interwoven with other assumptions about life to reach awareness. It is infrequent in our conscious thoughts, but never absent in the underground realms of the unconscious mind, whence so much of our consciousness wells. . . .

Homo sapiens is by birth and nature an intelligent animal, but is it also a rational one? Is the organization of the mind, the means by which one thinks consecutively and analytically, inherent and uniform for all humanity, or is logic something we absorb with the rest of our culture? Until the last twenty years or so, most anthropologists would have chosen the latter proposition and taken the view propounded by the psychologist B. F. Skinner that logic is the outcome of conditioning and the adjustment of learned reflexes to each other. Recently, however, there has been reintroduced into social thought the idea that certain structures, or modes of organization, of the mind are hereditary and common to all humankind. These structures do not by any means account for all of human rationality, but rather are the basic armature upon which this rationality is built. It is an idea very reminiscent of Immanuel Kant's "categories" of the mind, and it shares the same intellectual ancestry. . . .

In structural theory, human rationality is universally the same, and the working of the mind involves a continual process of sorting perceptions into paired opposites, which are then reconciled. In short, the mind works in a dialectical fashion. In the first place, the stream of consciousness becomes broken up into discrete events and things, which are usually reducible to words. We chop up and distort the flow of reality in this process, but words and language are the only ways in which we can think of our world and by which we can communicate these thoughts to others. We fracture and break up our perceptions, but we have no choice. How we do this is where the dualism of thought comes in. Fundamentally, we arrive at our delineation and definition of objects, which we express in words and symbols, by defining what an object is not, as well as what it is. The category of "night" is defined by darkness, but this only implies the absence of sunlight. Night, then, is the absence of day. It is nonday or antiday. In much the same way, a man is a human creature that is not a woman; and if the Democrats did not have the Republicans, they would have to invent them. Words and symbols, the very substance of our thought, are given definition by their otherness. This allows us to break up reality and reduce it to the hard, objective status of the word. At the same time, it does a certain violence to the human grasp on reality.

[Claude] Lévi-Strauss [defends] his theme of dualism by asserting that the same human mind that sets up these oppositions is also continually trying to mend them, to reconcile them. The antithesis between life and death is healed by belief in the immortality of the soul, and the opposition of the sexes is sealed by marriage. Lévi-Strauss feels that one of the great dualities, one from which others are spawned, is that between nature and culture, between the nonhuman part of the environment and the artificial and human-created order of culture. *Homo sapiens* has the peculiarity of being both an animal, and therefore part of nature, and the creator of culture, an ambiguity that makes us both ape and angel. Humans reconcile this duality and set themselves off from the animal world by many ways, including dress and adornment. The South American Indian practices of body painting are not, he tells us, an attempt to imitate the plumage and colors of the animal world, but rather to set humans apart from it through arbitrary and artificial decorations—through culture. Similarly, marriage bridges nature and culture, for it involves the natural functions of sex and procreation but is carried out through culturally imposed law.

Dualism finds expression in culture, for the same basic logic is found in all humankind and must, therefore, be accommodated by all cultures. In his monumental work *The Elementary Structures of Kinship*, Lévi-Strauss attempts to show how the dualism of opposition, and the triadic relations created when a mediating factor is introduced, are expressed in the institutions of marriage and kinship. In a four-volume analysis of the mythology of South and North American Indians, he finds these structures of the mind to be faithfully reproduced by the structure of myth. He has also suggested that these elemental and underlying structures are inherent within music, art, and literature.

Structuralism is a controversial theory, but its extreme complexity does not permit further discussion at this early phase of my narrative. I believe, however, that Lévi-Strauss has correctly identified a panhuman logic. In doing so, he has told us not only that all the varieties of humanity are rational, but that they are rational in the same way. The universality of human binary, dialectical reasoning has led Lévi-Strauss to speculate that the structure is rooted in the neurophysiology of the brain. This is entirely a guess on his part, but it is a hypothesis that may be totally superfluous. The very fact that we speak in words and that these words are not only inclusive of certain meanings but exclusive of others, as previously discussed, would predispose us to binary expression and thought. Moreover, there is much that is dual in our experience. The body is fundamentally symmetrical—we have two eyes, two ears, two arms, and so forth—and there are two types of body, male and female. Binary structures may exist in the brain, but human speech and human experience are sufficient in themselves to account for this characteristic.

Just as there is a basic human rationality, there is also a set of emotional predispositions that is common to all our species. In addition to being naturally endowed with superior intelligence, humans also have a long period of infantile and childhood dependency relative to their total life spans. The average life expectancy in the United States today is about seventy-four years, of which at least the first seventeen or eighteen are spent in learning and play, dependent for sustenance on the older generation. The dependency period for those entering certain professions may extend to the age of twenty-five or more, or over one-third of a lifetime. In simpler societies than our own, the lack of a formal schooling period may allow a boy to assume adult functions by fifteen or sixteen and a girl at thirteen or fourteen, but the life span is also much shorter. Primitives, too, must support their young for more than 25 percent of their lives.

Prolonged dependency is related to a number of important learning factors. We are born with a group of drives and physical requirements, such as hunger, thirst, sex, rest and sleep, play, elimination, and bodily warmth, but these are very limited in number and are felt as diffuse, broad, and nonspecific urges. They are not "instincts" in the sense we use the term for animal behavior; in the latter context the urge is seen as specific, and a part of the instinct is a set of innate behaviors for gratifying the urge. Except for the smiling and sucking reflexes in infants, this is not true of human behavior. We have to learn a good deal of our drive-satisfying activity.

Nature provides us with certain needs, but culture tells us how to fulfill them. Reminiscent of Lévi-Strauss's words on the separation of nature from culture, almost all of our natural functions are heavily governed by culture, including some highly formal rules of etiquette and a frequent sense of shame. Among most peoples defecation is done in private, and among Arabs and other Moslem groups, one uses only the left hand to clean oneself after elimination; the right is considered sacred, the left profane. This is reminiscent of our own custom of washing the hands after urination, a practice that many men follow only in public restrooms and neglect at home. Similarly, sex is natural enough, but its satisfaction is surrounded by taboos, sanctions, secrecy, and that most reliable of indicators of a sensitive area, false information. Similarly, everybody needs food, but we follow cultural dictates on what to eat, when and how much to eat, and whom to eat with. The act of eating, too, is heavily colored by manners and rules of propriety. We do not talk with our mouths full, and we have to learn how to use our cutlery. A Yurok Indian of California learns to eat with serious countenance while thinking of wealth, and a Brazilian Mundurucú does not engage in boisterous behavior while eating game meat lest he offend the spirit mothers of the animals. We engage in the same life-sustaining activities as lower animals do, but it is exactly while doing these things that we are enjoined not to "act like animals." If somebody wolfs his food in our society, we say that "he eats like an animal" (and note the use of the metaphor wolf). And when asked whether incest occurred among them, a Mundurucú Indian told me "only animals do that."

The period of prolonged dependency is a time in which we learn to satisfy our needs in socially approved ways and, since we are not equipped by nature to survive on our own, it is a period in which we learn to cope with the environment and gain subsistence from it. We mature slowly, but it is time well spent. The dependency of the young on their parents is also an important source of our social nature. We cannot survive as adults without the cooperation of others in gaining self-defense and livelihood, and we certainly require the nurturance of our elders when children. It is during this time that we establish close ties, which become the models of other relationships we acquire in life, and it is during this time that we learn to love.

LENGTH: 3,280 WORDS

27   Robert F. Murphy
Culture

SCORING: Reading time: _____ Rate from chart: _____ W.P.M.

RETENTION	number right _____ × 2 equals _____ points	
MAIN IDEA	number right _____ × 4 equals _____ points	
INTERPRETATION	number right _____ × 3 equals _____ points	
CONCLUSION	number right _____ × 3 equals _____ points	
APPLICATION	number right _____ × 3 equals _____ points	
VOCABULARY	number right _____ × 2 equals _____ points	

(Total points: 100) **total** _____ points

RETENTION   Based on the selection, which of the following statements are True (T), False (F), or Not answerable (N)?

1. _____ Our self-image is a product of how others treat us.

2. _____ The sucking reflex in an infant is an example of instinctive behavior.

3. _____ A dualistic logical structure has been found to be universal in all cultures.

4. _____ An object must be defined by what it is, not by what it is not.

5. _____ Murphy is convinced that chimpanzees can use language.

6. _____ All animals are born with the knowledge that they will someday die.

7. _____ A capacity for abstract thought is limited to man and the other higher primates such as chimpanzees.

8. _____ Man is an intelligent animal.

9. _____ The Russian scientist Pavlov conditioned a dog to use language.

10. _____ The development of culture has been studied by the Swiss psychologist Piaget.

11. _____ Words help us to keep our perception of reality an integrated whole.

12. _____ Not all varieties of humanity are rational.

13. _____ Culture makes social interaction possible.

14. _____ Human beings have a relatively short period of dependency on the older generation.

15. _____ It is during our period of dependency that we learn to love.

MAIN IDEA   Which of the following statements best represents the main point of the selection? _____

1. Culture is manifested in symbols and signs.
2. Culture is a result of a rational and emotional component in man that is universally the same in structure.
3. It is culture that sets man apart from the other lower-order animals.
4. Cultural anthropology studies the distinctive life-styles characteristic of different societies.
5. Unless he is a student of the culture in which he lives, man is prey to his baser instincts.

INTERPRETATION   Which of the following is the best interpretation of a key point in this selection? _____

1. Human beings begin to acquire the characteristics of the culture when they move outside the family into the larger world.
2. Dualism involves the ability to think of two things at the same time.
3. A dualistic, symmetrical body structure is universal throughout the animal kingdom.
4. Sharing a culture allows the members of a given society to live together more easily.
5. We are born with the ability to satisfy our drives and physical requirements.

CONCLUSION   Which of the following statements is the best conclusion that can be drawn from the selection? _____

1. The question of man's rational nature has been answered for all time by the theory of structuralism.
2. If man did not have the ego-other separation that characterizes him, he would probably not have a self-image.
3. The cultural life of animals has yet to be studied.
4. The lack of an awareness of death would probably not change man's cultural behavior.
5. The author is more interested in animal behavior than he is in human behavior.

APPLICATION Choose the best answer for each question.

1. _____ The most useful definition of culture for the purpose of this essay is:
   a. excellence in the arts.
   b. cultivation of the soil.
   c. the habits and routine behaviors of a given group.
   d. a set of symbols or signs that helps individuals communicate.

2. _____ Man's self-awareness is a product of his:
   a. abstract thinking process.
   b. use of language.
   c. large brain and complex central nervous system.
   d. self-consciousness.

3. _____ The first step in the process of human reason is:
   a. reducing things to words.
   b. breaking consciousness up into separate events.
   c. reconciling opposites.
   d. communicating to others.

4. _____ For Lévi-Strauss, which of the following would not be an example of the reconciliation of opposites?
   a. the definition of objects.
   b. marriage.
   c. body painting.
   d. a belief in the immortality of the soul.

5. _____ The idea of man's dualism is supported by:
   a. human speech and human experience.
   b. the binary structure of the brain.
   c. the universality of human experience.
   d. the psychologist Skinner.

6. _____ When advanced cultures are compared with primitive cultures, the former's period of childhood dependency is found to be:
   a. longer.
   b. nonexistent.
   c. the same.
   d. more brief.

7. _____ The taboo against talking with our mouths full is cited by Lévi-Strauss as an example of:
   a. sexual behavior.
   b. the triumph of culture over nature.
   c. inherited traditions.
   d. the way in which we are like animals.

8. _____ An individual human being would probably find his greatest similarity with:
   a. a member of the opposite sex.
   b. a human being of the same culture.
   c. a human being of any culture.
   d. higher-order animals such as chimpanzees.

9. _____ Culture minimizes the potential for social conflict because it:
   a. enables each individual to be in touch with his inner feelings.
   b. helps humans to adapt to their physical environment.
   c. establishes natural and absolute meanings for behavior.
   d. sets mutually agreed upon rules for social behavior.

10. _____ Our awareness of our impending death probably does not:
   a. accent our joy in living.
   b. always occupy our conscious minds.
   c. make us different from other animals.
   d. add anxiety to our lives.

VOCABULARY   Choose the best definition for each italic vocabulary entry.

1. _____ a *tautology* in the linguistic aspect of culture
   a. twist
   b. communication
   c. question
   d. repetition

2. _____ a whole category of life forms under one *rubric*
   a. roof
   b. life
   c. heading
   d. moral

3. _____ They are *sapient* and cultural.
   a. careful
   b. wise
   c. sensitive
   d. sticky

4. _____ This introduces a primary *dichotomy*.
   a. example
   b. characteristic
   c. division
   d. failure

5. _____ that serves as a *template*
   a. foundation
   b. pattern
   c. flat surface
   d. class

6. _____ It poses a *paradox*.
   a. truth
   b. question
   c. position
   d. self-contradiction

7. _____ It is an *existential* fear.
   a. actually unnecessary
   b. unqualified
   c. of a negative kind
   d. having to do with being

8. _____ the basic *armature*
   a. framework
   b. element
   c. freedom
   d. theory

9. _____ in a *dialectical* fashion
   a. spoken
   b. disjointed
   c. argumentative
   d. methodical

10. _____ *discrete* events and things
    a. cautious
    b. separate
    c. sophisticated
    d. thoughtful

11. _____ imitate the *plumage* and colors
    a. appearance
    b. feathers
    c. headdress
    d. sounds

12. _____ *binary* expression and thought
    a. two-part
    b. compartmentalized
    c. complicated
    d. harmonious

13. _____ The right is considered sacred, the left *profane*.
    a. not religious
    b. crude
    c. wicked
    d. confident

14. _____ engage in *boisterous* behavior
    a. manly
    b. hungry
    c. greedy
    d. noisy

15. _____ the *nurturance* of our elders
    a. support
    b. defense
    c. medical aid
    d. survival

28

DONALD LIGHT, JR.
SUZANNE KELLER

Elements of Culture

One of the most surprising things about culture is the way it influences our daily lives without our even being aware of it. This essay makes clear that, from brushing our teeth in the morning with brush and paste to having a pillow beneath our head at night, our habitual behaviors are governed by the culture in which we live.

"Come alive with Pepsi" proved a winning advertising slogan in the United States. But some residents of Taiwan found the translation — "Pepsi brings your ancestors back from the dead"—unappealing. General Motors Corporation ran into difficulty in Belgium when the firm promoted its "Body by Fisher" cars that translated into Flemish as "Corpse by Fisher." And some car buyers in Spanish-speaking countries were reluctant to purchase the Chevrolet Nova because *no va* means "it doesn't go." These examples all demonstrate a failure to understand language differences in a foreign environment.

A somewhat different problem arose in Salt Lake City, Utah, when a man came to purchase a Shetland pony advertised for sale. The owner asked what the man planned to do with the horse. "For my son's birthday," was the response. Gratified that the pony was going to a child, the owner closed the deal. But then the buyer took out a two-by-four, clubbed the pony over the head, dumped the carcass in his pickup truck, and drove off. The horrified seller notified the police. When the police arrived at the buyer's home, they found a birthday party underway. The pony was roasting in a "luau pit." The buyer, a recent immigrant from Tonga, a group of Polynesian Islands off New Zealand, explained that the Tongans do not ride horses but eat them. They had acquired their taste for horse meat from European missionaries who found horses the only readily available source of meat on the Pacific Islands.

All of the customs, beliefs, values, knowledge, and skills that guide a people's behavior along shared paths are part of their **culture**. Culture can be divided into material aspects (the products of a people's arts and technology) and nonmaterial aspects (a people's customs, beliefs, values, and patterns of communication). People throughout the world have different cultures. Thus their standards for behavior often differ. We tend to assume that certain behaviors have pretty much the same meaning around the world, and we anticipate that other people will act as we do. But this is clearly not the case. When we are thrust into a different culture, we may find ourselves in situations for which we are unprepared.

Not surprisingly, interaction among peoples of different cultures is often filled with uncertainties and even difficulties. Take the matter of the "language of space," identified by the anthropologist Edward T. Hall. He notes that Arabs tend to get very close to other people, close enough to breathe on them. When Arabs do not breathe on a person, it means that they are ashamed. But Americans insist on staying outside the range of other people's breath, viewing the odor as distasteful. Arabs ask, "Why are Americans so ashamed? They withhold their breath." Americans on the receiving end wonder, "Why are the Arabs so pushy?" Americans typically back away as an Arab comes close, and the Arab follows. Such differences can have serious consequences. For example, an Arab business representative may not trust an American who backs off. On the other hand, the American may distrust the Arab for seeming so pushy.

Culture is a taken-for-granted aspect of life, one we commonly overlook as we go about our daily activities. Yet it touches all aspects of our lives. Alexander Alland, Jr., provides the following analogy for culture:

> I remember watching a blind student several years ago walking across the campus of a large state university. He guided himself with a cane, tapping it against the sidewalk which ran in spokes from building to building. Although he knew the campus well, on that particular occasion he became distracted for a moment and wandered onto the grass, where he immediately lost all sense of direction. His movements became disorganized as he searched hopelessly for a bit of cement. He became visibly panicked until a passing student came up and led him back to the appropriate path. Once again he was able to continue toward his class unaided.
>
> I was struck by the similarity of this situation to the situation of all human beings who have grown up within a particular social milieu. Out of an incredibly large number of possible ways of living successfully, all normal human beings operate within a narrow framework of convention. The convention is sometimes limiting and perhaps to certain individuals unsatisfying, but it provides a set of rules which act as guidelines for action.

The anthropologist Edmund Carpenter confronted a situation similar to that described by Alland when he went to live among the Aivilik, an Eskimo people:

For months after I first arrived among the Aivilik, I felt empty, clumsy. I never knew what to do, even where to sit or stand. I was awkward in a busy world, as helpless as a child, yet a grown man. I felt like a mental defective.

The map of life that underlies both material and nonmaterial culture includes three elements: norms, values, and symbols. Let's consider what each contributes to social life.

Norms

In *Games People Play* Eric Berne describes the greeting ritual of the American:

> "Hi!" (Hello, good morning.)
> "Hi!" (Hello, good morning.)
> "Warm enough forya?" (How are you?)
> "Sure is. Looks like rain, though." (Fine. How are you?)
> "Well, take cara yourself." (Okay.)
> "I'll be seeing you."
> "So long."
> "So long."

This brief exchange is conspicuously lacking in content. If you were to measure the success of the conversation in terms of the information conveyed, you would have to rate it zero. Even so, both parties leave the scene feeling quite satisfied. In using the greeting ritual, they have made social contact and established a friendly atmosphere.

Norms are the guidelines people are supposed to follow in their relations with one another; they are shared rules that specify appropriate and inappropriate behavior. Not only do norms indicate what people should or should not do in a specific situation; they also enable people to anticipate how others will interpret and respond to their words and actions. Norms vary from society to society, from group to group within societies, and from situation to situation. Polite and appropriate behavior in one society may be disgraceful in another. For example:

> Among the Ila-speaking peoples of Africa, girls are given houses of their own at harvest time where they may play at being man and wife with boys of their choice. It is said that among these people virginity does not exist beyond the age of ten. [In contrast] among the Tepoztlan Indians of Mexico, from the time of a girl's first menstruation, her life becomes "crabbed, cribbed, confined." No boy is to be spoken to or encouraged in the least way. To do so would be to court disgrace, to show oneself to be crazy or mad. [Ember, C.R., & Ember, M. (1977) *Anthropology,* 2nd ed., Englewood Cliffs, N.J.: Prentice-Hall, p. 277.]

Some norms are situational—they apply to specific categories of people in specific settings. We consider it appropriate for a person to pray to God in church, or to speak to people who have long since "gone to the other side" during a séance (even if we think the séance is phony). But we usually find a person "peculiar" if he or she addresses God or invokes spirits on a bus.

Social norms shape our emotions and perceptions. For example, people are *supposed* to feel sad and be depressed when a family member dies. Similarly, people are supposed to pay attention to certain things but not to others. For example, we consider it bad taste to gawk at a couple who is quarreling bitterly or to eavesdrop on an intimate conversation, yet we occasionally do both. Thus we hold norms, but at times we violate them.

Most of the time people follow norms more or less automatically; alternatives never occur to them. This is particularly true of unspoken norms that seem self-evident, such as responding to a person who addresses you. People conform because it seems right, because to violate norms would damage their self-image (or "hurt their conscience"), and because they want approval and fear ridicule, ostracism, or, in some cases, punishment.

Folkways, Mores, and Laws

Norms vary in the importance that people assign to them and the leeway they permit violators. **Folkways** are everyday habits and conventions people obey without giving much thought to the matter. For example, Americans eat three meals a day and call other food "snacks." We have cereal for breakfast but not for other meals; we save sweets for the end of dinner. Even though we could easily begin a meal with cherry pie, we don't. Other customs we observe are covering our mouths when we yawn, shaking hands when introduced, closing zippers on pants or skirts, and *not* wearing evening clothes to class. People who violate folkways may be labeled eccentrics or slobs, but as a rule they are tolerated.

In contrast, violations of mores provoke intense reactions. **Mores** are the norms people consider vital to their well-being and to their most cherished values. Examples are the prohibitions against incest, cannibalism, and sexual abuse of children. People who violate mores are considered unfit for society and may be ostracized, beaten, locked up in a prison or a mental hospital, exiled, or executed. (Hence, most Americans would not condemn an individual who gave a child molester a severe beating.)

Some norms are formalized into laws. A **law** is a rule enacted by a political body and enforced by the power of the state. Whereas folkways and mores are typically enforced by the collective and spontaneous actions of the members of the community, laws are enforced by the police, the military, or some other special organization. Laws may formalize folkways (as some traffic regulations do) or back up mores (as laws against murder and treason do). Political authorities may also attempt to introduce new norms by enacting laws such as those governing the disposal of toxic wastes or the extension of civil rights to various minorities. In general, the laws that are most difficult to enforce are those that are not grounded in the folkways or mores—for example, laws against gambling or the use of marijuana.

Sanctions

Norms are only guides to behavior; by themselves they have no force. It is **sanctions**, or socially imposed rewards and punishments, that compel people to obey norms. Such sanctions may be formal or informal. Examples of formal sanctions that reward people are promotions, medals of honor, and paychecks. Formal sanctions that punish people include jail terms, job dismissals, failing grades, and traffic fines. Informal sanctions are those expressed by behavior in everyday situations—smiles, frowns, friendly nods, gossip, praise, insults, and even attention.

Societies vary in their use of sanctions. For instance, the Amish punish those who violate their norms with shunning, in which no one is allowed to speak to the offender. Such a punishment is less effective in the larger American society. In Japan slurping one's soup loudly is a positive sanction, indicating to a hostess that one has greatly enjoyed a meal. In the United States, such slurping is itself disapproved; instead, Americans are expected to compliment the cook verbally.

Values

Norms typically derive from a people's values. **Values** are the general ideas that individuals share about what is good or bad, right or wrong, desirable or undesirable. These notions transcend particular situations or interactions. Unlike norms (the rules that govern behavior in actual situations with other people), values are broad, abstract concepts. As such, they provide the foundation that underlies a people's entire way of life. Even the games they play reflect their values. A good illustration is formed among the Tangu, a people who live in a remote part of New Guinea and play a game called *taketak*.

In some respects taketak resembles bowling. The game is played with a toplike object fashioned from a dried fruit and with two groups of coconut stakes that look like bowling pins. The players divide into two teams. The members of the first team step to the line and take turns throwing the top into their batch of stakes; every stake they hit they remove. Then the members of the second team toss the top into their batch of stakes. The object of the game, surprisingly, is not to knock over as many stakes as possible. Rather, the game continues until both teams have removed the *same* number of stakes. The Tangu disapprove of winning while favoring value equivalence. The idea that one individual or group should win and another lose bothers them, for they believe winning generates ill will. In fact, when Europeans brought soccer to New Guinea, the Tangu altered the rules so that the object was for two teams to score the same number of goals.

Sometimes their soccer games went on for days! American games, in contrast, are highly competitive; there are always winners and losers.

Since values entail broad and abstract cultural principles, we frequently have difficulty identifying them. The sociologist Robin M. Williams, Jr., in an interpretation of American society, identifies fifteen major value orientations. These include the high value Americans place upon achievement and success, activity and work, humanitarianism, efficiency and practicality, progress, material comfort, equality, freedom, conformity, science and rationality, nationalism and patriotism, democracy, individuality, and racial and ethnic group superiority. Many of these values tend to be interrelated, including those having to do with achievement and success, activity and work, material comfort, and individuality. Others are in conflict, for example, stressing conformity and individuality or equality and racial and ethnic superiority. Moreover, values change. Thus in recent years many of America's more overt racist attitudes have faded. The 1983 annual survey of college freshmen found that, for the first time, a majority supported busing to achieve racial integration in the schools. In the same year, 69.3 percent of the freshmen said they believed that being well off was very important; in 1970 the figure stood at 39 percent. The distinct characteristics of American values become more apparent when we compare them with the values of another culture.

The Relation between Norms and Values

Values assume considerable importance because norms are usually based on them. Even so, there is not a one-to-one correspondence between norms and values. For instance, some American values favor individuality and competition, yet some norms run counter to these values. Affirmative-action laws, for example, have often allowed minorities to be hired in proportion to their numbers as a matter of fairness, while competitive standards of individual achievement are relaxed. Such a norm attempts to reconcile the values of individuality and competition with the values of justice and equality. Thus conflicts in values are often a source of social change that leads to new norms.

In our daily lives we frequently find that more than one value may also be operating in a given situation. If being honest also means being unkind to another person, we are caught in a conflict of values. You have probably faced situations where the truth will hurt someone and kindness means lying. Hinting gently at the truth or surrounding the hurtful truth with kindnesses or saying nothing at all are norms that attempt to reconcile two conflicting values.

It is important not to confuse norms with values. The distinction is highlighted by a young child's obedience: A child obeys the parent because failure to do so may result in punishment or jeopardize rewards (a norm). But the child as yet does not judge the behavior as desirable or undesirable in its own right (a value). Likewise, you may stop at a red light even when there is no traffic, yet you do not attach an underlying value to stopping for a red light under these circumstances. In sum, norms constitute rules for behavior; values provide the criteria or standards we use for evaluating the desirability of behavior.

LENGTH: 2,637 WORDS

28   Donald Light, Jr., and Suzanne Keller
Elements of Culture

SCORING: Reading time: _____ Rate from chart: _____ W.P.M.

      RETENTION   number right _____ × 2 equals _____ points

      MAIN IDEA   number right _____ × 4 equals _____ points

      INTERPRETATION number right _____ × 3 equals _____ points

      CONCLUSION   number right _____ × 3 equals _____ points

      APPLICATION   number right _____ × 3 equals _____ points

      VOCABULARY   number right _____ × 2 equals _____ points

(Total points: 100) **total** _____ points

RETENTION   Based on the selection, which of the following statements are True (T), False (F), or Not answerable (N)?

1. _____ Government sometimes tries to change norms by creating new folkways.

2. _____ Norms vary from situation to situation.

3. _____ The values in a given society remain stable.

4. _____ More than one value can operate at one time.

5. _____ Tongans eat roasted horse meat.

6. _____ Culture can be divided into two aspects, material and nonmaterial.

7. _____ Margaret Mead was one of the first to study courtship rituals among the Polynesians.

8. _____ Seeing a blind student become lost gave one anthropologist an idea of a way to explain culture to people.

9. _____ Because the influence of norms is so powerful, we cannot bring ourselves to violate them.

10. _____ The Amish tradition of shunning involves refusing to talk to people who are not Amish.

11. _____ Recreational activities such as games may reflect people's values.

12. _____ Because human beings are basically alike, advertisements that work in one country will work well in most countries.

13. _____ We tend to take our culture for granted.

14. _____ Eating three meals a day is an example of mores.

15. _____ A society's values are harmonious, working smoothly together to create a conflict-free world.

MAIN IDEA   Which of the following statements best represents the main point of the selection? _____

1. Culture means different things to different people; therefore, we should be careful in how we use the term.
2. The most important elements of culture are the norms and values that affect our daily lives.
3. The quality of each society can be evaluated on the basis of its cultural norms, mores, laws, and values.
4. Culture is made up of three elements: norms, values, and symbols, each of which quietly shapes our behavior.
5. Conformity to one's culture is necessary for mental health.

INTERPRETATION   Which of the following is the best interpretation of a key point in this selection? _____

1. By setting some limits, conventions free us to live in a large number of possible ways.
2. Although norms vary, the norms of one society will seldom be directly contradictory to those of another.
3. Laws and norms have nothing in common.
4. Norms and values are essentially the same thing.
5. Culture is like a map of life in that it provides guidelines and a sense of direction.

CONCLUSION   Which of the following statements is the best conclusion that can be drawn from the selection? _____

1. People are probably more likely to obey laws not grounded in mores because they are enforced by the state, not by the members of the community.
2. In their everyday interactions with each other, Americans usually say what they mean without any alternative meaning.
3. An experienced American advertiser is probably better at designing ads to use in a foreign country than an experienced foreigner.

4. Because of their studies of many cultures, anthropologists are probably exempt from feeling dislocated in a new culture.

5. The authors of this article probably went on to a discussion of symbols.

APPLICATION   Choose the best answer for each question.

1. _____ The authors told the story of the Shetland pony as an example of:
   a. what happens when people use different languages.
   b. how primitive American immigrants sometimes are.
   c. the variety of cultural behaviors.
   d. how not understanding others' cultures can lead to problems.

2. _____ Two participants in a greeting ritual will probably leave feeling satisfied because:
   a. the exchange is brief.
   b. they have made friendly contact.
   c. they have managed to communicate important information.
   d. they haven't had to make physical contact.

3. _____ An example of mores would be:
   a. eating lunch at noon.
   b. wearing clothing when out in public.
   c. paying your income tax.
   d. placing nonmaterial things over material things.

4. _____ If the Tangu people of New Guinea took up the American sport of football, they would probably:
   a. beat the opposing team to a pulp because of their size.
   b. take a long time to adjust to the sport.
   c. compete without wearing the padding Americans use.
   d. change the rules.

5. _____ If we look down on parents who refuse to take care of their children, we are exercising our:
   a. judgment.
   b. laws.
   c. values.
   d. rights.

6. _____ The "language of space" refers to:
   a. the significance placed on the distance of one person from another.
   b. the common code language used by both Russian and American astronauts.
   c. the right of every nation to have enough land space for its people.
   d. communication that involves long spaces between words.

7. _____ The most abstract, broadest element in culture is:
   a. folkways.
   b. laws.
   c. values.
   d. norms.

8. _____ A good example of a sanction would be:
   a. a law against gambling.
   b. a pat on the back.
   c. child abuse.
   d. an invitation to dinner.

9. _____ If I hear somebody burp after eating at a formal dinner party in
   another country I should probably:
   a. assume that they are impolite.
   b. point out their social error to them politely.
   c. talk fast and loud to cover up the noise.
   d. consider the possibility that burping is socially acceptable.

10. _____ An example of a material aspect of culture would be:
   a. drinking Coca-Cola.
   b. knocking on wood.
   c. answering the telephone.
   d. loathing child abuse.

VOCABULARY   Choose the best definition for each italic vocabulary entry.

1. _____ a winning advertising *slogan*
   a. warning
   b. saying
   c. picture
   d. promotion

2. _____ dumped the *carcass* in his pickup truck
   a. animal
   b. dead body
   c. pony
   d. saddle

3. _____ provides the following *analogy* for culture
   a. explanation
   b. warning note
   c. extended comparison
   d. cure for the symptoms of

4. _____ a particular social *milieu*
   a. mixture
   b. class
   c. environment
   d. custom

5. _____ *conspicuously* lacking in content
   a. thoughtfully
   b. consciously
   c. apparently
   d. obviously

6. _____ *invoke* spirits on a bus
   a. imitate
   b. make fun of
   c. anger
   d. call upon

7. _____ labeled *eccentrics* or slobs
   a. oddballs
   b. bores
   c. pigs
   d. lunatics

8. _____ *prohibitions* against incest
   a. unwritten laws
   b. angry outcries
   c. violations
   d. demonstrations

9. _____ Norms are *formalized* into laws.
   a. given a public structure
   b. changed in shape
   c. made strict
   d. altered beyond recognition

10. _____ *overt* racist attitudes
    a. usual
    b. intense
    c. open
    d. customary

11. _____ Some norms run *counter* to these values.
    a. as a support for
    b. parallel
    c. in numerical relation
    d. against

12. _____ to *reconcile* the values
    a. bring into agreement
    b. make more understandable
    c. give advice to
    d. separate

13. _____ The *distinction* is highlighted.
    a. honor
    b. incident
    c. confusion
    d. difference

14. _____ *jeopardize* rewards
    a. offer
    b. risk
    c. intensify
    d. cancel

15. _____ Norms *constitute* rules for behavior.
    a. judge
    b. override
    c. set up
    d. influence

29

CECIE STARR
RALPH TAGGART

The Brain

|M|ore complicated than a computer, more
fascinating than outer space, the brain is
only now revealing its mysteries to science.
As much as we grow in understanding,
however, one question remains: why do men
sometimes deliberately destroy with drugs
the very part of themselves that makes
them human?

Conscious Experience

|O|ur two cerebral hemispheres are strapped together deep inside the cleft between them by a thick tract of white matter, the **corpus callosum**. The corpus callosum consists of axons running from one hemisphere to the other.

Thus you might assume that it functions in communication between the two hemispheres. Indeed, experiments such as those performed by Roger Sperry and his coworkers showed that this is the case. They also demonstrated some intriguing differences in perception between the two halves!

The body's right and left sides have the same kinds of sensory nerves. These nerves enter the spinal cord or brainstem, then run in parallel to the brain. Similarly, sensory nerves from the left eye and ear run in parallel with sensory nerves from the right eye and ear toward the brain. The signals carried by these nerves reach the left or right cerebral hemisphere. But the signals are not all processed on the same side as the nerves. Instead, much of the information is projected onto the opposite hemisphere. In other words, *many of the nerve pathways leading into and from one hemisphere deal with the opposite side of the body.*

Knowing this, Sperry's group set out to treat severe cases of epilepsy. Persons afflicted with severe epilepsy are wracked with seizures, sometimes as often as every half hour of their lives. The seizures have a neurological basis, analogous to an electrical storm in the brain. What would happen if the corpus callosum of afflicted persons were cut? Would the electrical storm be confined to one cerebral hemisphere, leaving at least the other to function normally? Earlier studies of animals and of humans whose corpus callosum had been damaged suggested that this might be so.

The surgery was performed. And the electrical storms subsided, in both frequency and intensity. Apparently, cutting the neural bridge between the two hemispheres put an end to what must have been positive feedback loops of ever intensified electrical disturbances between them. Beyond this, the "split-brain" individuals were able to lead what seemed, on the surface, entirely normal lives.

But then Sperry devised some elegant experiments to determine whether the conscious experience of these individuals was indeed "normal." After all, the corpus callosum is a tract of no less than 200 million through-conducting axons; surely *something* was different. Something was. "The surgery," Sperry later reported, "left these people with two separate minds, that is, two spheres of consciousness. What is experienced in the right hemisphere seems to be entirely outside the realm of awareness of the left."

In Sperry's experiments, the left and right hemispheres of split-brain individuals were presented with different stimuli. Recall that visual connections to and from one hemisphere are mainly concerned with the opposite visual field. Sperry projected words—say, COWBOY—onto a screen. He did this in such a way that COW fell only on the left visual field, and BOY fell on the right. The subject reported seeing the word BOY. (The left hemisphere, which received the word, controls language.) However, when asked to write the perceived word with the left hand—a hand that was deliberately blocked from view—the subject wrote COW. The right hemisphere, which "knew" the other half of the word, had directed the left hand's motor response. But it couldn't tell the left hemisphere what was going on because of the severed corpus callosum. The subject knew that a word was being written, but could not say what it was!

The functioning of our two cerebral hemispheres has been the focus of many more experiments. Taken together, the results have revealed the following information about our conscious experience:

1. Each cerebral hemisphere can function separately, but it functions in response to signals mainly from the opposite side of the body.
2. The main association regions responsible for spoken language skills generally reside in the *left* hemisphere.
3. The main association regions responsible for nonverbal skills (music, mathematics, and other abstract abilities) generally reside in the *right* hemisphere.

Memory

Conscious experience is far removed from simple reflex action. It entails *thinking* about things—recalling objects and events encountered in the past, comparing them with newly encountered ones, and making rational connections based on the comparison of perceptions. Thus conscious experience entails a capacity for **memory**: the storage of individual bits of information somewhere in the brain.

The neural representation of information bits is known as a **memory trace**, although no one knows for sure in what form a memory trace occurs, or where it resides. So far, experiments strongly suggest that there are at least two stages involved in its formation. One is a *short-term* formative period, lasting only a few minutes or so; then, information becomes spatially and temporally organized in neural pathways. The other is *long-term* storage; then, information is put in a different neural representation that lasts more or less permanently.

Observations of people suffering from **retrograde amnesia** tell us something about memory. These people can't remember anything that happened during the half hour or so before experiencing electroconvulsive shock or before losing consciousness after a severe head blow. Yet memories of events before that time remain intact! Such disturbances temporarily suppress normal electrical activities in the brain. These observations may mean that whereas short-term memory is a fleeting stage of neural excitation, long-term memory depends on *chemical or structural* changes in the brain.

In addition, information seemingly forgotten can be recalled after being unused for decades. This means that individual memory traces must be encoded in a form somewhat immune to degradation. Most molecules and cells in your body are used up, wear out, or age and are constantly being replaced—yet memories can be retrieved in exquisite detail after many years of such wholesale turnovers. Nerve cells, recall, are among the few kinds that are *not* replaced. You are born with billions, and as you grow older some 50,000 die off steadily each day. Those nerve cells formed during embryonic development are the same ones present, whether damaged or otherwise modified, at the time of death.

The part about being "otherwise modified" is tantalizing. *There is evidence that neuron structure is not static, but rather can be modified in several ways.* Most likely, such modifications depend on electrical and chemical interactions with neighboring neurons. Electron micrographs show that some synapses regress as a result of disuse. Such regression weakens or breaks connections between neurons. The visual cortex of mice raised without visual stimulation showed such effects of disuse. Similarly, there is some evidence that intensively stimulated synapses may form stronger connections, grow in size, or sprout buds or spines to form more connections! The chemical and physical transformations that underlie changes in synaptic connections may correspond to memory storage.

Sleeping and Dreaming

Between the mindless drift of coma and total alertness are many *levels* of conscious experience, known by such names as sleeping, dozing, meditating, and daydreaming. Through this spectrum of consciousness, neurons in the brain are constantly chattering among themselves. This neural chatter shows up as wavelike patterns in an **electroencephalogram** (EEG). An EEG is an electrical recording of the frequency and strength of potentials from the brain's surface. Each recording shows the contribution of thousands of neurons.

EEG Patterns

The prominent wave pattern for someone who is relaxed, with eyes closed, is an *alpha rhythm*. In this relaxed state of wakefulness, potentials are recorded in trains of about ten per second. Alpha waves predominate during the state of meditation. With a transition to sleep, wave trains gradually become longer, slower, and more erratic. This *slow-wave sleep* pattern shows up about eighty percent of the total sleeping time for adults. It occurs when sensory input is low and the mind is more or less idling. Subjects awakened from slow-wave sleep usually report that they were not dreaming. If anything, they seemed to be mulling over recent, ordinary events. However, slow-wave sleep is punctuated by brief spells of *REM sleep*. The name refers to the Rapid Eye Movements accompanying this pattern (the eyes jerk about beneath closed lids). Also accompanying REM sleep are irregular breathing, faster heartbeat, and twitching fingers. Most people who are awakened from REM sleep say that they were experiencing vivid dreams.

With the transition from sleep (or deep relaxation) into wakefulness, EEG recordings show a shift to low-amplitude, higher frequency wave trains. Associated with this accelerated brain activity are increased blood flow and oxygen uptake in the cortex. The transition, called *EEG arousal*, occurs when individuals make a conscious effort to focus on external stimuli or even on their own thoughts.

The Reticular Formation

What brain regions govern changing levels of consciousness? Deep in the brainstem, buried within ascending and descending nerve pathways, lies a mass of nerve cells and processes called the **reticular formation**. This mass forms connections with the spinal cord, cerebellum, and cerebrum, as well as back with itself. It constantly samples messages flowing through the central nervous system. The flow of signals along these circuits—and the inhibitory or excitatory chemical changes accompanying them—has a great deal to do with whether you stay awake or drop off to sleep. For example, when certain areas of the reticular formation of sleeping animals are electrically stimulated, long, slow alpha rhythms are displaced by high-frequency potentials associated with arousal.

Similarly, damage to the reticular formation leads to unconsciousness and coma.

Within this formation are neurons collectively called the **reticular activating system** (RAS). Excitatory pathways connect the RAS to the thalamus (the forebrain's switching station). Messages routed from the RAS arouse the brain and maintain wakefulness.

Also in the reticular formation are *sleep centers*. One center contains neurons that release the transmitter substance serotonin. This chemical has an inhibitory effect on RAS neurons: high serotonin levels are associated with drowsiness and sleep. Another sleep center, in the part of the reticular formation that lies in the pons, has been linked to REM sleep. Chemicals released from the second center counteract the effects of serotonin. Hence its action allows the RAS to maintain the waking state.

Drug Action on Integration and Control

Each day can bring some minor frustration or disappointment, some pleasure or small triumph—and the brain responds to the shadings of environmental stimuli with delicate interplays among the activities of norepinephrine, dopamine, and the like. These interplays translate into changing emotional and behavioral states. When stress leads to physical or emotional pain, the brain apparently deploys other substances—**analgesics**, or pain relievers that the brain produces itself.

Receptors for natural analgesics have been identified on neural membranes in many parts of the nervous system, including the spinal cord and limbic system. (The limbic system includes structures bordering the cerebral hemispheres, at the top of the brainstem.) When bound to receptors, the pain relievers seem to inhibit neural activity. *Endorphins* (including *enkephalins*) are brain analgesics that may have this inhibitory effect. High concentrations of endorphins ("internally produced morphines") occur in brain regions concerned with our emotions and perception of pain.

Emotional states—joy, elation, anxiety, depression, fear, anger—are normal responses to changing conditions in the complex world around us. Sometimes, through imbalances in transmitter substances, one or another of these states becomes pronounced. For instance, schizophrenic persons become despairing; they withdraw from the social world and focus obsessively on themselves. In an extreme form of the disorder (paranoid schizophrenia), afflicted persons suffer delusions of persecution or grandeur. Yet by administering certain synthetic tranquilizers, the symptoms can be brought under control. It appears that the tranquilizers affect norepinephrine, dopamine, and serotonin levels in the brain, in ways that depress the activity of neurons utilizing these transmitter substances.

Tranquilizers, opiates, stimulants, hallucinogens—such drugs are known to inhibit, modify, or enhance the release or action of chemical messengers throughout the brain. Yet research into the effects of drugs on integration and control is in its infancy. For the most part, we don't understand much about how any one drug works. Given the complexity of the brain, it could scarcely be otherwise at this early stage of inquiry.

Despite our ignorance of drug effects, one of the major problems in the modern world is drug abuse—the self-destructive use of drugs that alter emotional and behavioral states. The consequences show up in unexpected places—among seven-year-old heroin addicts; among the highway wreckage left by individuals whose perceptions were skewed by alcohol or amphetamines; among victims of addicts who steal and sometimes kill to support the drug habit; among suicides on LSD trips who were deluded into believing that they could fly, and who flew off buildings and bridges.

Each of us possesses a body of great complexity. Its architecture, its functioning are legacies of millions of years of evolution. It is unique in the living world because of its nervous system—a system that is capable of processing far more than the experience of the individual. One of its most astonishing products is language—the encoding of *shared* experiences of groups of individuals in time and space. Through the evolution of our nervous system, the sense of history was born, and the sense of destiny. Through this system we can ask how we have come to be what we are, and where we are headed from here. Perhaps the sorriest consequence of drug abuse is its implicit denial of this legacy—the denial of self when we cease to ask, and cease to care.

LENGTH: 2,231 WORDS

29 Cecie Starr and Ralph Taggart
The Brain

SCORING: Reading time: _____ Rate from chart: _____ W.P.M.

RETENTION	number right ____ × 2 equals ____ points	
MAIN IDEA	number right ____ × 4 equals ____ points	
INTERPRETATION	number right ____ × 3 equals ____ points	
CONCLUSION	number right ____ × 3 equals ____ points	
APPLICATION	number right ____ × 3 equals ____ points	
VOCABULARY	number right ____ × 2 equals ____ points	

(Total points: 100) **total** ____ points

RETENTION   Based on the selection, which of the following statements are True (T), False (F), or Not answerable (N)?

1. _____ The main association regions responsible for spoken language skills generally reside in the right hemisphere.

2. _____ The sleep centers are in the reticular formation.

3. _____ Some people on LSD trips think that they can fly.

4. _____ Cutting the corpus callosum resulted in increased epileptic seizures.

5. _____ Even when we are in a coma, the neurons in our brains are constantly talking with one another.

6. _____ We understand how one stimulant, coffee, works.

7. _____ Nerve cells are among the few kinds of cells that can be replaced.

8. _____ Epileptic seizures can be controlled with drugs.

9. _____ The body's right and left sides have the same kinds of sensory nerves.

10. _____ Most people who are awakened from slow-wave sleep report that they were experiencing vivid dreams.

11. _____ Anxiety is a normal response to changing conditions in the world around us.

12. _____ The pituitary gland governs changing levels of consciousness.

13. _____ No one knows for sure in what form a memory trace occurs.

14. _____ Each cerebral hemisphere functions in response to signals from its own part of the body.

15. _____ The brain is actually capable of producing its own pain relievers.

MAIN IDEA   Which of the following statements best represents the main point of the selection? _____

1. The brain consists of two cerebral hemispheres.
2. The brain varies in its activity depending on whether we are asleep or awake, using drugs or not using drugs.
3. The brain, carrier of our conscious and unconscious experiences, is that part of us which makes us distinctively human.
4. The brain is a complex organ whose role and workings we are only beginning to understand.
5. Experimentation on the brain is difficult because of the repercussions involved in terms of the quality of life.

INTERPRETATION   Which of the following is the best interpretation of a key point in this selection? _____

1. Whether we are awake or asleep is a result of physical activity and time, not chemicals.
2. When the corpus callosum was cut, people's brains were to all intents and purposes cut in half, with one side not knowing what the other side was experiencing.
3. Long-term memory and short-term memory have basically the same structure.
4. Schizophrenia is a result of a normal response to change in our world.
5. REM sleep periods represent a deeper sleep than do sleep periods characterized by alpha waves.

CONCLUSION   Which of the following statements is the best conclusion that can be drawn from the selection? _____

1. If synapses can be strengthened, scientists may be able to improve an individual's memory by synapse stimulation.
2. Even if a person were placed in a different environment, the basic relative amounts of the substances put out by his brain would not change.
3. Cutting a person's corpus callosum would mean that they would see a word such as *backstop* as two different words, each being read separately by one side of the brain.

4. Alcoholism, while self-destructive, is not a form of drug abuse.

5. The author of this article does not believe in evolution.

<small>APPLICATION</small>   Choose the best answer for each question.

1. _____ If I touch a hot stove with my left hand, the signal will go to:
   a. the left hemisphere of my brain.
   b. both hemispheres.
   c. the right hemisphere.
   d. the corpus callosum.

2. _____ If the memory of my tenth birthday party is stored in my long-term memory:
   a. it has made chemical or structural changes in my brain.
   b. the party must have been an especially awful one.
   c. I probably received a shock or a head blow shortly after the party.
   d. it was probably not part of my conscious experience.

3. _____ A coma is probably the result of:
   a. an excessive desire for sleep.
   b. unconsciousness.
   c. synapse regression.
   d. damage to the reticular formation.

4. _____ A person having an electroencephalogram is:
   a. having trouble sleeping.
   b. having his brain waves measured.
   c. having his corpus callosum cut.
   d. replacing his alpha rhythms.

5. _____ A conscious effort to focus thoughts results in:
   a. a headache in the lower lumbar region.
   b. increased cortical oxygen uptake.
   c. longer, slower alpha waves.
   d. rapid eye movements.

6. _____ Paranoid schizophrenia is caused by:
   a. despair.
   b. synthetic tranquilizers.
   c. interruptions in the limbic system.
   d. imbalances in transmitter substances.

7. _____ Tranquilizers are an example of drugs that:
   a. are sold over the counter too frequently.
   b. have influenced the development of our nervous system.
   c. modify the release of chemical messengers in some way.
   d. have been responsible for delusions of grandeur.

8. _____ When a person is in a state of REM sleep:
   a. the effects of serotonin are being counteracted by chemicals released from a sleep center.
   b. her breathing is regular.
   c. the neural chatter throughout the spectrum of her consciousness has become unusually loud.
   d. she is probably not dreaming.

9. _____ Scientists reasoned that cutting the corpus callosum must make people different from the norm because:
   a. the operation had cured epileptics.
   b. it was such a thick tract of white matter.
   c. it has hundreds of millions of conducting axons.
   d. its function was to create positive feedback loops.

10. _____ The ability to share experiences through language is the result of:
   a. the human nervous system.
   b. improved technology.
   c. research into the structure of the brain.
   d. the transmitter substances deployed by the activated brain.

VOCABULARY   Choose the best definition for each italic vocabulary entry.

1. _____ the *cleft* between them
   a. mark
   b. split
   c. strap
   d. bridge

2. _____ *intriguing* differences in perception
   a. scheming
   b. extreme
   c. interesting
   d. self-defeating

3. _____ The seizures have a *neurological* basis.
   a. physical rather than mental
   b. unclear
   c. medical
   d. having to do with the nerves

4. _____ *analogous* to an electrical storm in the brain
   a. resembling
   b. appropriate
   c. opposite
   d. causing

5. ____ devised some *elegant* experiments
    a. tasteful
    b. large
    c. newly designed
    d. refined

6. ____ *entails* a capacity for memory
    a. finalizes
    b. destroys
    c. involves
    d. stores

7. ____ suffering from *retrograde* amnesia
    a. intense
    b. moving backward
    c. limited
    d. increasingly painful

8. ____ a form somewhat immune to *degradation*
    a. being encoded
    b. wearing away
    c. lasting forever
    d. shame

9. ____ Some synapses *regress* as a result of disuse.
    a. grow in size
    b. disappear
    c. move backward
    d. experience stimulation

10. ____ Alpha waves *predominate.*
    a. slow down
    b. become regal
    c. lose strength
    d. prevail

11. ____ become longer, slower, and more *erratic*
    a. even
    b. wandering
    c. faulty
    d. irregular

12. ____ *accelerated* brain activity
    a. quickened
    b. excellent
    c. pedaling
    d. overactive

13. _____ the *inhibitory* chemical changes
    a. restraining
    b. unnecessary
    c. exciting
    d. constant

14. _____ suffer *delusions* of persecution
    a. excessive amounts
    b. agonies
    c. false ideas
    d. disorders

15. _____ opiates, stimulants, *hallucinogens*
    a. sleeping potions
    b. causing illusions
    c. bringing about addiction
    d. mood alterers

30

RITA ATKINSON
RICHARD ATKINSON
EDWARD SMITH
ERNEST HILGARD

Hypnosis

Even today, many of us associate hypnosis
with theatre and night club acts. Others may
be aware that hypnosis is used in helping
people change such deep-seated habits as
smoking and overeating. The authors of this
essay explain the scientific origins of this
phenomenon.

Of all states of altered consciousness, none raises more questions
than the *hypnotic condition*. Once associated with the bizarre and the occult,
hypnosis has now become the subject of rigorous scientific investigation. As in
all fields of psychological investigation, uncertainties remain, but by now many
facts have been established. A definition of hypnosis proposed by Kihlstrom
serves as an introduction to the topic:

> Hypnosis may be defined as a social interaction in which one person
> (designated the subject) responds to suggestions offered by another
> person (designated the hypnotist) for experiences involving altera-
> tions in perception, memory, and voluntary action. In the classic
> case, these experiences and their accompanying behaviors are asso-
> ciated with subjective conviction bordering on delusion, and in-
> voluntariness bordering on compulsion. [Kihlstrom, J. F. (1985)
> "Hypnosis," *Annual Review of Psychology*, 36: 385–86.]

From INTRODUCTION TO PSYCHOLOGY, Ninth Edition, by Rita L. Atkinson, Richard C. Atkinson,
Edward E. Smith, and Ernest R. Hilgard. Copyright © 1987 by Harcourt Brace Jovanovich, Inc.
Reprinted by permission of the publisher.

Hypnotic Experience

In hypnosis, a willing and cooperative subject (the only kind that can be hypnotized under most circumstances) relinquishes some control over his or her behavior to the hypnotist and accepts some reality distortion. The hypnotist uses a variety of methods to induce this condition. For example, the subject may be asked to concentrate all thoughts on a small target (such as a thumbtack on the wall) while gradually becoming relaxed. A suggestion of sleepiness may be made because, like sleep, hypnosis is a relaxed state in which a person is out of touch with ordinary environmental demands. But sleep is only a metaphor. The subject is told that he or she will not really go to sleep but will continue to listen to the hypnotist.

The same state can be induced by methods other than relaxation. A hyperalert hypnotic trance is characterized by increased tension and alertness, and the trance-induction procedure is an active one. For example, in one study, subjects riding a stationary laboratory bicycle while receiving suggestions of strength and alertness were as responsive to hypnotic suggestions as were conventionally relaxed subjects. This result denies the common equation of hypnosis with relaxation but is consistent with the trance-induction methods of sects like the whirling dervishes.

Modern hypnotists do not use authoritarian commands. Indeed, with a little training, subjects can hypnotize themselves. The subject enters the hypnotic state when the conditions are right; the hypnotist merely helps set the conditions. The following changes are characteristic of the hypnotized state.

1. *Planfulness ceases.* A deeply hypnotized subject does not like to initiate activity and would rather wait for the hypnotist to suggest something to do.

2. *Attention becomes more selective than usual.* A subject who is told to listen only to the hypnotist's voice will ignore any other voices in the room.

3. *Enriched fantasy is readily evoked.* A subject may find herself or himself enjoying experiences at a place distant in time and space.

4. *Reality testing is reduced and reality distortion is accepted.* A subject may uncritically accept hallucinated experiences (for example, conversing with an imagined person believed to be sitting in a nearby chair) and will not check to determine whether that person is real.

5. *Suggestibility is increased.* A subject must accept suggestions in order to be hypnotized at all, but whether suggestibility is increased under hypnosis is a matter of some dispute. Careful studies have found some increase in suggestibility following hypnotic induction, although less than is commonly supposed.

6. *Posthypnotic amnesia is often present.* When instructed to do so, a highly responsive hypnotic subject will forget all or most of what transpired during the hypnotic session. When a prearranged release signal is given, the memories are restored.

Responsiveness to suggestions is typical of relatively superficial levels of hypnosis. When highly responsive subjects are encouraged to go deeper into hypnosis, they eventually reach a state in which they are unresponsive to the hypnotist's suggestions (except when a prearranged signal returns them to a level at which they can communicate). People who have been deeply hypnotized describe a sense of mind-body separation, a feeling of oneness with the universe, an impression of gaining knowledge of a kind that cannot be communicated. This state seems similar to the kind of mystical experience reported by those who have had extensive training in meditation, suggesting that meditation may be a kind of self-hypnosis.

Not all subjects are equally responsive to hypnotic procedures. Responsiveness seems to have both learned and genetic components. The capacity to set ordinary reality aside and become deeply absorbed in reading a book, watching a play, listening to music, or enjoying nature is an important predictor of hypnotizability. This is probably a learned capacity, developed in early childhood through experiences with parents rich in imagination. Support for a hereditary component comes from studies of twins. For example, when identical (monozygotic) twins were compared with fraternal (dizygotic) twins, there was a significant difference between the groups. The identical twins achieved more similar hypnotizability scores than did the fraternal twins.

Suggestions given to a hypnotized subject can result in a variety of behaviors and experiences. The person's motor control may be affected, new memories may be lost or old ones re-experienced, and current perceptions may be radically altered.

Control of Movement

Many hypnotic subjects respond to direct suggestion with involuntary movement. For example, if a person stands with arms outstretched and hands facing each other and the hypnotist suggests that the subject's hands are attracted to one another, the hands will soon begin to move, and the subject will feel that they are propelled by some force that she or he is not generating. Direct suggestion can also inhibit movement. If a suggestible subject is told that an arm is stiff (like a bar of iron or an arm in a splint) and then is asked to bend the arm, it will not bend, or more effort than usual will be needed to make it bend. This response is less common than suggested movement.

Subjects who have been roused from hypnosis may respond with movement to a prearranged signal from the hypnotist. This is called a *posthypnotic response*. Even if the suggestion has been forgotten, subjects will feel a compulsion to carry out the behavior. They may try to justify such behavior as rational, even though the urge to perform it is impulsive. For example, a young man searching for a rational explanation of why he opened a window when the hypnotist took off his glasses (the prearranged signal) remarked that the room felt a little stuffy.

Posthypnotic Amnesia

At the suggestion of the hypnotist, events occurring during hypnosis may be "forgotten" until a signal from the hypnotist enables the subject to recall them. This is called *posthypnotic amnesia*. Subjects differ widely in their susceptibility to posthypnotic amnesia. The items to be recalled in one study were ten actions the subjects performed while hypnotized. A few subjects forgot none or only one or two items; most subjects forgot four or five items. However, a sizable number of subjects forgot all ten items. This type of bimodal distribution, showing two distinct groups of subjects, has been found in many studies of posthypnotic amnesia. The group of subjects with the higher recall is larger and presumably represents the average hypnotic responders; the smaller group, the subjects who forgot all ten items, has been described as hypnotic virtuosos. Differences in recall between the two groups following posthypnotic suggestion do not appear to be related to differences in memory capacity: once the amnesia is canceled at a prearranged signal from the hypnotist, highly amnesic subjects remember as many items as those who are less amnesic. Some researchers have suggested that hypnosis temporarily interferes with the person's ability to search for a particular item in memory but does not affect actual memory storage.

Age Regression

In response to hypnotic suggestion, some individuals are able to relive episodes from earlier periods of life, such as a birthday at age 10. To some subjects, the episode seems to be pictured as if it were on a TV screen; the subjects are conscious of being present and viewing the event but do not feel as if they are producing it. In another type of regression, subjects feel as if they are re-experiencing the events. They may describe the clothing they are wearing, run a hand through their hair and describe its length, or recognize their elementary school classmates. Occasionally, a childhood language, long forgotten, emerges during regression. For example, an American-born boy whose parents were Japanese and who had spoken Japanese at an early age but had forgotten it began speaking the language fluently again while under hypnosis.

Positive and Negative Hallucinations

Some hypnotic experiences require a higher level of hypnotic talent than others. The vivid and convincing perceptual distortions of hallucinations, for instance, are relatively rare. Two types of suggested hallucinations have been documented: *positive hallucinations*, in which the subject sees an object or hears a voice that is not actually present; and *negative hallucinations*, in which the subject does not perceive something that normally would be perceived. Many hallucinations have both positive and negative components. In order not to see a person sitting in a chair (a negative hallucination), a subject must see the parts of the chair that would ordinarily be blocked from view (a positive hallucination).

Hallucinations can also occur as the result of posthypnotic suggestion. For example, subjects may be told that on arousal from the hypnotic state they will find themselves holding a rabbit that wants to be petted and that the rabbit will ask, "What time is it?" Seeing and petting the rabbit will seem natural to most of the subjects. But when they find themselves giving the correct time of day, they are surprised and try to provide an explanation for the behavior: "Did I hear someone ask the time? It's funny, it seemed to be the rabbit asking, but rabbits can't talk!" is a typical response.

Negative hallucinations can be used effectively to control pain. In many cases, hypnosis completely eliminates pain, even though the source of the pain—a severe burn or a bone fracture—continues. The failure to perceive something (pain) that would normally be perceived qualifies this response as a negative hallucination. The pain reduction need not be complete in order for hypnosis to be useful in giving relief. Reducing the pain by as little as 20 percent can make the patient's life more tolerable. Experimental studies have shown that the amount of pain reduction is closely related to the degree of measured hypnotizability. Pain reduction through hypnosis is useful in dentistry, obstetrics, and surgery, especially when chemical anesthetics are ill-advised because of the patient's condition.

Theories of Hypnosis

Experts have been arguing about what hypnosis is and how it works since the late 1700s, when Franz Mesmer claimed that it was caused by "animal magnetism." A hundred years later, the French neurologist Charcot suggested that hypnosis is a sign of hysteria and classified it as a neurological disturbance. His views were opposed by Bernheim, a physician who argued that hypnosis is the result of suggestion and insisted that normal people can be hypnotized. Although Bernheim won the argument, hypnosis remained a source of controversy.

Pavlov, famed for his work on conditioned reflexes, believed that hypnosis is a form of sleep, from which, in fact, its name derives. His theory has been largely discredited by physiological studies that show a difference between sleep and hypnosis in the EEG and by demonstrations of alert hypnosis. Nevertheless, the tie between hypnosis and relaxation is still prominent.

A psychoanalytic theory suggests that hypnosis is a state of *partial regression* in which the subject lacks the controls present in normal waking consciousness and therefore acts impulsively and engages in fantasy production. The idea is that hypnosis causes a regression in the thought processes to a more infantile stage; fantasies and hallucinations during hypnosis are indicators of a primitive mode of thought uncensored by higher levels of control.

A theory based on the dramatic nature of many hypnotic behaviors emphasizes a kind of involuntary *role enactment* as a response to social demands. This theory does *not* imply that the subject is playacting in a deliberate attempt to fool the hypnotist; it assumes that the subject becomes so deeply involved in a role that actions take place without conscious intent.

Yet another approach emphasizes the dissociative aspects of hypnosis. *Dissociation* involves a split of consciousness into several streams of thought, each somewhat independent of the others. Hypnosis theoretically induces a dissociative state in the subject so that he or she is not aware of all that is occurring in consciousness. The hypnotist, however, can tap into the various streams of thought. A special version of this theory, called *neodissociation theory*, has proved to be useful in analyzing hypnotic phenomena.

Competing theories of hypnosis were argued more vehemently in the 1960s and 1970s than they are today. With the facts and relationships now better understood, differences between explanations fade in importance. Each theory calls attention to some significant features of hypnosis, and as new data become available, differences are being resolved.

LENGTH: 2,266 WORDS

30 Rita Atkinson, Richard Atkinson, Edward Smith, and Ernest Hilgard
Hypnosis

SCORING: Reading time: _____ Rate from chart: _____ W.P.M.

RETENTION	number right _____ × 2 equals _____ points
MAIN IDEA	number right _____ × 4 equals _____ points
INTERPRETATION	number right _____ × 3 equals _____ points
CONCLUSION	number right _____ × 3 equals _____ points
APPLICATION	number right _____ × 3 equals _____ points
VOCABULARY	number right _____ × 2 equals _____ points

(Total points: 100) **total** _____ points

RETENTION   Based on the selection, which of the following statements are True (T), False (F), or Not answerable (N)?

1. _____ Some people can be trained to hypnotize themselves.

2. _____ People undergoing age regression may include other people in the picture they see of the past.

3. _____ After many years, posthypnotic suggestion wears off.

4. _____ After hypnosis, a subject will be aware that an action he performs may not be rational, but he doesn't worry about that.

5. _____ Hypnosis is a form of sleep.

6. _____ Usually only a person who wants to be hypnotized can be.

7. _____ People are pretty much the same in their responsiveness to hypnosis.

8. _____ Hallucinations are fairly common under hypnosis.

9. _____ Franz Mesmer started a controversy over hypnotism in the late 1700s.

10. _____ After hypnosis, a subject may forget what happened during the hypnotic session.

11. ____ Responsiveness to hypnotism may be at least partially inherited.

12. ____ Negative hallucination cannot be used to control pain, although positive hallucination can be.

13. ____ It is possible that in hypnosis some mental aspects are separated from others.

14. ____ One requirement for inducing a hypnotic trance is that the subject must be relaxed.

15. ____ Hypnotism can affect a subject's motor control.

MAIN IDEA   Which of the following statements best represents the main point of the selection? _____

1. Hypnosis is a state of altered consciousness that is little understood.
2. The hypnotic experience is varied according to the hypnotist and the subject.
3. Scientific investigation of hypnosis has increased our understanding of how it works.
4. Hypnosis has many potential scientific applications that will benefit mankind.
5. There are many scientific theories of hypnosis, all of which cannot be true.

INTERPRETATION   Which of the following is the best interpretation of a key point in this selection? _____

1. Responsiveness to hypnotism is more inherited than learned.
2. People with good memories will remember more of what happened under hypnosis.
3. Hypnosis has been found to be associated with mental disorders.
4. A hypnotized subject is more likely to be passive rather than active in his interactions with the hypnotist.
5. A person in a hypnotic trance is asleep.

CONCLUSION   Which of the following statements is the best conclusion that can be drawn from the selection? _____

1. Research into hypnosis is usually carried on by anthropologists.
2. Hypnosis raises an unusual number of questions for a mind-altered state.
3. Research into hypnosis cannot help us in understanding the workings of the mind, since hypnosis is a mind-altered state.
4. The differing theories of hypnosis are bound to multiply as time goes on.
5. Under hypnosis, a person's perceptions of reality are heightened.

APPLICATION   Choose the best answer for each question.

1. _____ A Hindu fakir who lies on a bed of nails for hours might be:
   a. sprayed with a local anesthetic all over his body.
   b. in a hyperalert hypnotic trance.
   c. hallucinating.
   d. extremely disciplined.

2. _____ An Irish-American who begins to speak Gaelic after hypnosis is probably experiencing:
   a. age regression.
   b. an out-of-the-body experience.
   c. reincarnation.
   d. amnesia.

3. _____ Under the deepest form of hypnosis, a subject may:
   a. respond to posthypnotic suggestion.
   b. remember what his life was like when he was young.
   c. do something that is against his will.
   d. experience a sense of oneness with the universe.

4. _____ If I am running on a treadmill during a hyperalert hypnotic session, I am probably:
   a. not really hypnotized.
   b. responsive to hypnotic suggestions.
   c. not responsive to hypnotic suggestions.
   d. experiencing decreased tension and alertness.

5. _____ A subject who sees a rabbit sitting in the chair where the hypnotist is actually sitting is experiencing:
   a. a negative hallucination.
   b. a positive hallucination.
   c. both a negative and a positive hallucination.
   d. a neutralized hallucination.

6. _____ In comparison to a person who is easily hypnotized, one who is less susceptible will experience:
   a. less pain reduction.
   b. more pain reduction.
   c. the same amount of pain reduction.
   d. no pain reduction at all.

7. _____ A subject will forget what happened under hypnosis:
   a. when a prearranged signal is given.
   b. as a general rule.
   c. after having been instructed to do so.
   d. if she is normally a forgetful person.

8. _____ If I perform an act such as touching my nose after hypnosis, I am most likely:
   a. being rational.
   b. in control of my movements.
   c. experiencing age regression.
   d. responding to some indirect signal.

9. _____ When a group of subjects is used in a hypnotic study, it is most possible that:
   a. half of them will not be able to be hypnotized.
   b. few of them will be able to be hypnotized.
   c. they will divide into two basic groups on the basis of their susceptibility to posthypnotic amnesia.
   d. most of them will forget only a few items on a memorized list.

10. _____ The authors of this article probably do not:
   a. work together on a regular basis.
   b. believe in hypnosis as a scientific phenomenon.
   c. consider themselves experts on the subject of hypnosis.
   d. accept change in hypnotic theory.

VOCABULARY   Choose the best definition for each italic vocabulary entry.

1. _____ once associated with the *bizarre*
   a. strange
   b. hidden
   c. market
   d. magicians

2. _____ accepts some reality *distortion*
   a. therapy
   b. warping
   c. enhancement
   d. control

3. _____ use *authoritarian* commands
   a. intellectual
   b. historical
   c. obedient
   d. dominating

4. _____ most of what *transpired*
   a. breathed
   b. increased
   c. was arranged
   d. took place

5. ＿＿＿ associated with the bizarre and the *occult*
   a. newsworthy
   b. strange
   c. mysterious
   d. dangerous

6. ＿＿＿ support for a hereditary *component*
   a. study
   b. movement
   c. element
   d. idea

7. ＿＿＿ respond to direct suggestion with *involuntary* movement
   a. unresponsive
   b. automatic
   c. swift
   d. awkward

8. ＿＿＿ Subjects will feel a *compulsion.*
   a. uncontrollable urge
   b. fear of
   c. disgust with
   d. suggestion

9. ＿＿＿ Subjects differ widely in their *susceptibility.*
   a. ability to be aroused
   b. ability to be affected
   c. rationality
   d. athletic skill

10. ＿＿＿ hypnotic *virtuosos*
    a. scorers
    b. masters
    c. fools
    d. subjects

11. ＿＿＿ once the *amnesic* subjects are questioned
    a. thoughtful
    b. willing
    c. hypnotized
    d. forgetful

12. ＿＿＿ and therefore acts *impulsively*
    a. forcefully
    b. without thinking
    c. deliberately
    d. with evil intention

13. _____ Subjects differ in their *posthypnotic* suggestibility.
    a. long-distance hypnotizability
    b. natural hypnotizability
    c. a period after hypnosis
    d. duration of the hypnosis

14. _____ Theories were argued more *vehemently*.
    a. quietly
    b. truthfully
    c. hotly
    d. swiftly

15. _____ One approach emphasizes the *dissociative* aspects of hypnosis.
    a. referring to a split in consciousness
    b. separating the hypnotist from the subject
    c. relating one detail to another similar detail
    d. the normal response of the highly amnesic subject

31

PETER ROSE
DONALD FRASER

Banks

Most of us take banks for granted, treating them as institutions that have always been there. But banks are imaginative inventions which took a long, evolutionary period of growth to become the assistants of both economic and political development. Their origin is obscured by the fact that they have been with us so long that people have no idea when they began. Yet, in their modern form, as institutions that safeguard, lend, and move money, they have a more recoverable history. The changing nature of banks and banking is likely to affect us all.

Types of Banks

What is a bank? The name *bank* is used very loosely today to describe a wide variety of institutions. For example, there are so-called *investment banks*, which specialize in underwriting corporate and government securities. These banks purchase securities from the issuer and attempt to resell them in the open market at a reasonable profit. There are *industrial banks*, which accept smaller consumer savings deposits and make certain types of loans, principally cash loans to wage earners. And there are *savings banks*, which draw upon individual and family savings as their principal source of funds and invest those funds mainly in mortgages, corporate bonds, and occasionally common stock.

Complicating the issue of what a bank is are rapid changes now occurring in the financial services industry. Many financial firms, particularly insurance companies, brokerage firms, and mutual funds, are today offering traditional

From *Financial Institutions,* 2nd ed., by Peter Rose and Donald Fraser (Business Publications, Inc., 1985). Reprinted by permission of the publisher.

banking services. These services include liquid savings accounts and transactions accounts (checkable deposits) which can be drafted to make payments. Shares in a money market mutual fund are a well-known example of a recent service innovation by brokerage firms and mutual funds which compete directly with bank savings and transactions accounts. Basically, a bank *is* what a bank *does*, regardless of the name given the institution by its owners or others.

When students in the field of financial institutions use the term *bank* they usually have a specific meaning in mind, however. A bank in the usual and traditional sense is a financial institution offering two major services to the public—(1) transactions accounts, which may be used to make payments for purchases of goods and services and are widely accepted by the public for that purpose; and (2) direct loans to businesses, individuals, and other institutions. The financial institution which comes closest to this definition is the *commercial bank*. Commercial bank checking accounts are the principal means of payment in the economy and are widely accepted as money. While commercial banks do purchase investment securities (such as corporate and government bonds) traded in the open market, their principal asset is *loans* made directly to business firms, individuals and families, securities dealers, and a host of other borrowers.

To be sure, banks offer many other services than just transactions accounts and loans. Commercial banks offer such diverse financial services as time and savings deposits, lease financing, financial advice and counseling, portfolio management, the safekeeping of valuables, transfer of securities, bookkeeping, and the guaranteeing of credit received from other lenders. Indeed, so numerous are the services offered today by commercial banks that these institutions are often called financial department stores. However, the essence of banking— what separates this particular financial institution from all the others—is the making of loans and the selling of transactions (or payments) accounts.

Incidentally, why is the adjective *commercial* used when referring to a bank? As we will see in the next section, when commercial banks got their start, they dealt almost exclusively with business firms, accepting deposits of money and other valuables from local merchants and discounting their commercial notes. Only in the 20th century did the commercial banking industry begin to aggressively compete for consumer accounts. Today, consumers are a principle source of deposits and represent one of the more rapidly growing sources of loans. In fact, commercial banks today are the leading consumer installment lending institution in the United States.

The Origins of Modern Banking

No one knows for sure when the business of banking began. One popular account traces the industry's origins to the shops of medieval goldsmiths. These merchants accepted deposits of gold coins and other valuables for safekeeping and, in many cases, paid interest on those deposits. When a customer made a deposit of gold, a receipt was issued, indicating the amount and kind of metal left in the goldsmith's vault. Soon, gold depositors found it more convenient and safe to pay for goods and services using goldsmith receipts rather than gold itself. Thus the goldsmith's receipts—his promise to pay—began to circulate as money, the forerunner of modern-day checks.

Goldsmiths soon discovered that the deposits left with them were relatively stable—while some customers were always withdrawing their funds from the goldsmith's vault, others were bringing in new deposits. At this point, so the story goes, an enterprising goldsmith discovered that, with stable deposits, he could make loans by issuing more receipts than he had gold reserves in the vault. It was at this point that the goldsmith became a banker because he was literally creating money. The concept of fractional-reserve banking was born.

While this is one appealing account of banking's origins, the history of banking actually goes back even earlier, to the money merchants who frequented the town markets of Asia, Europe, and the Middle East in ancient times. The Assyrians, Babylonians, ancient Greeks, and later the Romans employed money merchants to facilitate trade and commerce. Money merchants provided an essential service—changing one form of money into another—in an age when money consisted largely of metallic coins and every major nation and city-state issued its own coins. If an individual traveled to a large city (such as Alexandria, Athens, Jerusalem, or Rome) and wished to purchase food, clothing, or items for trading, this usually meant converting foreign coin into domestic coin. In some busy markets the business of exchanging coins became a full-time occupation and a few merchants began to specialize in financial services, including not only money changing but also accepting deposits for safekeeping and discounting notes from other merchants. In ancient Rome some money merchants specialized even further as bankers who made loans and bankers who traded foreign coin.

Banking institutions similar to the kind we recognize today first made their appearance in Italy during the Middle Ages and thereafter spread into Western Europe. As in the ancient world, the first European bankers were probably merchants changing one form of money for another as a sideline to their other commercial ventures. Frequently, these merchants would occupy a simple wooden bench in the market square and wait for customers to come by. Some scholars suggest that the term *bank* had its origins in the Italian word *banco*, meaning a bench. Others doubt the authenticity of this account, but it is at least a plausible story. Equally intriguing is the oft-heard suggestion that the foreboding term *bankrupt*—destroying a merchant's bench—came from the same source. Presumably, if one of the early bankers failed to serve his clients honestly and faithfully, he might well have found himself without customers and without any furniture either!

At some point during the Middle Ages the great potential of banks for creating (not just exchanging) money must have been noticed, particularly by beleaguered governments. Indeed, as we will soon note, there has always been a close link between governments and banks, principally because banks exercise such a potent influence on the economy through their credit-granting and money-creating activities. There is historical evidence that a number of Italian cities (most notably Genoa and Venice) set up banks to accept deposits from local merchants, discount commercial notes, and, most importantly for some cities, make credit available for governmental activities (including preparation for war).

Slowly the practice of banking, especially the acceptance of deposits and the making of loans, began to spread from nation to nation. It did not happen overnight. Instead, the industry grew in a slow but steady evolution, reaching Western Europe in its more recognizable modern form about the time of the Industrial Revolution. This is not too surprising, because that revolution brought with it tremendous needs for both short- and long-term venture capital. At the same time a middle-class of consumers and savers began to emerge who, in later years, would supply a major share of bank funds.

Most authorities are agreed that the institutional father of modern banking was the Bank of England, chartered in 1694. This great institution was actually both a merchants' bank, accepting commercial deposits and lending against commercial notes, and an agent of the British government.* Today it plays an extremely important role in the conduct of economic policy in the British Isles, assisting in the management of government debt, control of that nation's money supply, and influencing interest rates through changes in its own discount rate. (In some ways the central bank of the United States—the Federal Reserve System—was modeled after practices followed by the Bank of England.)

Banking in the United States began much as it had in Europe. First, local merchants began offering money changing and safekeeping services as a sideline. Later, some merchants began to specialize in accepting funds for deposit and making loans with those funds. Eventually the colonial governments became involved in establishing banks to promote commerce, expand the supply of credit, and assist in government financing. Just as their predecessors in Europe and the Middle East had been, U.S. banks were initially commercial-oriented, offering credit and deposit services primarily to business firms. But, govern-

---

*Some historians believe that banking in Great Britain began as a historical accident. The story here goes back to mid-17th century, when London merchants kept gold in the Tower of London for safekeeping. Allegedly, King Charles I, in need of more government revenue, began to tap the merchants' gold reserves. While the king only intended to borrow the money for a brief period, wary merchants appointed clerks or overseers to keep track of their deposits. The clerks, however, took a lesson from the king and began loaning the gold deposits out at interest to goldsmiths who turned around and made their own loans at a higher interest rate. In this way the goldsmiths stumbled on a key service of modern banking (especially among the largest, commercially oriented banks)—the brokering of money, borrowing from one individual or institution and lending to another at a profitable spread. Soon, the story goes, the goldsmiths dropped their secret borrowing from gold reserves in the Tower of London and turned to the more pedestrian practice of borrowing directly from the public through deposits that bore interest, promising safe return of the public's funds.

ments, too, had critical financing needs, especially during the American Revolution. The Bank of North America—the first major banking institution in U.S. history—was chartered by the Continental Congress in 1781 in order to financially support the American War for Independence. After the Constitution was ratified by the states in 1789, Congress moved quickly to establish the First Bank of the United States in 1791 to promote a sound money and credit system in the early years of the American Republic. This federally chartered bank issued paper notes, which gave the nation a convenient source of circulating currency, and promoted the growth of private industry in order to reduce the nation's dependence on foreign imports. Later, in 1816, after the First Bank of the United States failed to win renewal of its charter, Congress chartered the Second Bank of the United States, to bring about orderly growth in the nation's supply of money and credit.

Unfortunately, banks have never been among the most politically popular institutions in the United States. Many prominent banking laws in U.S. history owe their origins to a misunderstanding of what banks do and fear of the financial power they seem to possess. This was certainly true of the First and Second Banks of the United States, both of which pursued policies calling for orderly and stable growth of money and credit at a time when the nation saw rapid growth and expansion (especially the development of western territories) as essential for its survival and prosperity. Accordingly, both of these government-sponsored banks failed to win Congressional renewal of their charters. By the 1830s the federal government had ceased to be active in the chartering and regulation of banks, leaving the door open for the states to manage the nation's banking system. And the states made the most of this opportunity by chartering a large number of banking institutions, most of which issued their own paper currency and provided a more ample supply of credit than had been true in the early years of the nation's history. Supported by aggressive bank lending policies, farming and ranching industries grew rapidly as did the manufacture of farm equipment, the railroads, and commercial shipping.

The era of exclusive state control over U.S. banking affairs ended with the Civil War, however. Many of the states failed to regulate the issue of paper bank notes carefully enough and neglected to actively supervise banking industry practices. In some areas, anyone with money or influence could secure a charter for a new bank, even if they possessed little or no experience at running a bank. Thousands of different bank notes appeared, many of which declined rapidly in value, making exchange difficult. Public outcry for reform, coupled with severe pressures on Congress to raise sufficient funds to finance the Civil War, brought the federal government back into the picture as an active regulator of the nation's banking system. In 1863 Congress passed the National Banking Act and initiated further amendments in that law a year later.

The National Banking Acts of 1863 and 1864 were landmark pieces of legislation which have continued to shape the character of American banking down to the present day. The acts created a new type of bank—federally chartered associations, known today as national banks—whose authority to operate came from a new federal office, the Comptroller of the Currency. The new national banks were required to pledge significant amounts of owners' (equity) capital to begin operations, to submit regular financial reports, and to undergo examination by members of the Comptroller's staff at least once each year. Determined to force as many of the state-chartered banks as possible into this new federal system, Congress levied a stiff tax against any notes issued by state banks, eliminating much of the profit from making loans. In turn, the new national banks could issue their own paper notes free of tax, provided they pledged U.S. government securities to back them up. The new federal bank notes were uniform in appearance and, with federal IOUs securing them, grew rapidly in popularity as a safe and convenient money medium. Moreover, the requirement that national banks buy government bonds to back bank notes gave the federal government an ample supply of funds to finance the Civil War.

For a time the federal bank note tax had the desired effect as scores of banks surrendered their state charters and became national banks. It looked as if the role of the states in regulating and supervising the nation's banking system might become a relic of history. However, the states came back into the picture during the latter part of the 19th century as deposit banking became increasingly popular with the average citizen. People were now more willing to accept and use deposits in a bank account as money instead of relying exclusively on bank notes. Checks became increasingly accepted as a medium of exchange. This made it possible for state-chartered banks to make loans, thereby creating deposits, without issuing taxable notes. The number of state-chartered banks grew rapidly again and eventually eclipsed the number of national banks.

This dramatic recovery of the state banking system has left us with an important legacy today—a dual banking system. Federal authorities (most notably the Comptroller of the Currency) have the primary responsibility for regulating and supervising national banks, while state authorities (usually in the form of state banking commissions) have primary responsibility for regulating and supervising state-chartered banking institutions. Yet, both federal and state authorities have overlapping powers and responsibilities. A system of checks and balances seems to prevail today in which each unit of government—state and federal—possesses important powers which limit the decisions and actions of the other.

For example, the states may charter new banks at will, but no bank is likely to open its doors today without deposit insurance from the Federal Deposit Insurance Corporation in Washington, D.C., thus giving that federal agency an important measure of influence over the growth of state-chartered banks. Similarly, the states are empowered to set limits over the establishment of branch offices and the creation and growth of bank holding companies within their borders. While this particular state authority is being challenged today at the federal level, it is currently an immensely powerful tool in the hands of state banking authorities (and, therefore, the state legislatures) in shaping the size and structure of the nation's banking system.

LENGTH: 2,754 WORDS

31 Peter Rose and Donald Fraser
Banks

SCORING: Reading time: _____ Rate from chart: _____ W.P.M.

RETENTION	number right ____ × 2 equals ____ points	
MAIN IDEA	number right ____ × 4 equals ____ points	
INTERPRETATION	number right ____ × 3 equals ____ points	
CONCLUSION	number right ____ × 3 equals ____ points	
APPLICATION	number right ____ × 3 equals ____ points	
VOCABULARY	number right ____ × 2 equals ____ points	

(Total points: 100) **total** ____ points

RETENTION   Based on the selection, which of the following statements are True (T), False (F), or Not answerable (N)?

1. _____ The Civil War saw the end of exclusive state control over banking.

2. _____ Most authorities agree that the Bank of America is the institutional father of modern banking.

3. _____ Banks have usually been politically popular institutions in the United States.

4. _____ The Federal Reserve System is the central bank of the United States.

5. _____ The National Banking Acts of 1863 and 1864 have only recently ended their period of shaping banking practices.

6. _____ After the Civil War the various new national banks issued banknotes which were the same in appearance.

7. _____ The first important U.S. bank was established to help finance the American Revolution.

8. _____ Today the states have essentially no power over U.S. banking and its practices.

9. _____ It would be unlikely for a bank to open today unless its deposits were protected by federal insurance.

10. _____ The forerunner of modern checks seems to be the goldsmith's receipts.

11. _____ Savings banks are today's leading consumer installment lenders.

12. _____ Banking and bankruptcy developed simultaneously.

13. _____ Italy seems to have produced the earliest institutions that resemble what we think of as banks today.

14. _____ Commercial bank checking accounts are the principal means of payment in today's economy.

15. _____ Commercial bonds are the principal assets of commercial banks.

MAIN IDEA   Which of the following statements best represents the main point of the selection? _____

1. A bank is so diverse it must be thought of as a financial department store.
2. Banking is the brainchild of convenience.
3. A bank is what it does, regardless of the name of the institution.
4. Without governments, we would not have banks, and we would not need them.
5. Banking is shaped and reshaped according to the needs of commerce and government.

INTERPRETATION   Which of the following is the best interpretation of a key point in this selection? _____

1. Early banks in the U.S. were entirely the brainchildren of the government and its needs.
2. The first two Banks of the United States did not respond to the credit needs of a rapidly expanding economy.
3. The first two Banks of the United States were not rechartered because the government did not want them to grow too strong.
4. State banks replaced the first two Banks of the United States because they did not trust the dominance of federal power.
5. The failure of the first two Banks of the United States demonstrated that the federal government simply did not understand banking.

CONCLUSION   Which of the following statements is the best conclusion that can be drawn from the selection? _____

1. The current system of checks and balances between state and federal banks suggests that our dual banking system will serve our needs for some time.
2. Other nations would do well to emulate our dual banking system, since it has been the key element in fostering the kind of economic growth we currently prize.

3. The dual banking system of the U.S. is one of the thorns in the side of the noncapitalist nations, since it should fail theoretically, but obviously works remarkably well.
4. The dual banking system is an accident that not only surprised its creators, but taught them something about the fundamentals of banking.
5. The dual banking system was inherent in the founding of our republic, but it did not really flourish until the pressure of war.

APPLICATION   Choose the best answer for each question.

1. _____ The essence of banking is:
    a. loaning money and paying accounts.
    b. making securities available to government.
    c. underwriting securities of corporations.
    d. keeping accounts and securing personal wealth.

2. _____ A transactions account is essentially equivalent to:
    a. a bond transfer.
    b. accepting unsecured loans.
    c. a checking account.
    d. a direct loan.

3. _____ When states exclusively controlled the banks:
    a. business was brisk.
    b. anyone with money and influence could become a banker.
    c. farmers were the dominant group that used their services.
    d. the federal government suffered.

4. _____ The federal government financed the Civil War through having national banks:
    a. buy war bonds.
    b. back their bank notes with purchases of government bonds.
    c. face the choice of supplying unlimited loans or go out of business.
    d. force the state banks out of business.

5. _____ The Industrial Revolution shaped the institution of banking into a recognizable modern form through:
    a. the incredible increase in the size of companies and their assets.
    b. a kind of sharing of excitement, intensity, and the growth of business.
    c. the interrelationship of the bankers and the boards of directors of the new industrial giants.
    d. a sudden increase in the demand for venture capital to underwrite industrial expansion.

6. _____ In America as in Europe, banking developed out of a merchant's:
   a. sideline.
   b. surplus.
   c. indignation.
   d. personal grief.

7. _____ When the early goldsmiths began issuing more receipts than they had actual gold, they began creating:
   a. growth.
   b. money.
   c. the economy.
   d. good faith.

8. _____ Fractional-reserve banking is based on:
   a. holding more gold than there are receipts for.
   b. receiving more gold than there are receipts for.
   c. issuing more receipts than there is gold for.
   d. maintaining an equal balance of gold and receipts.

9. _____ States have the power to limit the creation of bank holding companies within their borders, although:
   a. there are currently no bank holding companies in any state.
   b. state influence extends only to individual banks over a certain size.
   c. there is currently a legal struggle with the federal government about that.
   d. states are currently anxious to help develop more bank holding companies at that level.

10. _____ Defining what a bank is has been complicated by:
   a. knowing what a bank does.
   b. the rapid changes occurring in the entire industry of banking.
   c. the interaction of state and federal influences on the nature of banking.
   d. a failure to understand banking's Asian, Middle Eastern, and European origins.

VOCABULARY   Choose the best definition for each italic vocabulary entry.

1. _____ banks which specialize in *underwriting* corporate securities
   a. agreeing to buy
   b. insuring
   c. establishing
   d. furnishing

2. _____ These services include *liquid* savings accounts.
   a. wet
   b. readily available
   c. fluent
   d. piddling

3. _____ accounts that can be *drafted* to make payments
   a. taken, but only on credit
   b. assumed to be completely secure
   c. written on, as a check
   d. forced

4. _____ Money market mutual funds are a service *innovation* in banking.
   a. specialty
   b. something new
   c. product
   d. implication

5. _____ The industry began to *aggressively* compete for business.
   a. vigorously
   b. ruthlessly
   c. forcefully
   d. brutally

6. _____ Romans used money merchants to *facilitate* trade with others.
   a. ease
   b. stifle
   c. pretend to
   d. boost

7. _____ Merchants *discounted* notes from other merchants.
   a. purchased
   b. denied the value of
   c. purchased for under face value
   d. coordinated their notes with

8. _____ The power of banks was discovered by *beleaguered* governments.
   a. threatened
   b. recently banded together
   c. unstable
   d. imaginative

9. _____ European banks did what their *predecessors* in the Middle East did.
   a. competitors
   b. tutors
   c. forerunners
   d. mentors

10. _____ when the Constitution was *ratified* by the states
    a. drafted
    b. approved
    c. finalized
    d. conceived

11. _____ The national banking laws were *landmark* acts of legislation.
    a. fundamental
    b. noticeable
    c. topographic
    d. unusual

12. _____ Federal notes became a safe and popular money *medium*.
    a. compromise
    b. instrument
    c. shape
    d. choice

13. _____ That guarantee gave the government *ample* funds for war.
    a. just enough
    b. more than enough
    c. sufficient
    d. an array of

14. _____ It looked as if their role in supervising banks would become a *relic* of history.
    a. ruin
    b. recollection
    c. mere memory
    d. hint

15. _____ The bank system has left us an important *legacy* today.
    a. structure
    b. model
    c. gift
    d. inheritance

32

HORST DE LA CROIX
RICHARD G. TANSEY

Cave Art

The authors of this leading text in the
history of art offer us a glimpse into the
background of the prehistoric European cave
paintings. They date back to 15,000 B.C. and
are spread over a wide area in France and
Spain, where natural limestone formations
encourage the kinds of caves which these
mysterious people may have used for religious ceremonies and worship. The mystery
of the caves may never be solved, but we are
beginning to grasp some of the essentials.

What Genesis is to the biblical account of the fall and redemption of
man, early cave art is to the history of his intelligence, imagination, and creative
power. In the caves of southern France and of northern Spain, discovered only
about a century ago and still being explored, we may witness the birth of that
characteristically human capability that has made man master of his environment—the making of images and symbols. By this original and tremendous feat
of abstraction upper Paleolithic men were able to fix the world of their experience, rendering the continuous processes of life in discrete and unmoving shapes
that had identity and meaning as the living animals that were their prey. Like
Adam, Paleolithic man gathered and named the animals, and the faculty of
imagination came into being along with the concepts of identity and meaning.

In that remote time during the last advance and retreat of the great glaciers
man made the critical breakthrough and became wholly human. Our intellectual and imaginative processes function through the recognition and construction of images and symbols; we see and understand the world pretty much as we
are taught to by the representations of it familiar to our time and place. The
immense achievement of Stone Age man, the invention of representation, cannot
be exaggerated.

The Later Old Stone Age
(Upper Paleolithic)

The physical environment of the cave peoples during the long thousands of years would not, one imagines, be favorable to the creation of an art of quality and sophistication since survival alone would seem to have required most of their energies. Though the Aurignacian period began between the early and main advances of the last glaciers and for a while was temperate, it grew cold toward its end. The great ice sheet advanced south from Scandinavia over the plains of north central Europe, and glaciers spread down from the Alps and other mountain ranges to produce a tundra and forest-tundra climate. With the end of the Magdalenian period began the final recession of the ice and the onset of temperate weather. In the cold periods, man, the hunter and food-gatherer, took refuge in caves, and it was here that Cro-Magnon man, who first appeared during the Aurignacian period, replacing Neanderthal man, took the remarkable turn that made him not simply a fabricator of stone tools, but an artist.

Cave Art

The first example of cave art was discovered—by amateurs and by accident—in 1879 near Santander in northern Spain. Marcelino de Sautuola, a local resident interested in the antiquity of man, was exploring the Altamira Caves on his estate, in which he had already found specimens of flint and carved bone. With him was his little daughter. Since the ceiling of the debris-filled cavern was only a few inches above the father's head, it was the child who was first able to discern, from her lower vantage point, the shadowy forms of painted beasts on the cave roof. De Sautuola was the first modern man to explore this cave and he was certain that these paintings dated back to prehistoric times. Archeologists, however, were highly dubious of their authenticity, and at the Lisbon Congress on Prehistoric Archeology in 1880 the Altamira paintings were officially dismissed as forgeries. But in 1896, at Pair-non-Pair in the Gironde district of France, paintings were discovered partially covered by calcareous deposits that would have taken thousands of years to accumulate; these paintings were the first to be recognized as authentic by experts. The conviction grew that these remarkable works were of an antiquity far greater than man had ever dreamed. In 1901 Abbé Breuil, dean of archeologists of the prehistoric, discovered and verified the cave art of Font-de-Gaume in Dordogne, France. The skeptics were finally convinced.

The caves at Lascaux, near Montignac, also in the Dordogne region of France, were discovered accidentally in 1940 by two young boys who were playing in a field. Their dog, following a ball, disappeared into a hole, and the boys, hearing barking from below, followed the animal down into the caves. Their lighted matches revealed magnificent drawings of animals, now generally regarded as the most outstanding of all known prehistoric art.

While these paintings survived more than 15,000 years in the sealed and dry subterranean chambers, many have deteriorated rapidly since the caves were opened to the public in recent decades. At Lascaux, for example, it was found that moisture and carbon dioxide exhaled by hordes of visitors settled on the walls and encouraged the growth of fungi destructive to the paintings. To avoid further damage, the cave has been closed to the public.

The Lascaux caverns, like the others, had been subterranean water channels, a few hundred to some four thousand feet long. They are often choked, sometimes almost impassably, by faults or by deposits such as stalactites and stalagmites. Far inside these caverns, well removed from the cave mouths that he chose for habitation, the hunter-artist engraved and painted on the walls pictures of animals—mammoth, bison, reindeer, horse, boar, wolf. For light he must have used tiny stone lamps filled with marrow or fat, with a wick, perhaps of moss. For drawing he used chunks of red and yellow ocher, and for painting he ground these same ochers into powder that he blew onto the walls or mixed with some medium, perhaps animal fat, before applying. A large flat bone may have served him as a palette; he could make brushes from reeds or bristles; he could use a blowpipe of reeds to trace outlines of figures and to put pigments on out-of-reach surfaces; and he had stone scrapers for smoothing the wall and sharp flint points for engraving. Such were the artist's tools. Rudimentary as they were, they were sufficient to produce the art that astonishes us today.

The artist's approach to the figures, as seen at Lascaux and at other sites, is naturalistic; he attempts to represent as convincing a pose and action as possible. Each painting reflects the keen observation and extraordinary memory of the hunter-artist, whose accuracy in capturing fleeting poses is hardly surpassed by today's camera. Yet this observation was selective, the artist seeing and recording only those aspects essential in interpreting the appearance and the character of the animal—its grace or awkwardness, its cunning, dignity, or ferocity. It is almost as if the artist were constructing a pictorial definition of the animal, capturing its very essence.

Any modern interpretation of this cave art must, of course, remain pure speculation. Properties common to all these paintings, however, provide researchers with some fairly definite clues to what they meant to their creators. For instance, the fact that the paintings are never found in those parts of the caves that were inhabited or near daylight rules out any purely decorative purpose. At Font-de-Gaume the first paintings were encountered about seventy yards behind the cave mouth, and in the cave at Niaux the painted animals in the "Salon Noir" are found some 850 tortuous yards from the entrance. The remoteness and difficulty of access of many of these sites and the fact that they appear to have been used for centuries strongly suggest that the prehistoric hunter attributed magical properties to them. And so the paintings themselves most likely had magical meaning to their creators. As Abbé Breuil has suggested, "by confining the animal within the limits of a painting, one subjected it to one's power in the hunting grounds." And, within this context, the artist's aim to be realistic may be explained by his probable conviction that the painting's magical power was directly related to its lifelikeness.

The naturalistic pictures of animals are often accompanied by geometric signs, some of which seem to represent man-made structures, or *tectiforms*, while others consist of checkers, dots, squares, or other arrangements of lines. Several observers have seen a primitive form of writing in these representations of nonliving things, but more likely they, too, had only magical significance. The ones that look like traps or snares, for example, may have been drawn to ensure success in hunting with these devices. In many places there appear representations of human hands, most of them "negative," where the hunter placed his hand against the wall and then painted or blew pigment around it. Occasionally he would dip his hand in paint and then press it against the wall, leaving a "positive" imprint. These, too, may have had magical significance, or may simply have been the "signatures" left by whole generations of visitors to these sacred places, much as the modern tourist leaves some memento of his presence.

The figures are in themselves marvelous approximations of optical fact, but their arrangement upon the cave walls shows little concern for any consistency of placement in relationship to each other or to the wall space, though this has been claimed. Certainly we find no compositional adjustment to suggest the perspective effect and no notion of separation and enframement. Figures, far from being proportionally related, are often superimposed at random and are of quite different sizes. Generations of artists, working in the same sanctuaries, covered and recovered the crowded walls, though often pains seem to have been taken not to break through the outlines of an earlier figure. It seems that attention to a single figure, the rendering of a single image, in itself fulfilled the purpose of the artist.

The hunter-artist made frequent and skillful use of the naturally irregular surfaces of the walls, of their projections, recessions, fissures, and ridges, to help give the illusion of real presence to his forms. A swelling outward of the wall could be used within the outline of a charging bison to suggest the bulging volume of the beast's body. The spotted horse at Pech-Merle may have been inspired by a rock formation that resembles a horse's head and neck, although the artist's eventual version of the head is much smaller than the formation and highly abstract. Natural forms like those of foliage or clouds, the profile of a mountain, or the shapes of eroded earth and rock can represent for any of us—sometimes quite startlingly—the features of men, animals, or objects. Thus man's first representations may have followed some primal experience of resemblance between a chance configuration of cave wall and the animal he had just been hunting. This might have had for him the effect of an awesome apparition of the very animal, a miraculous and magical reappearance of its vanished life. With the impulse to give the apparition even more presence he could have "finished" the form by cutting an outline around the relief and continuing it until a silhouette more or less complete and familiar had emerged. The addition of color would enhance the reality of the image.

The Magical Function

We have evidence that the hunters in the caves, perhaps in a frenzy stimulated by magical rites and dances, treated the painted animals as if they were alive. Not only was the quarry painted as pierced by arrows, as in the *Chinese Horse* at Lascaux, but hunters may have thrown spears at the images—as sharp gouges in the side of the bison at Niaux suggest—predestinating and magically commanding the death of the animals. This practice would be analogous to that kind of magic, still cultivated in parts of the world today, that has as a basis the belief that harm can be done to an enemy by abusing an image of him.

This art produced in dark caverns deep in the earth must have had, as most scholars are now convinced, some profound magical functions. Familiar in religious architecture, which had its beginning thousands of years after the era of the caves, are the cavelike spaces of the sanctuary where the most sacred and hidden mysteries are kept and where the god dwells in silence. The sacred has meant the mysterious, and this means in many cases a place of darkness, lit only by fitful light, where, at the culmination of rituals, absolute silence reigns. These features of the sacred environment were already present in the "architecture" of the caves, and the central theme has never been lost despite its myriad variations.

It is significant that the miracle of abstraction—the creation of image and symbol—should have taken place in just such secret and magical caverns. For abstraction is representation, a human device of fundamental power, by which not only art but ultimately science comes into existence, and both art and science are methods for the control of human experience and the mastery of the environment. And that too was the end purpose of the hunter-magician—to control the world of the beasts he hunted. The making of the image was, by itself, a form of magic; by painting an animal, the hunter fixed and controlled its soul within the prison of an outline, and from this initial magic all the rest must follow. Rites before the paintings may have served to improve the hunter's luck. At the same time, prehistoric man must have been anxious to preserve his food supply, and the many representations of pregnant animals suggest that these cavalcades of painted beasts may also have served magically to assure the survival of the actual herds.

The Representation of Man

The figure of man is almost completely excluded from representation among the vivid troops of painted animals. There are at least two notable exceptions. A very puzzling picture at Lascaux shows a stick-figure man, falling or fallen, before a huge bison that has been disemboweled, probably by the rhinoceros at the left, which slouches away from the scene. The two animals are rendered with all that skilled attention to animal detail we are accustomed to in cave art; the rhinoceros heavy and lumbering, the buffalo tense and bristling with rage, its bowels hanging from it in a heavy coil. But the birdfaced (masked?) man is rendered with the crude and clumsy touch of the unskilled at any time or place. His position is ambiguous. Is he dead or in an ecstatic trance? The meaning of the bird on the staff and of the spear and throw stick is no more obvious. We shall not add here to the already abundant speculation on the meaning of this picture. More important is the question, Why the difference in treatment of the man and the animal figures? Does man in this dawn of magic distinguish himself so much from the beast that he can find no image suitable to self-depiction? Or is he afraid to cast a spell on himself, as he casts it upon the animals, by rendering his image visible?

At Trois Frères in the Pyrenees there is a very strange humanoid creature, masked and wearing the antlers of a reindeer—the so-called *Sorcerer*. Is this the memory sketch of a shaman or witch-doctor? If so, one can imagine how the fearsome composite apparition—the paws of a bear, tail of a wolf, beard of a man, corporal parts of a lion—could have struck terror into the heart of its audience. The chamber in which the figure appears is crowded with beasts, and Breuil has suggested that the figure may be their god, who has descended into the witch-doctor and filled him with his bestial power. It has also been suggested that this is only a hunter camouflaged to stalk deer, but it would again appear that, for Paleolithic man, mankind simply is not to be counted among the animals; at least his figure must be so disguised—perhaps to avoid magical self-involvement—as to be unrecognizable as a man.

Quality

In explaining the great accomplishment of Stone Age man—who pictured the world in order to magically control it—we must not forget that his art is *art*. It is not simply that he made images but that he made them skillfully and beautifully. Ancient and modern art have produced, along with masterpieces, images that are dull, prosaic, and of indifferent quality. The art of the caves is of an extraordinary level of quality. The splendid horse in the Axial Gallery at Lascaux has been called the *Chinese Horse* because its style strangely resembles that of Chinese painting of the best period. Not only do the outlines have the elastic strength and fluency that we find in Chinese calligraphy and brushwork, but the tone is so managed as to suggest both the turning under of the belly of the pregnant animal and the change of the color of the coat. At Font-de-Gaume there is a painted reindeer executed with deft elegance in the contours and remarkable subtlety in the modeling tones. The grace of the antlers is effortlessly translated into an upward-sweeping line that renders the natural shapes with both strength and delicacy. Breuil, while copying the originals, discerned some highly sophisticated pictorial devices that one expects to find only in the art of far later times; for example, the darkening of the forward contour of the left hind leg so as to bring it nearer to the observer than the right leg.

The pictures of cattle at Lascaux and elsewhere show a convention of representation of the horns that has been called *twisted perspective*, since we see the heads in profile but the horns from a different angle. Thus, the approach of the artist is not strictly or consistently optical—that is, organized from a fixed-viewpoint perspective. Rather, the approach is descriptive of the fact that cattle have two horns. Two horns would be part of the concepts "cow" and "bull." In strict optical-perspective profile only one horn would be visible, but to paint the animal in such a way would, as it were, amount to an incomplete definition of it. And for the cave artist this would have been a defective image, without magic.

LENGTH: 2,980 WORDS

32 Horst de la Croix and Richard G. Tansey
Cave Art

SCORING: Reading time: _____ Rate from chart: _____ W.P.M.

RETENTION	number right _____ × 2 equals _____ points		
MAIN IDEA	number right _____ × 4 equals _____ points		
INTERPRETATION	number right _____ × 3 equals _____ points		
CONCLUSION	number right _____ × 3 equals _____ points		
APPLICATION	number right _____ × 3 equals _____ points		
VOCABULARY	number right _____ × 2 equals _____ points		

(Total points: 100) **total** _____ points

RETENTION   Based on the selection, which of the following statements are True (T), False (F), or Not answerable (N)?

1. _____ Survival rather than art would have seemed the priority at the time the cave paintings were made.

2. _____ The Abbé Breuil copied some originals and detected their unusually advanced artistic techniques.

3. _____ The representation of animals seems aimed at capturing their essence.

4. _____ Most of the great paintings are nearest to the entrances of the caves.

5. _____ The geometric forms on the cave walls are all related to specific objects, such as snares.

6. _____ The animals are portrayed in a symbolic manner, rather than being simply realistic.

7. _____ Oddly, the artists ignored the underlying bumps and mounds on the walls' surfaces when painting the animals.

8. _____ The so-called Sorcerer may be a witch doctor or a god.

9. _____ The aim of the paintings may have been to assure the survival of the people, but certainly not the survival of the herds.

10. ____ Apparently the images were so sacred that no prehistoric person would touch or deface them.

11. ____ The first examples of cave art were discovered by accident in 1492.

12. ____ The first cave art verified as authentically ancient was discovered in 1901 by Abbé Breuil.

13. ____ Modern tourists were denied admission to the caves because they were defacing them with their initials and with new paint.

14. ____ The cave artists did their work by the light of day.

15. ____ Symbols and images are what help humans master their environment.

MAIN IDEA Which of the following statements best represents the main point of the selection? ____

1. The changeover from Neanderthal to Cro-Magnon signaled the beginning of a new world.
2. Magic is a force that is very close to religion.
3. The cave paintings are worth a trip, despite their inaccessibility.
4. The cave painters represent the genesis of human intelligence and artistic sensibility.
5. There is no chance that these paintings could be forgeries, although that was one of the chief worries of their discoverers.

INTERPRETATION Which of the following is the best interpretation of a key point in this selection? ____

1. Without the power of higher-level abstraction, we might still be making paintings on cave walls.
2. The power of abstraction is essential for higher-level human thought.
3. Science depends on the power of abstraction, but ignores the artistic implications of naturalistic drawing.
4. Until they developed the power of abstraction, people were really feeling around in the dark, afraid.
5. The natural, childlike delight in abstraction seems to be present as much in these caves as in a modern nursery.

CONCLUSION Which of the following statements is the best conclusion that can be drawn from the selection? ____

1. The art produced in the caves is an antidote to magic.
2. Magic seems to be one of the strongest motivations for the cave paintings.

3. Religion is essentially the same thing as magic, as we can see from the cave paintings.
4. The cave paintings are like modern nature illustrations: they are designed for the closer study of species of animals.
5. Hunting magic of this type exists to this day.

APPLICATION   Choose the best answer for each question.

1. _____ The representations we see of people, animals, and things:
   a. are what excite us to art.
   b. essentially control the way we understand the world.
   c. are identical to those of the cave painters.
   d. have not changed since the great glacial period of the caves.

2. _____ If the glaciers spread down to north central Europe to create a forest-tundra climate, then a tundra must be:
   a. cold, barren, but able to sustain life.
   b. cloudy.
   c. rocky, hilly, and rolling country.
   d. a permanent winter causing people to live indoors.

3. _____ Neanderthal man was replaced by Cro-Magnon man, who was:
   a. possessed of a larger cranium and greater intelligence.
   b. unable to fabricate tools until well into the Aurignacian period.
   c. a born tool maker.
   d. not just a tool maker, but an artist.

4. _____ The hunter-artists painted their scenes deep in the caves, but:
   a. usually decorated the entrances with magic symbols.
   b. sometimes lived in the entrances.
   c. never painted anything outside the caves.
   d. were surprised when the animals were lured into their caverns.

5. _____ Although absolute interpretation of the cave paintings is impossible, some things can be deduced because:
   a. many paintings have the same properties in common.
   b. so many things today are exactly as they were then.
   c. human impulses are so similar that human nature helps us know.
   d. what we sense to be appropriate is probably close to what was appropriate for these people.

6. _____ One thing that suggests the paintings may have magical qualities is:
   a. the fact that they were used constantly for centuries.
   b. implied in the beauty and realism of the works.
   c. suggested by the fact that we use similar symbols today.
   d. part of the power of abstraction and imagination.

7. _____ The great efforts to make the paintings realistic are probably connected to:
   a. the artist's sense of duty.
   b. the demands of the current styles.
   c. a fear that if the images were stylized, no one would know them.
   d. a sense that realism produced greater magic.

8. _____ If the animals were painted from a fixed-viewpoint perspective:
   a. sometimes the image would not reveal all the important details.
   b. the caves would have had to be vastly larger than they are, and there would have been fewer representations.
   c. the artists would have had to have the skills of a modern painter.
   d. possibly the magical powers would have been absent from the painting.

9. _____ The authors think the caverns may have had magical, religious significances because:
   a. we still are afraid of dark, damp places.
   b. cellars were the first places of worship in the Western world.
   c. the sacred parts of churches have often been dark and secret.
   d. sacred caves are still found among ancient peoples in Europe.

10. _____ There are no highly realistic representations of people in the caves apparently because:
   a. they didn't hunt people.
   b. the human form was too complex for these artists.
   c. they may have feared that the representation of a human would have cast a spell on that person.
   d. everyone knew what people looked like; they needed to know what their most important prey looked like.

VOCABULARY   Choose the best definition for each italic vocabulary entry.

1. _____ rendering the continuous processes of life in *discrete* and unmoving shapes
   a. distinct
   b. exceptional
   c. separate
   d. thoughtful

2. _____ With the end of the Magdalenian period came the final *recession* of the ice.
   a. achievement
   b. depression
   c. arrival
   d. withdrawal

3. _____ The caves would not have seemed favorable to an art of quality and *sophistication*.
    a. self-awareness
    b. maturity
    c. beauty
    d. knowledgeableness

4. _____ In the cold periods man took *refuge* in the caves.
    a. periods of hibernation
    b. safe conduct
    c. to hiding
    d. shelter

5. _____ The child was first able to *discern* the shapes from her lower vantage point.
    a. notice
    b. make out
    c. have
    d. discuss

6. _____ the inner chambers well removed from the cave mouths that he used for *habitation*
    a. cooking
    b. living
    c. instruction
    d. fabrication

7. _____ *Rudimentary* as they were, the tools were sufficient to produce great art.
    a. simple
    b. ungainly
    c. unlikely
    d. wieldy

8. _____ The prehistoric hunter may have *attributed* magical powers to them.
    a. suggested
    b. associated
    c. assigned
    d. interpreted

9. _____ Far from being proportionately correct, figures are often *superimposed* at random.
    a. placed one on top of another
    b. designed as part of the composition
    c. assumed to be correct
    d. placed

10. _____ This would have the effect of an awesome *apparition* of the animal.
   a. ghostly appearance
   b. representation
   c. foreshadowing
   d. presentiment

11. _____ The addition of color would *enhance* the reality of the image.
   a. vivify
   b. heighten
   c. abet
   d. approximate

12. _____ This practice would be *analogous* to modern magic.
   a. like
   b. different from
   c. stimulating
   d. supportive

13. _____ It has one theme with *myriad* variations.
   a. more than one
   b. impressive
   c. notable
   d. innumerable

14. _____ *Paleolithic* man is not to be counted among the animals.
   a. human
   b. glacially experienced
   c. hunter-artist
   d. of the old Stone Age

15. _____ There is a reindeer executed with *deft* elegance.
   a. uncanny
   b. amazing
   c. startling
   d. skilled

33

OSCAR G. BROCKETT

The Origins of
the Theatre

It is easy for us to take theatre for granted.
It is all about us, on the stage, on the movie
screen, on television. Naturally, its beginnings
are wrapped in the darkness of prehistory,
but in recent years anthropologists have
made some strides to help the historian
of drama understand its origins. We are
proceeding tentatively; however, if
contemporary theories are generally accurate,
then it is clear that theatre is tied in with
ritual ceremonies connected with early
religious practices.

The basic elements of theatre and drama are found in every society
no matter how primitive or advanced. They may be seen in the dances and
ceremonies of primitive peoples, just as they can be found today in such diverse
activities as religious services, political campaigns, parades, sports, and children's make-believe. But most of these activities are not intentionally theatrical,
even though they may use such theatrical elements as spectacle, dialogue, or
conflict. Thus, it is essential to distinguish between *the theatrical in daily life* and
the theatre as a form of art. It would be impossible to construct a coherent
history of all the theatrical elements found in mankind's diverse activities
through the ages. This discussion, consequently, will be concerned with the
theatre as an institution; its origins, and its subsequent development.

In exploring the beginnings of the theatre, it has been customary to use
evidence drawn from primitive societies. Anthropologists of the late 19th and
early 20th centuries argued that all cultures go through similar patterns of
development, and consequently that a study of primitive groups which still exist
can supply valuable clues to the origin of drama 2500 years ago. As a result most

accounts of the beginnings of theatre and drama are based upon studies of modern primitive societies, although more recent anthropologists have seriously questioned this procedure.

The pattern of development which has been deduced from the study of primitive groups can only be summarized here. In the beginning, man gradually becomes aware of forces which appear to control his food supply and the other determinants of his existence. Having no understanding of natural causes, he attributes occurrences to supernatural forces and assigns human motivations, such as anger and jealousy, to them. Next, he begins to search for means by which he may win the favor of these powers. Over a period of time, he perceives a supposed connection between certain of his attempts and the desired ends. These acts are then refined and formalized into a ritual. At this early stage, rites are usually performed by the entire tribe, while the "audience" is the supernatural force.

Once a ritual is clearly established, the demand soon arises that it always be performed precisely and without deviation. A failure to achieve success in battle, hunt, or harvest is often attributed to the displeasure of the god because of some mistake made in the performance of the ritual. Since all members of the tribe cannot perform the ceremony properly, the most effective are chosen as representatives of the entire group. The rest now participate only at second hand. Thus, the tribe is divided into "actors" and "audience."

By this time stories or myths—which explain, illustrate, or idealize the rites—have usually appeared. Often they draw on real events or persons, although these may be considerably transformed in the stories. Frequently the myths include as characters those supernatural forces which the rites celebrate or hope to influence. Performers may then come to impersonate the mythical characters in the enactment of rituals or in accompanying celebrations.

As a tribe becomes more sophisticated, its conceptions of supernatural forces and of causal relationships change. As a result, some rites are abandoned or modified. The myths which have grown up around the rites may be retained, however, as a part of the tribe's oral tradition. At some later time, stories based on these myths may be acted out as a kind of primitive drama divorced from all ceremonial concerns. When this occurs, the first step has been taken toward the theatre as a specialized activity.

Many tribes never take this decisive step. In most primitive cultures performances remain parts of rituals and thus are utilitarian, being intended to bring about some practical goal. To primitive man, the crucial problem is to survive in a world which he understands only dimly, and which often appears hostile. Thus, when he wears a disguise and impersonates a god, it is not, as a rule, for the sake of giving pleasure but rather of gaining some material reward, such as an adequate supply of food or success in war. His rituals are as "scientific" as his knowledge permits, and probably seem no more theatrical to him than the use of fertilizers or contour farming do to us.

In those societies which have developed drama, the precise evolutionary stages are still obscure. One sign of the change can be seen in the introduction of comedy, which was late in appearing in ritual drama. Comedy requires a greater degree of objectivity than does serious drama, for it depends upon the ability to see deviations from norms as ridiculous rather than as serious threats to the welfare of the whole tribe. Other probable sources of an independent theatre can be found in those dances which are primarily rhythmical and gymnastic, and in imitations of animal movements and sounds, both of which, completely divorced from any utilitarian functions, are to be found among many primitive tribes. In these cases, it is the virtuosity and grace of the performers which are admired.

A very few primitive tribes—in Australia, the Philippines, and Africa—have evolved "pleasure plays" (that is, short dramas intended primarily as entertainment). Most of these plays, however, seem to have been motivated by the attempt to ward off evil by ridiculing unfriendly spirits, unsuccessful war or hunting tactics, or socially unacceptable behavior. Such works are interesting in part because of their very rarity. A single pleasure play seems to be the most that any primitive tribe can produce, and these dramas have become as fixed and traditional as rituals. In every case, they are inconsequential when compared with the drama of advanced societies.

Within primitive societies, dramatic ritual serves a number of purposes. First, it is intended to influence events through "sympathetic magic." One of the fundamental premises of primitive magic is that a desired effect—such as success in battle or adequate rainfall—can be achieved by acting it out. Many rituals of this kind are related to seasonal changes. Primitive man does not always perceive that the years recur in a fixed pattern. Therefore, he may feel it essential to enact rites to insure the return of spring and the continuance of fertility. At times he may resort to sexual orgies to induce fertility in the earth; at others, he stages ritual combats between the representatives of winter/death and spring/life, ending with the triumph of the latter.

Second, dramatic ritual may be used to educate. Since one mark of a primitive society is the absence of a written language, dramatic ritual serves as a means for passing on traditions. Many primitive tribes use initiation rites, some occupying only a few days but others extending over a period of years, to acquaint the young with sacred beliefs, taboos, mores, and history. Such rites are still common among Australian and African tribes and were traditional with American Indian tribes.

Third, dramatic ritual is often used to glorify—a supernatural power, a victory in a hunt or war, the tribal past, a hero, or a tribal totem (an animal, plant, or natural element with which a tribe thinks itself closely related). Fourth, ritual drama may entertain and give pleasure. Even in the most serious ceremony there may be an element of pleasure which derives from the spectacle, the repetition of a formal pattern, or the skillful performance. The emphasis upon pleasure as an end in itself, however, is not usually developed in primitive societies.

Although our specific goals may differ considerably from those of primitive man, the modern theatre still serves the last three purposes. Similarly, ritual drama and theatre employ the same basic elements—music, dance, speech, masks, costumes, performers, audience, and auditorium. In almost all dramatic ritual, pantomimic dance with rhythmical and musical accompaniment is more fundamental than speech, which may nevertheless be used. Masks and costumes are usual accessories, for most primitive people believe that a spirit can be controlled by making a likeness of it or by assuming its likeness. Masks and costumes, consequently, are means of embodying the god to be propitiated, the animal to be killed, the event to be brought about. Makeup—in the form of paint, ashes, or juices—may supplement masks and costumes by covering parts of the body. There must also be "actors," highly skilled and disciplined ones when no deviations in the ritual are permitted. When rites have become fixed, the tribal elders, priests, or witch doctors may exercise strict control over the performances and serve in a capacity comparable to that of a theatrical director.

An "acting area" and, if there are spectators, an "auditorium" are needed. The most typical spatial arrangement for dramatic rituals is the circular performance area surrounded by spectators. In other instances, as in certain Australian ceremonies which use painted-bark or cloth panels as a background, the audience sits or stands on three sides of the performance area. Thus in dramatic ritual all of the basic elements of theatre are present, and it is usually assumed that they were gradually transformed into an independent drama.

But the theory that drama evolved from ritual has not gone unchallenged. Many anthropologists have questioned the premise that all primitive societies follow the same developmental patterns, and thus have cast doubt on the validity of evidence drawn from modern primitive groups in explaining the appearance of drama in antiquity. Furthermore, the exclusive concern for ritualistic origins is overly simplistic. In the beginning ritual also included religion, art, philosophy, history, science, and all of man's attempts to cope with human experience, since he could not as yet distinguish among various kinds of knowledge. An advanced society is differentiated in large part from the primitive by the degree to which specialized knowledge and skills have emerged. As a primitive society enters a more advanced state, it separates ritual from history, science, and other concerns. Consequently, on the surface it might seem that theatre as a specialized activity would inevitably appear; but not all societies, even advanced ones, produced a drama. Why, then, have some emerging societies created a theatre while others have not? Furthermore, why does drama continue to be valued after it ceases to fulfill any immediately practical or ritualistic purpose?

A partial explanation is suggested by Aristotle's argument that man is by nature an imitative creature—that he takes pleasure in imitating persons, things, and actions, and in seeing imitations. Aristotle states that drama is an imitation of human deeds, feelings, and thoughts, and gives pleasure because it helps man to understand his world and organize his responses to it. Thus it can be both entertainment and a form of knowledge.

Even this, however, is not a complete explanation, for the "imitative instinct" does not necessarily lead to drama. At least two other conditions seem to be essential: first, the appearance of men who can organize the theatrical elements into an experience of a high order, and second, a society which can recognize the value of theatre and drama as independent specialized activities. Only then can the ever-present potentialities be realized.

It is for these reasons that the Greeks must be considered the primary inventors of theatre and drama, for, regardless of all antecedents, it was they who first recognized the possibilities which had existed for centuries.

LENGTH: 1,895 WORDS

33 Oscar G. Brockett
The Origins of the Theatre

SCORING: Reading time: _____ Rate from chart: _____ W.P.M.

RETENTION	number right ____ × 2 equals ____ points	
MAIN IDEA	number right ____ × 4 equals ____ points	
INTERPRETATION	number right ____ × 3 equals ____ points	
CONCLUSION	number right ____ × 3 equals ____ points	
APPLICATION	number right ____ × 3 equals ____ points	
VOCABULARY	number right ____ × 2 equals ____ points	

(Total points: 100) **total** ____ points

RETENTION   Based on the selection, which of the following statements are True (T), False (F), or Not answerable (N)?

1. _____ Apparently, the "imitative instinct" leads directly to drama.

2. _____ The modern theatre serves the same purposes for modern man as it did for primitive man.

3. _____ The role of theatrical director in primitive tribes is sometimes taken by the priests.

4. _____ Even in an advanced state, primitive societies do not separate ritual from history and science.

5. _____ Pleasure plays seem to have developed primarily as entertainment.

6. _____ In those societies that have developed drama, the precise evolutionary stages are known.

7. _____ One thing primitive drama does not seem to do is educate its audiences.

8. _____ Most performances in primitive cultures are expected to be directly useful to the culture.

9. _____ Sympathetic magic is not thought by primitive societies to have a specific effect on events.

10. _____ The basic elements of theatre and drama are found only in a few societies.

11. _____ Primitive man ritualizes every gesture related to fertility.

12. _____ Once established, primitive rituals are usually performed in the same way, precisely and without deviation.

13. _____ In a primitive society all members of the group perform the rituals equally well.

14. _____ Myths and stories arise after the clear establishment of rituals.

15. _____ Primitive myth never alludes to or relates to supernatural powers or tribal totems.

MAIN IDEA   Which of the following statements best represents the main point of the selection? _____

1. Religions seem to be the basis for many kinds of art, including drama.
2. Patterns of development of drama in primitive societies could give us knowledge of how drama began.
3. Tribal patterns are the same, whether in Australia, New Guinea, or modern New York.
4. No one has any idea how theatre began.
5. Theatre developed in a summary fashion, beginning with religion and ending with comedy.

INTERPRETATION   Which of the following is the best interpretation of a key point in this selection? _____

1. A modern anthropologist might seriously question the theories in this selection.
2. Anthropologists before the nineteenth century really had no concepts of how primitive peoples developed ritual.
3. Contemporary anthropologists have had no chance to investigate primitive peoples directly.
4. Anthropologists are in general agreement on the theories of how ritual becomes drama, whether in primitive or modern societies.
5. There are two kinds of anthropologists: theoreticians, who agree with Brockett, and practitioners, who find that practice defies theory.

CONCLUSION   Which of the following statements is the best conclusion that can be drawn from the selection? _____

1. The origins of drama have defied investigators since the nineteenth century.

2. The origins of drama are of no interest to the anthropologist.
3. The origins of drama are the same everywhere.
4. The origins of drama are very speculative.
5. The origins of drama are relatively clear.

APPLICATION   Choose the best answer for each question.

1. _____ In order for drama to develop, a society has to see theatre's:
   a. connection with primitive man.
   b. relationship to religion.
   c. necessary connection to priestly functions.
   d. value as a specialized activity.

2. _____ Studies of ritual and ceremony in primitive society lead us to separate that which is theatrical in life from:
   a. that which is theatrical in death.
   b. living theatre.
   c. theatre as an art form.
   d. things that are not theatrical.

3. _____ The reason that primitive people assign special powers to supernatural forces is:
   a. a sign of humanity's instinctive understanding of nature.
   b. unrelated to the intensity of the daily experience of living.
   c. that they have a keen regard for the power of those forces.
   d. they do not understand natural forces.

4. _____ The division of primitive participants in ritual into "actors" and "audience" stems from:
   a. an anxiety of influence.
   b. the need to perform the ritual correctly.
   c. a sympathetic magic extending to controlling events.
   d. a problem in space, particularly in using small theatres.

5. _____ Performers will sometimes impersonate:
   a. mythical characters.
   b. dead animals.
   c. their ancestors.
   d. the spirit of their tribe.

6. _____ Comedy needs more objectivity than serious drama because:
   a. tragedy is very subjective.
   b. objectivity is the heart and soul of drama.
   c. it takes a very confident society to accept comic laughter at itself.
   d. comedy depends on laughing at eccentric things, not fearing them.

7. _____ One of the primary purposes in the primitive acting out of an event is:
   a. to ward off the event.
   b. so the event can be changed.
   c. inherent in the establishment of standards for performance.
   d. to make the event happen.

8. _____ Primitive dramatic rituals help pass on traditions because:
   a. traditions do not pass on easily.
   b. traditions are not written down and ritual preserves them.
   c. people will pay much more attention to them if they are dramatized.
   d. everyone, no matter what society, enjoys the three dimensions of drama.

9. _____ One thing anthropologists have questioned vigorously is:
   a. the theory that all primitive societies follow the same development patterns.
   b. that there are any development patterns at all.
   c. a view of mankind that would omit pleasure as the first principle.
   d. the connection between ritual drama and ceremonial religion.

10. _____ One of the curiosities of the investigation into the origins of the theatre is the question of:
    a. how theatre was able to survive through cultural shock.
    b. why priests became directors, but not writers of drama.
    c. why some societies have produced theatre and some have not.
    d. how anyone could get information about primitive societies in the first place.

VOCABULARY Choose the best definition for each italic vocabulary entry.

1. _____ They use such theatrical elements as *spectacle*, dialogue, or conflict.
   a. sight-seeing
   b. visual splendor
   c. alarm
   d. religious vision

2. _____ It is impossible to construct a *coherent* history of theatrical events.
   a. complete
   b. intelligible
   c. consistent
   d. thorough

3. _____ He attributes occurrences to *supernatural* forces.
   a. divine
   b. holy
   c. beyond nature
   d. evil

4. _____ Myths explain, illustrate, and *idealize* the rites.
   a. reform
   b. perfect
   c. realize
   d. shape

5. _____ These performances remain rituals and are therefore *utilitarian*.
   a. practical and useful
   b. unusual but pleasant
   c. conservative and pragmatic
   d. part of Protestant religion

6. _____ His rituals are as "*scientific*" as knowledge permits.
   a. meaningful
   b. true
   c. belabored
   d. sensible

7. _____ He perceives certain *deviations* from the norm.
   a. oddities
   b. turning away
   c. clues
   d. duplicities

8. _____ influence events through *sympathetic* magic
   a. nice
   b. concerned
   c. in agreement with
   d. powerful

9. _____ In these cases the *virtuosity* of the performers is admired.
   a. skill
   b. impression
   c. sensitivity
   d. brilliance

10. _____ Masks embody the gods to be *propitiated*.
    a. harmed
    b. helped
    c. assuaged
    d. reviled

11. _____ the theory that drama *evolved* from ritual
    a. came slowly
    b. separated completely
    c. developed slowly
    d. turned away from

12. _____ The concern for ritualistic origins is overly *simplistic*.
    a. ingenious
    b. emotional
    c. unrealistic
    d. eccentric

13. _____ No deviations in the *ritual* are permitted.
    a. ceremonies
    b. play
    c. events
    d. righteous behavior

14. _____ The Greeks, regardless of all *antecedents*, invented theatre.
    a. ancestors
    b. predecessors
    c. anterior events
    d. anthropological evidence

15. _____ An advanced society is *differentiated* from the primitive.
    a. separated
    b. disconnected
    c. distinguished
    d. no different

34

MORTIMER CHAMBERS
RAYMOND GREW
DAVID HERLIHY
THEODORE RABB
ISSER WOLOCH

Explanations of Imperialism

The most intense period of European empire building in Africa and Asia occurred over a span of seventy-five years, from 1875 to 1950. During this time, European investors amassed huge fortunes, and European governments became more and more drawn into the affairs of these adventure-capitalists. While European nations threatened each other with war over their holdings, the territories they seized or invaded became more and more westernized. They lost much of their regional culture while absorbing more and more the ways of Europe. The story is marked by an unusual collaboration of individual, state, and church.

In 1875, after centuries of close contact with Africa, European powers laid claim to no more than a tenth of Africa's land. Twenty years later, seven nations had through fierce competition established dominion over almost the entire continent. And they had carried their rivalry to most of Asia and the small islands of the Pacific Ocean. Won in open conquest, through protectorates, and by treaties granting special trading privileges, most of the newly acquired lands at first had few European settlers (the primary means of exploiting local wealth in the past) and most of them lay in tropical zones Europeans had heretofore found unappealing and unhealthy.

Such rapid and dramatic developments demand explanation, and by the turn of the century, the opponents of imperialism in particular sought to explain the pervasive imperial fever. In 1902 J. A. Hobson, a British economist, published *Imperialism: A Study*, a critical tract that has been heavily attacked by subsequent scholars but that remains the starting point of modern analysis. Writing during the Boer War, Hobson was eager to show that imperialism offered little to restless populations or to commerce. Emigrants, he noted, preferred to go to the Americas, and Britain's trade with the European continent and the Americas was far greater and growing faster than her trade with her colonies.

The economic explanation of imperialism Hobson found in financiers, small numbers of men controlling great wealth and looking for quick profits. They used their social and political connections to induce the government to protect their investments through political dominance over undeveloped lands. Similarly their social position enabled them to exploit the missionaries, soldiers, and patriotic dreamers who glorified empire. Imperialism thus stemmed from the manipulation of public opinion in the interests of certain capitalists.

Hobson's analysis inspired the still more influential theory of Lenin. The leader of Russia's Marxist revolutionaries, Lenin provided a Marxist interpretation of a subject on which Marx had written little. In *Imperialism: The Last Stage of Capitalism* (1916), Lenin agreed that the stimulus behind empire building was basically economic and that the essence of colonialism was exploitation. But for Lenin imperialist ventures grew from the very dynamics of capitalism itself. Competition produced both monopolies and lowered profits, and surplus capital was forced to seek overseas investments. The alternative, to enlarge the domestic market by raising wages, would increase competition, thus further reducing profit. Imperialism was therefore the last "stage" of capitalism, the product of its internal contradictions. Lenin would add in 1916 that imperial rivalries, involving whole nations, led to wars that further hastened the end of capitalism. "Imperialist" became an epithet for a system considered decadent as well as immoral.

Although influenced by these views, most historians have remained uncomfortable with them. They contribute little to an understanding of the actual process of imperial conquest, in which capitalists were often reluctant participants. They do not explain why imperialists called for political control beyond treaty rights or for the swift spread of European power into areas that offered small financial return; investment, like trade, remained heavier in more developed noncolonial countries. Nor do economic arguments tell us much about the role of the popular press, explorers, earnest missionaries, and ambitious soldiers in pressing hesitant politicians to imperial conquest.

Many factors help explain the sudden increase in the pace and importance of European imperialism, although all analysts today would agree that economic interests, at least in the long run, were among the most important. By the late nineteenth century, a society familiar with self-made men was readier to believe that new lands offered the chance to make a quick fortune. A general increase in trade and the growing demand for rubber, oil, and rare metals spurred the search for natural resources. Stiffening competition in international commerce and rising tariffs taught businessmen to seek the backing of their governments. Technology too played a part. Not only was regular trade with distant places made easier, but dynamite lessened the difficulty of building roads, while modern medicine reduced the dangers of the tropics. Coaling stations and telegraph posts acquired strategic as well as commercial importance, a fact that argued for military and political protection.

Beyond such rational calculations, however, imperialism was rooted in the values Europeans held and in their domestic society and politics. Mass-circulation newspapers gloried in imperialism, writing of adventure and wealth, Christianity and progress in the virile language of force. To the people of the late nineteenth century, exploration and conquest were high and noble adventure. Press reports made popular heroes of daring men like Henry M. Stanley, who followed the rivers of South Africa and penetrated the interior of the Congo, and Pierre de Brazza, who traveled up the Congo River, overcoming hardship and danger and dismantling a steamship so it could be carried around the rapids. Exploration seemed in itself an expression of progress, the brave adventurer the personification of individual initiative. If the explorer also gained wealth, that completed the parable.

The missionaries who risked their lives to build a chapel in the jungle and convert the heathen were as symbolically appealing as the explorer. For churches often at odds with the culture of their day and in conflict with the state, here was a dramatic outlet and a welcome reassurance of their importance in modern life. Hundreds of Social Darwinists preached the inevitable conflict of race with race and hailed the resultant spread of civilization, by which they meant of course their own. Geographical societies became prominent in every European country, proudly acclaiming yet another association of new knowledge with increased power.

Where class tensions were high and domestic conflict serious, colonial expansion offered all citizens a share in national glory and gain. Rudyard Kipling's poems of imperial derring-do in exotic lands hail the simple cockney soldier; whatever his lot at home, he was a ruler abroad. Thus in politics imperialism, like nationalism, cut across social divisions. It was an important part, especially in Great Britain and Germany, of the political resurgence of the right, allowing conservative groups strong in the army, the church, and the aristocracy to ally themselves with commercial interests in a program of popular appeal. Employment as well as glory was promised as the fruit of a policy of strength. Significantly imperialism never achieved comparable political effect in France, the nation with the second largest of the European empires, though hers too was built principally by soldiers and priests. The right fumbled its effort at mass appeal in the Dreyfus affair; patriots were preoccupied with avenging the loss of Alsace and Lorraine to Germany; and French nationalism retained ideas associated with the Revolution that often conflicted with those of imperialism. But everywhere empire offered the appeal of individual daring and dramatic action in a society becoming more organized into large institutions. It gave openings to groups such as the military and the clergy often disparaged at home, and it supplemented popular theories with concrete tales of risk, gain, glory, and conquest.

Patterns of Imperialism

Despite the general popularity of imperialist ideas, few whole-hearted imperialists held high political office even in Great Britain. The history of colonial conquest in this period was less one of long-range schemes than of individual acts and decisions that appear almost accidental when viewed singly. Frequently individual explorers, traders, or officers established their claims in a given region through treaties with native leaders and then, usually later, obtained recognition from their home government. In the process of enforcing contracts and maintaining order, they tended to exceed their original authorization and to extend their territorial claims. Governments anxious not to appear weak before their public or other powers then supported such moves; trading concessions and protectorates became colonies. This pattern of expansion required little premeditation. Applying their own laws and practices to other cultures, Europeans were shocked when natives failed to honor Western rules, and they responded with increased force.

Even Europeans attracted by non-Western cultures or devoted to helping local populations, in the name of Western religion and medicine, undermined their host societies by introducing alien ideas, institutions, and technology as well as by sheer wealth and power. There is in fact a whole other history of imperialism just now being written from the perspective of the indigenous peoples that shows how native political, economic, and religious organization was disrupted by the arrival of outsiders. To the confident men of empire, such conditions left no alternative but further European control.

Africa

In the 1870s European involvement in Africa began a rapid spread inland from a few coastal posts that would end in the partition of the entire continent by 1895. Early signs of the domination to come were the collapse of Egyptian finances, the energetic exploration of the Congo sponsored by King Leopold II of Belgium, and the increasing conflicts between the British and the Boers.

The Suez Canal was completed in 1869, the shares in its ownership held by French investors and the khedive of Egypt, who ruled as a monarch representing the nominal suzerainty of the Ottomans. When the debt-plagued khedive sold his shares in 1875, they were purchased by the British government in one of

Disraeli's most dramatic coups. Determined to protect their investments, the British and French then established joint control over Egyptian finances. In 1882, however, a nationalist revolt by the Egyptian army against both the khedive and foreign influence threatened this arrangement. The British government decided to mount a show of strength (in which the French Parlement refused to allow France a part) and the Royal Navy bombarded Alexandria to teach Egyptians that contracts must be met. In the resulting chaos the British attempted to restore order, a process that quickly led to their occupying Egypt, and the country remained under their rule until after World War II. In Tunisia a similar pattern of increased foreign investments followed by a financial crisis and intricate diplomatic maneuverings brought about French occupation in 1881. Both events accelerated the competition for African empire.

Although reluctant to accept responsibility for all their countrymen did, European governments nevertheless found themselves drawn piecemeal into scores of treaties that prescribed for societies little understood and fixed boundaries in areas whose geography was barely known. The International Association for the Exploration and Civilization of Central Africa, founded in Brussels in 1876, quickly became a private operation of Leopold II. The association paid less attention to its lofty aims of furthering science and ending slavery than to the vast territorial claims it might make by sponsoring Stanley's explorations. From their outposts along the west coasts, the French, the English, Spaniards, and Portuguese hurried to push into the hinterlands of what are now Senegal and Nigeria.

French gains in West Africa were the most extensive of all, and in 1898 a group of soldiers who had pushed two-thirds of the way across the continent at its widest point arrived at Fashoda, on the Nile, a few days before the British, who were moving into the Sudan. Both nations considered the encounter of their troops at Fashoda a matter of national honor, and imperialists plotted on maps how dominance over Africa was at stake. The French imagined holdings stretching from west to east across the continent, controlling the headwaters of the Nile. The British talked in terms of territory and maybe even a railway from the Cape of Good Hope to Cairo, a north-south axis through the continent. Thus the obscure outpost at Fashoda sought by no general staff brought Great Britain and France close to war for weeks. The confrontation ended when the French, divided at home over the Dreyfus Affair, chose to give way.

In South Africa Cecil Rhodes typified the interconnection of local politics, private interest, and visions of empire. Confident of white and indeed Anglo-Saxon superiority, he schemed and propagandized relentlessly, stretching old claims and using trading companies and his own wealth to establish new ones. He died during the Boer War, but the British victory paved the way for the establishment of the Union of South Africa in 1910, a partial fulfillment of Rhodes' ambitions.

As the European states were drawn into the scramble, they sought through diplomacy to lessen the clear danger that clashes in Africa would lead to war in

Europe. At Berlin in 1885 the powers established rules for each other. The most important was that coastal settlement by a European nation would give it claim to the hinterlands beyond. Straight lines drawn from haphazard coastal conquests cut across the little-known indigenous cultures, but they restrained the anarchy of European ambition. The powers also agreed at Berlin to prohibit slavery; and five years later they banned liquor and limited arms in the zone between the Sahara and the Cape Colony. Humanitarian considerations were not wholly forgotten, and by the turn of the century, the ruthless exploitation of the Belgian Congo was considered an international scandal. The men who bravely planted their flags and wrote out treaties for chieftains to sign did not doubt that theirs was a beneficial achievement to be measured by mission hospitals and schools, new roads and political order as well as profit. By 1912 only Liberia and Ethiopia were formally free of European domination. The social, cultural, religious, and political life of Africans was everywhere submerged under an imposed European order.

Asia

For more than a century the decline of the Ottoman Empire had been a major theme of international relations, one clearly demarked by the independence of Greece early in the century, the Crimean War at midcentury, and then by the growing turmoil in the Balkans and the British occupation of Egypt. As British, French, Russian, and German interests competed for political privileges and economic concessions (that the Germans won the right to build a railroad from the Bosporus to Baghdad was recognized as a major diplomatic triumph and a troubling challenge), it almost seemed as if those rivalries were what held the Ottoman Empire together.

In the East beyond the Ottoman Empire, Great Britain and Russia were again the main contenders for influence. Persia had felt their competition since the 1830s and by the 1870s had conceded control of the Imperial Bank of Persia to British interests. Russia competed by exerting military pressure along Persia's northern frontier and in the 1890s by offering a large loan and related concessions in an effort to reduce Britain's dominance. As part of a general entente reached in 1907, the two European powers agreed on spheres of influence: the British sphere would include the area of the Persian Gulf, in the south, and Russia's the north. Their competition, by limiting the intrusions of either power, had helped the Persian state preserve a nominal independence, but their presence increased its instability, and revolution erupted in 1905. The technique of playing off Russian and British ambitions was less successful in Afghanistan, however, where the emir's efforts to use the Russians as a counterweight to British influence could not match Britain's determination through her presence to guarantee the security of India on Afghanistan's southeast border.

India remained the jewel of the British Empire, the envy of all imperial powers. As a British trading partner, India stood on a par with France (only the

United States ranked higher). Her wealth and the prestige of her culture made India the very symbol of empire, a special status recognized in the proclamation of Queen Victoria as empress of India in 1877. Many of the leading figures of British political life made their reputations in the India service, and their techniques of administration through local lords and British courts were often proclaimed as models of enlightened rule. Yet the growth of trade and industry did not prevent devastating famines in the 1890s, and concessions to local government only stimulated increasingly organized and nationwide demands for a native voice in political life.

East of India and south of China only Siam (Thailand) preserved her independence of European control through a willingness to modernize—that is, to adopt European forms of political and economic organization—and thanks to the countervailing pressures of the three European powers present in neighboring realms, who in effect constrained each other. The British annexed upper Burma in 1886 and part of Malaya in 1896; the Dutch were on the island of Borneo; and French influence had steadily increased in Cambodia and Cochin-China (both parts of Indochina) during the 1860s, despite the indifference of the governments in Paris. Whenever Christians were attacked or a trader murdered, the local commander pressed native rulers for further political concessions without waiting for instructions from home. The French themselves seemed unable to constrain the extension of their authority. Even the modest goal of providing their enclave a secure frontier—a European conception that ignored social realities—usually led to war and expansion into another ancient realm. France in this way eventually found herself at war with China in 1883; and though Parlement voted down the government of Premier Jules Ferry, France's leading imperialist, the war nevertheless resulted in a French protectorate, reorganized in 1887 as French Indochina.

The weakness of China and the strengthening of Japan were the central realities of Southeast Asian history in the second half of the nineteenth century. Both proud nations had sought to keep intruding Europeans at a distance, and both failed, but with contrasting results. For the huge Chinese Empire, its administrative system threatened by inefficiency and provincial warlords, Western missionaries and traders were especially disruptive. When the Chinese attempted to restrict the importation of opium, which was as expensive and demoralizing for them as it was profitable for the British traders who brought the opium from India, the result was a brief war that led to the cession of Hong Kong to Britain (1841) and special foreign trading rights in a number of Chinese cities. The impact of missionaries contributed to the Taiping Rebellion (1850–1864), in which a Chinese-led millenarian movement incorporating elements of Christianity and social discontent produced revolts that threatened the empire. Battling for survival, the government was forced to grant new concessions to Britain, the United States, France, and Russia for trade, the protection of missionaries, and extraterritorial rights. In 1860 British and French forces occupied Peking and burned the summer palace in retaliation for the seizure of their envoys, and Russia took Vladivostok—a step recognized by China's Department of Foreign Affairs, a ministry not needed before.

Thus the French gains in Indochina, the extension of Russian interests in Manchuria, the arrival of more and more missionaries, and further trading concessions were all part of a continuing process. Again and again, a local riot, a missionary murdered, or a contract broken would lead to renewed demands and military pressure from Western powers. In 1898 inland waters were opened to foreign shipping (mainly British), and the Germans laid claim to Kiaochow Bay, as Germany and Japan now joined the competition for claims on China. Chinese efforts to raise revenues, reform administration, and stimulate railroads required in turn further loans from and concessions to Western nations. The Boxer Rebellion of 1900–1901, a complicated response by local militias outraged by foreigners and the weakness of their own government, brought another round of violence. Scores of Western missionaries, agents, and some diplomats were killed, prompting heavy military intervention, especially by Russia and Germany. When order was restored, China agreed to a large indemnity. The only defense against European imperialism even in a great and ancient nation appeared to be a westernization that deepened European influence. For China, that also meant the revolution of 1911, led by Sun Yat-sen, and the establishment of the Chinese Republic.

Japan, which for centuries had preserved its isolation, was in 1853 successfully pressed by Commodore Matthew Perry of the United States to permit commerce with the West, an opening quickly followed by a series of treaties permitting trade and protecting the rights of foreigners. There followed the familiar pattern of misunderstandings, broken agreements, antiforeign feeling, and renewed Western demands; but domestic political transformation came quickly in Japan. A new generation of leaders joined with the emperor, after a brief civil war, in carrying out the Meiji Restoration (1868). The essentially feudal system that had lasted seven centuries was ended, and Japan embarked on a systematic policy of adapting Western industry, technology, education, laws, and governmental institutions, including a constitutional system (much influenced by Germany's) in 1889. The resultant economic growth, efficient administration, and modern army enabled Japan, like the nations of the West, to attack China and win easy victories in the war of 1894–1895. Japan's gains included Formosa and the control of Korea. As in her victory over Russia (1904–1905), Japan showed that successful imperialism, like the Western ambitions and power from which it stemmed, need not be limited to Europeans. With the United States in control of the Philippines, as a result of the Spanish-American War (1898), the Western system of power relations dominated Southeast Asia and encircled the globe.

LENGTH: 3,476 WORDS

34 Mortimer Chambers, Raymond Grew, David Herlihy, Theodore Rabb, and Isser Woloch Explanations of Imperialism

SCORING: Reading time: _____ Rate from chart: _____ W.P.M.

RETENTION number right _____ × 2 equals _____ points

MAIN IDEA number right _____ × 4 equals _____ points

INTERPRETATION number right _____ × 3 equals _____ points

CONCLUSION number right _____ × 3 equals _____ points

APPLICATION number right _____ × 3 equals _____ points

VOCABULARY number right _____ × 2 equals _____ points

(Total points: 100) **total** _____ points

RETENTION Based on the selection, which of the following statements are True (T), False (F), or Not answerable (N)?

1. _____ Japan was opened to foreign commerce by Commodore Perry of the United States Navy in 1853.

2. _____ Japan was actually very slow in adapting to western ways after Commodore Perry left.

3. _____ In Asia, Thailand was able to remain independent in large measure because of its willingness to westernize.

4. _____ In the second half of the nineteenth century China was strengthening in power and Japan was weakening.

5. _____ Japan's experience showed that successful imperialism was limited to European nations.

6. _____ India was accorded a special status by the British in part because of its culture and its wealth.

7. _____ Liberia and Ethiopia were two of the first African countries to be absorbed as European colonies.

8. _____ The 1885 conference at Berlin permitted slavery in some of the African colonies.

9. _____ Humanitarian concerns were irrelevant to the imperialists, as shown by the ruthless exploitation of the Belgian Congo.

10. _____ The rural outpost of Fashoda near the Sudan almost triggered a war between major European powers.

11. _____ Egypt was exceptionally passive in face of foreign domination, permitting Britain to occupy and dominate it almost at will.

12. _____ In most European countries imperialists were at the head of government.

13. _____ The most dominant desire among the colonized territories was to acquire colonies of their own, and therefore become imperialists by default.

14. _____ For the Europeans, colonialism tended to ignore class lines: even an ordinary man was a prince in the colonies.

15. _____ Before 1875 there had been little or no European contact with Africa.

MAIN IDEA   Which of the following statements best represents the main point of the selection? _____

1. Imperialism was a result of the innocence of colonized peoples who expected Europeans to be wholesome and altruistic in their dealings.
2. It was the underlying selfishness and grasping qualities of colonized peoples that made them easy pickings for the Europeans.
3. Imperialism resulted from natural forces that permitted the weak to be dominated by the strong.
4. Imperialism resulted from a combination of media manipulation of public opinion and the natural expansive forces of capitalism.
5. Imperialism resulted from a combination of energies: economic, missionary, technological, and the popular imagination.

INTERPRETATION   Which of the following is the best interpretation of a key point in this selection? _____

1. Imperialism fueled the political powers of the European right because a policy of strength guaranteed jobs for ordinary citizens as well as the rich.
2. Imperialism was essentially forwarded at a greater rate because of a resurgence of the political right.
3. Lenin's rightist views were surprisingly shorn of support for imperialism until it was clear that Russia would benefit from increased power in Afghanistan.

4. Imperialism was so popular in European nations that it was totally un-affected by whether the right was in power or the left.
5. France's imperial policies were rightist from the start because of the hold-over of influence from the French Revolution, which began as a rightist ground swell.

CONCLUSION   Which of the following statements is the best conclusion that can be drawn from the selection? _____

1. Imperialism was an inevitable event whose result has been to draw diverse populations much closer together.
2. The long-term effect of imperialism is the breakdown of local political, economic, and religious practices, thereby leaving many former colonies in a shattered condition.
3. Imperialism is no longer practiced because of a resurgence of conscience among the European colonizers.
4. Imperialism could never have been carried out without the anxious coop-eration of the local businessmen, who saw an opportunity to profit by emulating the ways of the Europeans.
5. Imperialism must be blamed on mass media exploitation which spilled over into the popular enthusiasm of the day, creating adventurers and then colonizers.

APPLICATION   Choose the best answer for each question.

1. _____ J. A. Hobson's *Imperialism: A Study* pleased Lenin because:
   a. Lenin had been opposed to imperialism from the first.
   b. it blamed imperialism on capitalism, which Lenin hated.
   c. Hobson praised the Russian reluctance to develop colonies.
   d. Hobson was a Marxist revolutionary.

2. _____ Lenin felt that imperialism was the last stage of capitalism:
   a. until he read Hobson's book, which told him it was an intermedi-ary stage.
   b. since it occurred only after domestic markets were saturated, and when imperialism saturated overseas markets capitalism was dead.
   c. prior to the wars which were certain, he felt, to eradicate capital-ism from modern life.
   d. and his regret was that imperialism ended before he could fashion the thoroughgoing political statement which was to have crowned his final years.

3. _____ One of the interesting spurs to imperialism in Europe was the positive value accorded to:
   a. excitement.
   b. the unknown.
   c. individual attainment.
   d. exploration and progress.

4. _____ India was considered the jewel of the British Empire, but its enlightened policy of government did not prevent:
   a. Japan from marching into Manchuria in 1903.
   b. Russia from changing its approach to northern tribal conflicts.
   c. disorder and protests against British policies.
   d. the East India Company from acting as if it were a government.

5. _____ As a result of their conflicts with national governments in Europe, churches enthusiastically established colonial missionaries in order to:
   a. bring themselves into favor with the government again.
   b. reestablish their own sense of importance.
   c. study the native religions so as to discover more about the spiritual nature of man.
   d. develop a source of funds for expansion in Europe.

6. _____ The history of imperialism is not marked by coherent national policies on the part of the European governments, but by:
   a. incoherent national policies administered from above.
   b. the political infighting of the political parties jockeying for power.
   c. virtually accidental responses to individual actions on the part of businessmen.
   d. actions in response to misunderstandings and blunders regarding treaties and obligations of traders.

7. _____ European colonists undermined the native culture by:
   a. their very presence.
   b. introducing ways that were alien to the colonies.
   c. insisting on cocktails and other forms of alcohol.
   d. declaring it invalid.

8. _____ One unexpected result of missionary activity in China was:
   a. the establishment of a Christian bank to loan money to the government.
   b. a resurgence of interest in Buddhism, which until that time was in a steep decline.

c. the easing of policies toward Europeans who wished to trade further inland than the coast.

d. to inspire a revolution which had the assistance of a Christian theoretical base.

9. _____ The Chinese government tried to halt the importation of opium by the British traders, but failed because:

a. the Chinese government was inefficient and weak.

b. British gunboat diplomacy protected the opium traders.

c. Britain knew opium would weaken the Chinese will to resist.

d. the Chinese were the primary figures behind the opium trade.

10. _____ Ultimately, the final defense of Japan against western imperialism was:

a. a refusal to discuss economics with the West.

b. outright war.

c. learning to beat the Europeans at their own game.

d. voluntary westernization.

VOCABULARY   Choose the best definition for each italic vocabulary entry.

1. _____ Seven nations established *dominion* over the entire continent.

a. government

b. power

c. control

d. rights of passage

2. _____ Theorists sought to explain the *pervasive* imperial fever.

a. ubiquitous

b. insidious

c. prodigal

d. invasive

3. _____ Imperialism grew from the very *dynamics* of capitalism itself.

a. influence

b. nature

c. forces

d. suddenness

4. _____ "Imperialist" became an *epithet* for a system considered decadent.

a. opprobrious word

b. saying

c. aphorism

d. term

5. _____ "Imperialist" became an epithet for a system considered *decadent*.
   a. immoral, worn out
   b. weakened
   c. opportunistic, vicious
   d. outmoded, obsolete

6. _____ progress in the *virile* language of force
   a. manly, forceful
   b. guileless
   c. unmistakable
   d. permanent, solid

7. _____ The brave adventurer was the *personification* of initiative.
   a. symbol
   b. presentation
   c. embodiment
   d. sign

8. _____ Trading *concessions* and protectorates became colonies.
   a. plotted territories
   b. possessions
   c. hegemonies
   d. leased land

9. _____ This pattern of expansion required little *premeditation*.
   a. planning
   b. thought
   c. care
   d. instrumentality

10. _____ History is being written from the perspective of *indigenous* peoples.
    a. colonies
    b. native
    c. surviving
    d. the remaining

11. _____ The khedive represented the nominal *suzerainty* of the Ottomans.
    a. influence
    b. power
    c. governance
    d. appearance

12. _____ The khedive represented the *nominal* suzerainty of the Ottomans.
    a. so-called
    b. public
    c. private
    d. essential

13. _____ It was one of Disraeli's most dramatic *coups*.
   a. stunts
   b. achievements
   c. plans
   d. purchases

14. _____ The powers reached a general *entente* in 1907.
   a. division of the spoils
   b. arrangement to explore jointly
   c. political agreement
   d. treaty discussion

15. _____ They halted thanks to *countervailing* pressures that constrained all
   three of them.
   a. working
   b. opposing
   c. overwhelming
   d. balancing

Charts for Measuring Speed of Reading

To find the speed at which a given selection is read, divide the total number of words (given at the end of each selection and in the following charts) by the time you take in seconds to read the entire piece. Then multiply that figure by 60 in order to get the speed in words per minute (W. P. M.). For example: if you read selection 1 in 90 seconds, or 1.5 minutes, you could calculate your speed in this way:

$$716 \div 90 = 7.95 \times 60 = 477 \text{ W.P.M.}$$

For your convenience, the following charts provide reading speeds (to the nearest half minute) for each selection.

SECTION I

| | SELECTIONS | | | | | |
TIME IN MINS.	1	2	3	4	5	6
1	716	1000	1200	1125	1063	2916
1.5	477	666	800	750	708	1944
2	358	500	600	562	531	1458
2.5	286	400	480	450	425	1166
3	238	333	400	375	354	972
3.5	204	285	342	321	303	833
4	179	250	300	281	265	729
4.5	159	222	266	250	236	648
5	143	200	240	225	212	583
5.5	130	181	218	204	193	530
6	119	166	200	187	177	486
6.5	110	153	184	173	163	448
7	102	142	171	160	151	416
7.5	95	133	160	150	141	388
8	89	125	150	140	132	364
8.5	84	117	141	132	125	343
9	79	111	133	125	118	324
9.5	75	105	126	118	111	306
10	71	100	120	112	106	291
10.5	68	95	114	107	101	277
11	65	90	109	102	96	265
11.5	62	86	104	97	92	253
12	59	83	100	93	88	243
12.5	57	80	96	90	85	233
13	55	76	92	86	81	224

SELECTIONS

TIME IN MINS.	7	8	9	10	11	12
1	1555	2408	1072	3149	3272	1562
1.5	1036	1605	714	2099	2181	1041
2	777	1204	536	1574	1636	781
2.5	622	963	428	1259	1308	624
3	518	802	357	1049	1090	520
3.5	444	688	306	899	934	446
4	388	602	268	787	818	390
4.5	345	535	238	699	727	347
5	311	481	214	629	654	312
5.5	282	437	194	572	594	284
6	259	401	178	524	545	260
6.5	239	370	164	484	503	240
7	222	344	153	449	467	223
7.5	207	321	142	419	436	208
8	194	301	134	393	409	195
8.5	182	283	126	370	384	183
9	172	267	119	349	363	173
9.5	163	253	112	331	344	164
10	155	240	107	314	327	156
10.5	148	229	102	299	311	148
11	141	218	97	286	297	142
11.5	135	209	93	273	284	135
12	129	200	89	262	272	130
12.5	124	192	85	251	261	124
13	119	185	82	242	251	120
13.5	115	178	79	233	242	115
14	111	172	76	224	233	111
14.5	107	166	73	217	225	107
15	103	160	71	209	218	104

SELECTIONS

TIME IN MINS.	13	14	15	16	17	18	19
1	919	1175	2897	1630	1931	1345	3140
1.5	612	783	1931	1086	1287	896	2093
2	459	587	1448	815	965	672	1570
2.5	367	470	1158	652	772	538	1256
3	306	391	965	543	643	448	1046
3.5	262	335	827	465	551	384	897
4	229	293	724	407	482	336	785
4.5	204	261	643	362	429	298	697
5	183	235	579	326	386	269	628
5.5	167	213	526	296	351	244	570
6	153	195	482	271	321	224	523
6.5	141	180	445	250	297	206	483
7	131	167	413	232	275	192	448
7.5	122	156	386	217	257	179	418
8	114	146	362	203	241	168	392
8.5	108	138	340	191	227	158	369
9	102	130	321	181	214	149	348
9.5	96	123	304	171	203	141	330
10	91	117	289	163	193	134	314
10.5	87	111	275	155	183	128	299
11	83	106	263	148	175	122	285
11.5	79	102	251	141	167	116	273
12	76	97	241	135	160	112	261
12.5	73	94	231	130	154	107	251
13	70	90	222	125	148	103	241
13.5	68	87	214	120	143	99	232
14	65	83	206	116	137	96	224
14.5	63	81	199	112	133	92	216
15	61	78	193	108	128	89	209

	SELECTIONS					
TIME IN MINS.	20	21	22	23	24	25
1	1816	1539	1485	1246	2608	2770
1.5	1210	1026	990	830	1738	1846
2	908	769	742	623	1304	1385
2.5	726	615	594	498	1043	1108
3	605	513	495	415	869	923
3.5	518	439	424	356	745	791
4	454	384	371	311	652	692
4.5	403	342	330	276	579	615
5	363	307	297	249	521	554
5.5	330	279	270	226	474	503
6	302	256	247	207	434	461
6.5	279	236	228	191	401	426
7	259	219	212	178	372	395
7.5	242	205	198	166	347	369
8	227	192	185	155	326	346
8.5	213	181	174	146	306	325
9	201	171	165	138	289	307
9.5	191	162	156	131	274	291
10	181	153	148	124	260	277
10.5	172	146	141	118	248	263
11	165	139	135	113	237	251
11.5	157	133	129	108	226	240
12	151	128	123	103	217	230
12.5	145	123	118	99	208	221
13	139	118	114	95	200	213
13.5	134	114	110	92	193	205
14	129	109	106	89	186	197
14.5	125	106	102	85	179	191
15	121	102	99	83	173	184

SELECTIONS

TIME IN MINS.	26	27	28	29	30	31	32	33	34
1	3261	3280	2637	2231	2266	2754	2980	1895	3476
1.5	2174	2186	1758	1487	1510	1836	1986	1263	2317
2	1630	1640	1318	1115	1133	1377	1490	947	1738
2.5	1304	1312	1054	892	906	1101	1192	758	1390
3	1087	1093	879	743	755	918	993	631	1158
3.5	931	937	753	637	647	786	851	541	993
4	815	820	659	557	566	688	745	473	869
4.5	724	728	586	495	503	612	662	421	772
5	652	656	527	446	453	550	596	379	695
5.5	592	596	479	405	412	500	541	344	632
6	543	546	439	371	377	459	496	315	579
6.5	501	504	405	343	348	423	458	291	534
7	465	468	376	318	323	393	425	270	496
7.5	434	437	351	297	302	367	397	252	463
8	407	410	329	278	283	344	372	236	434
8.5	383	385	310	262	266	324	350	222	408
9	362	364	293	247	251	306	331	210	386
9.5	343	345	277	234	238	289	313	199	365
10	326	328	263	223	226	275	298	189	347
10.5	310	312	251	212	215	262	283	180	331
11	296	298	239	202	206	250	270	172	316
11.5	283	285	229	194	197	239	259	164	302
12	271	273	219	185	188	229	248	157	289
12.5	260	262	210	178	181	220	238	151	278
13	250	252	202	171	174	211	229	145	267
13.5	241	242	195	165	167	204	220	140	257
14	232	234	188	159	161	196	212	135	248
14.5	224	226	181	153	156	189	205	130	239
15	217	218	175	148	151	183	198	126	231

How to Measure Reading Efficiency

Measuring your reading efficiency means considering the speed by which you read a selection as a measurable function of your total score. You may do so by using the following formula:

Speed in W. P. M. × total score on selection exercise expressed in percentage

The result will be a comparable figure for measuring your increase in speed even if your exercise score should decrease somewhat. An example will show how this works. Two people may read the same selection and get the same score on the exercise, but one person may take much longer to do the reading. The difference can be measured in terms of efficiency as shown here:

Person A: reads selection 1 at the rate of 193 words per minute and scores 70 points. He computes his reading efficiency thus: 193 × .70 = 135 reading efficiency score.
Person B: reads selection 1 at the rate of 90 words per minute and scores 70 points. She computes her reading efficiency thus: 90 × .70 = 63 reading efficiency score.

Table of Reading Efficiency

Speed in W. P. M. × Point Score in Percentage = Reading Efficiency Score

SECTION I

1. _____ × _____ = _____

2. _____ × _____ = _____

3. _____ × _____ = _____

4. _____ × _____ = _____

5. _____ × _____ = _____

6. _____ × _____ = _____

SECTION II

7. _____ × _____ = _____

8. _____ × _____ = _____

9. _____ × _____ = _____

10. _____ × _____ = _____

11. _____ × _____ = _____

12. _____ × _____ = _____

Speed in W.P.M. × Point Score in Percentage = Reading Efficiency Score

SECTION III

13. _____ × _____ = _____
14. _____ × _____ = _____
15. _____ × _____ = _____
16. _____ × _____ = _____
17. _____ × _____ = _____
18. _____ × _____ = _____
19. _____ × _____ = _____

SECTION IV

20. _____ × _____ = _____
21. _____ × _____ = _____
22. _____ × _____ = _____
23. _____ × _____ = _____
24. _____ × _____ = _____
25. _____ × _____ = _____

SECTION V

26. _____ × _____ = _____
27. _____ × _____ = _____
28. _____ × _____ = _____
29. _____ × _____ = _____
30. _____ × _____ = _____
31. _____ × _____ = _____
32. _____ × _____ = _____
33. _____ × _____ = _____
34. _____ × _____ = _____

Graph for Measuring Progress in Reading Speed in Words per Minute

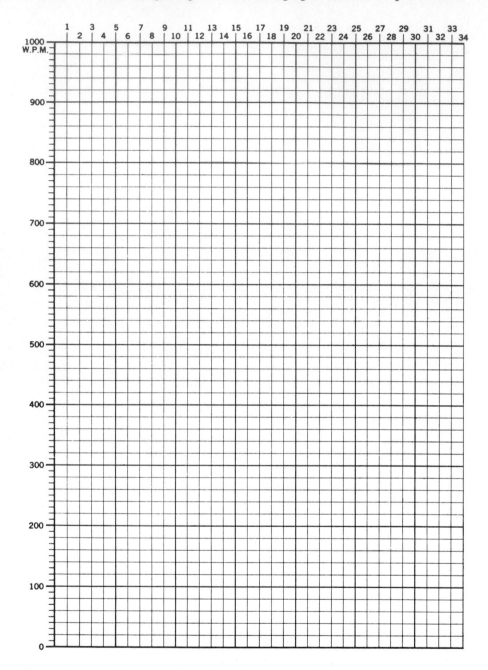

The numbers on the horizontal line refer to the selection; the numbers on the vertical line refer to reading speed in words per minute. Make a dot at your speed for each selection and connect the dots with a line.

Progress Chart

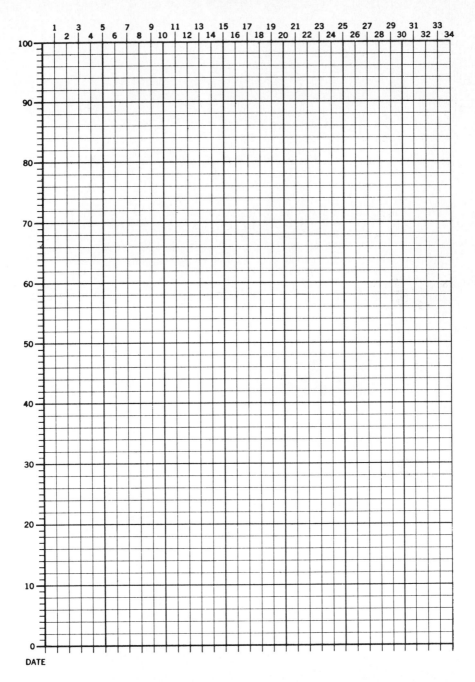

DATE

The numbers on the horizontal line refer to the selection; the numbers on the vertical line refer to the point score of each selection. Make a dot at your score for each selection and connect the dots with a line. Put the date of each exercise at the bottom of the graph.

A 7
B 8
C 9
D 0
E 1
F 2
G 3
H 4
I 5
J 6